AN EDITOR'S ESSAYS

OF TWO DECADES

BOOKS BY ALAN SWALLOW

XI Poems

The Practice of Poetry

The Remembered Land

The War Poems

The Beginning Writer

Two Stories

The Nameless Sight: Poems 1937-1956

An Editor's Essays of Two Decades

EDITOR

Three Young Poets
Three Lyric Poets
American Writing: 1942
American Writing: 1943
American Writing: 1944
(with Helen Ferguson Caukin)
Anchor in the Sea: An Anthology of Psychological Fiction
New Signatures 1948
Some Poems of Sir Thomas Wyatt
The Rinehart Book of Verse
Anthology for Basic Communication
(with Iris Pavey Gilmore
and Marion Huxoll Talmadge)
The Brand Book of the Denver Westerners, 1955
Twenty-Five: An Anniversary Anthology
The Wild Bunch

AN EDITOR'S ESSAYS
OF TWO DECADES

ALAN SWALLOW

SEATTLE AND DENVER
EXPERIMENT PRESS

Copyright 1962 by Alan Swallow

Library of Congress Catalog Card No.: 62-12521

Experiment Press books are distributed
to the trade by Alan Swallow, Publisher,
2679 South York Street, Denver 10, Colorado

For Mae

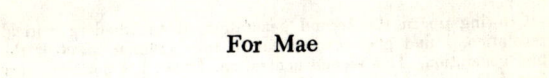

FOREWORD

A book such as this properly should be offered with diffidence. A collection of such scattered interests hardly provides the unity of a good *book*. As a publisher and editor, I look upon such books with a jaundiced eye.

But, as writer, I have been pleased that some friends have wished for it and that the editors of the Experiment group have wished to see it in print. In this case, the editor/publisher feeling will have to bow to the vanity of the writer. The unity is not in subject matter; it can lie only in the developing point of view of the person.

Growing up in the second generation of the modern critical revolution, I find great excitement in the germinal ideas of the first generation. This second generation, I fear, has not been very forceful, making few contributions to the exciting concepts and theories they inherited. In my own case, my interest has especially been upon a particular concern: the relationship between idea and method, the interdependence of "philosophy and literary method." If I have made any minute contribution to critical theory, it is in this area and would be found under the first two sections of this collection, the first entitled "Philosophy and Literary Method" and the second "On Critical Theory." The third section, "Essays on English Literature," incorporates two studies of more traditional scholarship from my particular interest in the English Renaissance; and it should be noted that, actually, the work of the first section was developed at the time of the study in the Renaissance.

As I look at the table of contents for the fourth and fifth sections, I realize strongly the faults of a collection of essays. Here are repetitiveness, special interest, great gaps in what one might have written about. But, committed to the plan of the volume, one has to leave the matter stand. Some remarks about the two sections may be helpful.

Of the fourth section, "On Contemporary Literature," I am aware that the essay "The Mavericks" ought to be in this section. But by the time that I realized this, the book was in page proof and the expense of changing about was too great to be considered.

Of the section as now constituted, the reader will perhaps be disconcerted to find three of the five items about Yvor Winters. There are a number of reasons for this: (1) The first essay of the three, "The Sage of Palo Alto," will demonstrate that my interest in Winters was extremely early, even before he had published much of his famous criticism. As perhaps the most neglected writer of our time, in relationship to his greatness, my innate tendency to assert conviction in the face of what I consider foolishness led me to write especially about this very great poet/critic. (2) That first essay ought properly not to be included, in consideration of any inherent value it may have. It is a rather stupid essay of a young man who thought he understood much when he understood rather little. However, I have included the essay primarily for historic purposes. I *can* say, with pride, that it was one of the earliest efforts to write about the Winters criticism, before a great deal of it was available, and that surely it was "on the right track," however filled with stupidity. Further, Winters was kind enough to write to me about the essay without the scorn it deserved. The correspondence developed, and this fact, plus my ever increasing respect for the criticism as it continued to develop, led to the situation, which I consider fortunate, whereby the Winters work became one of the main assertions of the Swallow publishing list. (3) Indeed, I have not included in this section, despite the reprinting of three pieces, all of the writing I have done about Winters. I am proud of the fact that when Winters' own edition of his *Poems* appeared in 1940 and he did not send out regular review copies, I was one of only two (to my knowledge) who reviewed the book. This review appeared in *New Mexico Quarterly Review* and asserted then, in its early stages, my conviction of the greatness of this poetry. Then during the school year 1961-1962, the undergraduate magazine *Sequoia* published a special memorial issue to Winters, and I was happy to contribute to that issue what I consider the mature convictions reached after more than twenty years of familiarity with the work of Winters, both critical and creative. Inasmuch as this essay followed the "period" for this collection and, as a matter of fact, this book was already in type at that time, the *Sequoia* essay is not included.

In section four, I considered for some time including a selection of my reviews upon poetry which I did (as many as eighty volumes a year) for *New Mexico Quarterly Review* during the 1940's. These were concerned particularly with the poets of the generation preceding my own and those of my own generation. To keep a scattered book from becoming more scattered, I decided against this reprinting. Perhaps the remarks concluding this Foreword may in part suggest some of my interests beyond the specific material included in section four.

In section five, the repetitiveness of remarks about the little magazines and about publishing may seem to have no excuse. But these, of course, have been central concerns to me for more than the two decades of the writing; and perhaps in this section the repetitiveness may be justified in that, within this repetitiveness, the interested reader may also find the developing attitudes as well as the consistency within the flux.

Of these essays in section five, I reprint the one "Directions in Publishing" with most apology. As I read it now, I see that it was too "young"; after all, I had been publishing only some seven or eight years (and two years among them had seen no new volumes issued because of army service), and I had just had my first glimpses of larger-scale publishing. I see now that the essay was unduly alarmist. However, to the critical reader, the essay does suggest certain concerns which time has deepened, both in me and in the publishing picture: that is the only excuse for reprinting it here. Further, the developing economy and some new factors in publishing, only dimly previsioned in the essay, have made a somewhat different picture, more ably discussed in the last essay.

On the last essay, I may remark that only three years, since composition, have borne out distressingly, as I see it, some of the trends conjectured there. What is happening in the paperback "revolution" is particularly pertinent.

I may most briefly state some matters upon which I should like to write at much greater length. In an age, literary movements follow each other swiftly; the generations of writers, as we might call them, come at approximately ten and fifteen year intervals; only a longer perspective will foreshorten this view and make one age, in a sense, of what we see as several. I am aware that my remarks upon contemporary literature (which I mean to include twentieth-century literature) in this volume are most selective. I should like to say just a bit in the way of overview.

1. The first generation of writers in this literature were men born in the nineteenth century, with 1888 (Eliot and Ransom) as something of a late date. This generation, by the foreshortening already upon us, included, however, older men such as Robinson, Hardy, Bridges, and Yeats, men who, like the younger ones, reached much of their fruition in the new century. A corrective is already proceeding upon these men, and the relative significance and greatness of Robinson, Hardy, Bridges, and Wallace Stevens being asserted.

2. The next generation is of men born at the turn of the century. Of these men, who had much vitality as a group, it seems to me that towering above them all in basic genius as poets were Hart Crane, Allen Tate, and Yvor Winters. These men had ideas, a rhetorical ability which puts into shadow the flamboyant rhetoric of a Dylan Thomas, and potential such as is seldom seen in any generation. I have included in this volume my considered essay upon Hart Crane, a great but fragmentary poet, a "sad case" of

personal and ideational problems. Allen Tate, a great mind as well as a great poetic sensibility, has been earning attention as a "man of letters" who embodies all that the term applies. I have a feeling sometimes that the attention is partly misdirected, that actually he is more worthy than this. He has ventured strongly in criticism, with some of the most exciting ideas anyone ever offered. His greatest fault as a critic lies in the fact that his criticism still remains a collection of essays, of individual insights, however brilliant they may be. He invites, by this, reading for those ideas. It is a pity that he did not face, also, the problem of making a book in which the flashes of insight, second to none at any time, anywhere, were gathered together and a full, complete, coherent critical theory stated. Apparently it will remain for this "systematization" to be done by his commentators. His one novel is considerable, and his poetry has greatness, indeed. He, of course, has lived to fulfill much of the potential with which he was endowed. Of the three, Yvor Winters has lived to fulfill to the greatest degree the potential he had, his criticism, as I have remarked, performing uniquely in our time the function of the "whole" critic; and his poetry has developed in the last thirty years to become one of the greatest bodies of poetry we can offer to the future.

3. The concept of "generations" is, of course, a poor one. Next in time is something of a half-generation, those born in something like the 1905-1910 period. These have included some most interesting talents, notably Robert Penn Warren, J. V. Cunningham, and Theodore Roethke. Warren has had attention, and he is to be honored personally. My personal debt to him is tremendous. He has worked strongly in the various roles of teacher, poet, writer of fiction, and critic. J. V. Cunningham is just the opposite; he is not expansive but tight, compressed. One of the finest minds in America, he has produced a volume of criticism which is perhaps the only very "new" conceptualization in criticism since the generation before him; and his poetry has attained greatness beyond that of his peers.

4. The next generation is of those born approximately during World War I. As this is my own generation, it is naturally difficult for me to sort out among many impressions of my fellows. For long, I felt that the persons of greatest innate genius among this group, as indicated by their early work and the excitement of discovery of this basic attribute, were Robert Lowell, Thomas McGrath, Karl Shapiro, and John Ciardi. Among them is not sufficient evidence of the ability of the Crane-Tate-Winters triumvirate, but this may be in part because of circumstance and lack of evidence of ten years of work. It is, I am sorry to say, a group of which I cannot be so proud as I hoped I might be—for the representatives

of my generation. Lowell's ability is unquestioned, surely one of the largest we have seen in a long time. He has been beset by too many problems, perhaps, to live out as yet the potential he has. Like Lowell, McGrath is a great rhetorician. His work has been spotty in that he has so often tackled so many different things, and his problems have been special among the group. And he has been most ambitious; and there are many who consider him almost saintly in his genius and devotion. Fortunately, among the whole group he seems to be working strongest now and to have hold of a future to be built on the selected best work he has done in the past. I confess I can feel little except pity for Shapiro and Ciardi —men of great ability, not so great perhaps as Lowell and McGrath in that respect—who started so promisingly. Shapiro's early notoriety ought not to happen to a poet, I suspect: as I once remarked in a review, when one has been called a "great poet" when he is very young, what is he to do the rest of his life? Here has been a great waste of talent for a decade and a half, and a near-desperation of effort. I certainly wish him the ability to overcome and to go on. Ciardi is not so sad, because he has chosen with his eyes wide open to dispell his talents in momentary activities; the choice is such that one cannot quibble except by the mere sadness that he did not choose otherwise.

5. Of the next generation, born in the 1920's, approximately, we have reason to expect, by their early work, a great deal. They are too close; there are too many of them with promising first or second books—it would be foolhardy to make any judgments, however preliminary. And one cannot have read them all, I suppose. I will remark that the first book by Edgar Bowers was perhaps the most startling, satisfying first book of poems published in America for a very long time and that, although, to his good fortune, it did not win any big awards or that sort of nonsensical attention, it won him very serious attention of the best kind. Here is one who has offered much and can offer more. With him one must place Alan Stephens, who is working so very strongly now; here is one whose reputation is smaller than that of Bowers so far, almost an enviable situation, since he can demonstrate his worth in the slowly developing way which seems best for most poets—and prove to those who have recognized the worth of his work that the conviction of worth was entirely justified. But there are many others, Richard Wilbur, for one, with an amazing ability to risk rather well a good many styles and manners. I fully believe that this generation, once removed from the "second generation" position of my own, will have more to offer. The next *twenty* years promise much, if we can survive and be allowed to do our work.

June 1962

ALAN SWALLOW

CONTENTS

Foreword   6

I: Philosophy and Literary Method

Introduction   14
Allegory as Literary Method *1940*   16
Induction as Poetic Method *1941*   28
Subjectivism as Poetic Method *1943*   44

II: On Critical Theory

A Reading of the Romantic Odes *1953*   72
Defoe and the Art of Fiction *1950*   76
/ An Essay in the Theory of Traditional Metrics *1955*   91

III: Essays on English Literature

John Skelton: The Structure of the Poem *1953*   108
The Pentameter Lines in Skelton and Wyatt *1950*   131

IV: On Contemporary Literature

Hart Crane *1949*   160
The Sage of Palo Alto *1940*   194
/ An Examination of Modern Critics: Yvor Winters *1947*   202
Winters' "A Summer Commentary" *1951*   215
Some Technical Aspects of Recent Poetry   220

V: On Publishing and Other Topics

The Little Magazines 1942	232
Postwar Little Magazines 1949	245
Why the Little Magazines? 1952	256
Poet, Publisher, and the Tribal Chant 1949	264
The Problems of Publishing Poetry 1957	280
Directions in Publishing 1948	293
The Liberal in the College	314
A Magazine for the West?	324
The Mavericks	330
Professional Letters and the Teaching of English	361
American Publishing and the American Writer	372
1960	

I
PHILOSOPHY
AND LITERARY
METHOD

INTRODUCTION

In terms of a broad metaphor, we may speak of the *intellectual climate* of an age. Of course no age is singular or simple: the Middle Ages cannot be entirely opposed to the Renaissance; the Age of Pope contained strong elements of Romanticism. But the literary historian justifiably speaks of intellectual tendencies and of the dominance of one tendency over another at any particular time; and the philosopher may indicate, in each age, a dominant rationalization of the world and of man's place in the world. Various critics, particularly the Marxist and sociological critics, have pointed out origins of such intellectual climate in the social and economic organization of the periods considered. They have also demonstrated that the artist is necessarily influenced by the thought of his time and that the intellectual scope, at least, of the artist's work is governed by that thought.

So far, then, we have attained a certain view of historical influences upon the creative process, a view which moves from the material organization of society, through the *intellectual* organization of that social order, through the artist's dependence upon the thought of his age, to the intellectual element in the art work. Obviously this is an incomplete picture. For one thing, it shows little or nothing concerning the element of technique or method in the art work. But just as each age may be characterized by a dominant intellectual climate, so it may also be characterized by a dominant general literary method: the poet of the twentieth century, for example, does not write as the Victorian poet did; and the method of Shakespeare's tragedies is not the method of the medieval fall-of-princes tragedy. I propose to demonstrate that such a general literary method is inherently related to the intellectual climate of an age and, indeed, rises out of that climate.

ALLEGORY AS LITERARY METHOD
New Mexico Quarterly, August, 1940

The student must look beneath the dry surface which allegory presents to the modern mind and understand that allegory was, for the people of the Middle Ages, a mode of thinking, a method by which they apprehended truths which were vital to them in their day-to-day lives. Allegory came with the Middle Ages and had its rise, according to C. S. Lewis in *The Allegory of Love*, in the conditions which attended the triumph of the Christian over the pagan religion. The gods of the pagans had been anthropomorphic gods, superhuman individuals possessing human appetites to be satisfied. But in the last days of the pagan religion, the gods became a strange mixture of abstractions and concrete individuals; often appeared an abstraction to be worshipped, not appeased. These Romans worshipped Fides and Concordia side by side with Jupiter and Mars.

With the rise of the Christian religion, people became aware of the unity of things, of the single God, of the One. What were the old multiple gods good for under such a religion? Lewis suggests that they became "aspects, manifestations, temporary or partial embodiments of the single power." In other words, they became the personified figures in the allegorical struggles which appeared in the literature of the Christian era, became Wrath, or Reason, or Love.

The Christian is much concerned with conduct. According to Christian doctrine, sin led to punishment, and good deeds to the rewards of a just God. Thus, the early Christians were deeply conscious of the divided will, the will to good and the will to evil. Such a conflict in the inner, psychological world may be easily dramatized in an allegorical fashion. The various whims, desires, and forces in that inner world can become personified, and through the struggle between these personifications, the introspective life of man can be represented. Thus, as Lewis points out, allegorical conflict became the natural method of dealing with psychology in this period. One will recognize the convenience of such a method if he remembers that a faculty psychology has only rather recently given over to a more empirical one.

Allegory is a means of expressing the immaterial in a drama of some kind. The figures of the drama may be either abstractions or real persons, but in all allegories there are two meanings or levels. There is the literal level of the conflict represented; then there is another level which the author had consciously in mind, something else which he meant by the movements of his characters. By what habit of mind, though, could these writers mean one thing when they were talking about another?

Allegory is a natural tool to that mind which holds

to a dualistic philosophy in which the spiritual, or God, is assumed to be in some measure immanent in the material world; and this doctrine is a fundamental of Christian philosophy, which held that in Christ two worlds had been united, the world of God and the world of matter. To the Middle Ages these two worlds were permanently connected. In logic, though the medieval philosophers said that every event and every phenomenon had four causes, the two with which they were most concerned were the efficient and the final causes. They conceived of the world as a vast machine, and the efficient cause, which was the immediate, materialistic cause, functioned within this machine. But what, they asked, set this vast machine in motion, and toward what end did it move? This they accounted for by the final cause, the cause described by de Wulf as "the attraction exerted on every efficient cause by some good towards which it tends." That good is God: God created both worlds, and the purposes of the Creation was to build and, finally, to consummate the City of God.

Medieval philosophers went one step further. Not only were the spiritual and the material worlds governed by one will, which was the divine will of God, but also the two worlds were similar and correspondent. And since the two worlds were correspondent, knowledge of one gave knowledge of the other. For example, it was evident that God was a Trinity, or Three in One. So man combined the spiritual, the intellectual, and the material in one body. Further, God was the head and ruler of the universe; thus, the principles of headship and obedient subordination were the patterns for human societies: monarchy was the best form of government; the father was the supreme head of the family.

The philosophy permits also the opposite argument, from the material world to the spiritual. A study of material phenomena will tell something of the spiritual world. As St. Thomas Aquinas said, "From material things we can rise to some kind of knowledge of immaterial things"; and, "we know God through creatures, according to the Apostle (Rom. 1, 20), *the invisible things of God are clearly seen, being understood by the things that are made.*"

Allegory was the method of such a philosophy and of such a psychology. The people of the Middle Ages admitted that events had a literal meaning of their own. But every event in the natural world and every product of human effort was an allegory; in fact, medieval thinkers commonly traced four meanings, the literal, the allegorical, the moral, and the anagogical. The last three meanings were classified by St. Thomas as spiritual. The presence of four meanings in the same work was expected, and was defended by St. Thomas: "Inasmuch as the Author of the Scriptures embraceth all things at once in his intelligence, why should not the same sacred letter. . . contain several senses founded on the literal?. . . The multiplicity of sense in the Writ produceth neither obscurity nor ambiguity; for these senses are multiple . . . not because the words have several meanings, but because the things exprest by the words are themselves the expression of other things."

The temper of the Middle Ages was such, then, that an allegorical meaning in any natural or literal account was expected, looked for, and considered true. The allegorical meaning was considered the better meaning because it was the spiritual, and thus the more nearly true, meaning. And the method of allegory provided a means of expressing the inexpressible and unknown in terms of the expressible and known, the abstract and spiritual in the form of the concrete and material.

II

Dante was a medievalist, and to him the things concerning which he wrote were loaded with overtones of spiritual meaning. Those spiritual meanings were not entirely precise, for the merely human mind could not know exactly the reality of the spiritual world. But he could conduct temporary explorations into that domain by writing an allegory. Dante surely did not believe that the state of souls after death, in hell, purgatory, and heaven, was literally as he conceived it. And that, as he wrote a patron (at least the letter is attributed to Dante), was the literal subject of *The Divine Comedy*. And surely he did not believe that the exact rewards and punishments he pictured were the rewards and punishments of God, which was his allegorical subject, as he explained in the same letter.

Dante's imagination, as T. S. Eliot has said, is visual. "It is a visual imagination in a different sense from that of a modern painter of still life; it is visual in the sense that he lived in an age in which men still saw visions." And for Dante, his vision was saying some truth about life after death; although he, being human and using material objects, was not saying the complete truth, the possibilities of his statement must have been for him almost limitless. So he made no effort deliberately to control and to point out a specific allegorical interpretation. The allegorical meanings were naturally there and never questioned.

Dante's *problem* as well as his imagination, I shoud like to suggest, was primarily a visual one. His problem was to give an exact transcript of his vision; and the more sharp and at the same time complicated it appeared at the literal level, the more the allegorical meaning would be extended and become rich. It is for this reason, I believe, that there is in Dante a use of metaphor and simile which is not characteristic of the later use of allegory. When his problem was to see as precisely as possible, he had to use metaphor to describe, on the literal level, as exactly as possible. Thus, we have such famous similes as the one singled out by Eliot, and by Arnold before him, of the crowd in Hell, who "sharpened their vision (knitted their brows) at us, like an old tailor peering at the eye of his needle"; and the simile of the stooping Antaeus as Carisenda, the leaning tower of Bologna.

In later writers of allegory, such as the Renaissance Spenser, the medieval philosophy and psychology had been subverted, and the use of allegory had changed. In them allegory is used as a cloak for abstract thinking. But in Dante there is the reverse process, as nearly, I believe, as it can be distinguished. He is thinking on a literal level, and that literal account has an expected and an accepted allegorical meaning behind it. The elements of *The Divine Comedy* are symbols, for the material expresses something of the immaterial. Dante, the man of the Middle Ages, was interested in both meanings of his work; Spenser, an abstract thinker, as we shall see, was mostly interested in the allegorical meaning of his work; the literal level is frequently shadowy and fantastic.

III

In the court of love tradition, allegory was used as psychological method. It provided a means of exploring and representing the subtle psychological states of the person in love. By this method, the courtly love poets transformed feeling, desire, and emotion into the sensible and dramatic. In the *Romance of the Rose*, for instance, the lady does not appear at all. She is distributed among her personified "faculties," which include Bialacoil, or good-address, Trespass, Shame, Chastity, Pity, Danger, and so on. The lover who woos her never encounters her in person; rather, he encounters these personifications, and thus the intangibles of the courtship are made tangible in drama. The object of the lover's action is to achieve the rose (*i. e.*, the consent of the lady); and in this effort he is aided by some of the personified faculties of the lady, and is hindered by others.

But in the period from the *Romance of the Rose* to Spenser, allegory lost its vitality as method. It was no longer used for symbolical purposes, as in Dante, or as a means of psychological analysis and exploration, as in the *Romance of the Rose*. Instead, certain externals of the allegorical poem became conventionalized decorations of poems whose real method was not allegorical at all. One of those conventions was the dream framework: once that framework was set up, the poet of this period launched out on the real work which he was doing. Within the dream framework of *Confessio Amantis*, for example, Gower set three types of work: the didactic lesson about virtues and vices, over a hundred stories told for their exemplary purposes, and an encyclopedic account of the knowledge of his time.

Stephen Hawes, in the early sixteenth century, combined the didactic, erotic, and encyclopedic uses of allegory and added to them the Italian romance, necessary in *The Passetyme of Pleasure* as a narrative thread upon which to string the various uses of allegory. Thus, he prepared the way for Spenser. But Hawes' descriptions of allegorical personages take on, as Berdan has commented, the character of tapestry work. His figures are not symbols nor are they used for psychological purposes; instead, allegory has provided him with decoration and with a stock means of getting his poem under way.

During the early Renaissance, allegory lost its vitality because its philosophic and psychological base was gone. With Aristotelian Christianity in the twelfth and following centuries, great values had been discovered in the secular and naturalistic world, and after that discovery had come a gradual shifting of attention away from the exclusively spiritual. The realm of values which was given most attention had shifted from the spiritual to the natural, from heaven to earth.

At the end of the sixteenth century, Bacon was protesting vigorously against final causes, the investigation of which he considered a deterrent to "the severe and diligent inquiry of all real and physical causes":

> For to say that the hairs of the eyelids are for a quickset and fence about the sight; or that the firmness of the skins and hides of living creatures is to defend them from the extremities of heat or cold; or that the bones are for the columns or beams, whereupon the frames of the bodies of living creatures are built; or that the leaves of trees are for protecting the fruit; or that the solidness of the earth is for the station and mansion of living creatures

and the like, is well enquired in Metaphysic; but in Physic they are impertinent.

And Bacon knew what method was needed for the study of material causes: the observation of facts; that information should come before generalization.

This method contrasted greatly with the allegorical. The sensible world was to be investigated for its own causes or in its relations to man, not for what it symbolized. It meant a new method in literary composition. The Renaissance poet tended more and more to analyze and represent the psychological world not in terms of abstractions of man's "faculties," but in terms of metaphor, conceit, and the dramatic relationship between persons. In tragedy, whereas mutability of man's fortunes had formerly been considered the result of a wheel of fortune over which man had no control, the Renaissance dramatist interpreted mutability of fortune in terms of human causes, in the terms suggested by Shakespeare's Cassius:

> Men at times are masters of their fates:
> The fault, dear Brutus, is not in our stars,
> But in ourselves, that we are underlings.

Thus Spenser, a man of the Renaissance, not of the Middle Ages, chose the allegorical method quite arbitrarily. The philosophical and psychological climate of his time did not require that method: it called, if for anything, for a quite different method. His problem in *The Faerie Queene* seems somewhat clear. He desired a method which would bring together and fuse several materials. Those materials may be classified as moral and historical. The large plan of the poem is moral: there were to be twelve knights-errant who personified the twelve moral virtues, and in addition there was to be Prince Arthur, or Magnificence, who was to combine all the virtues in one character. In addition to this moral plan Spenser, like many Elizabethans, wished to have historical references in his work. He wished to justify Elizabeth's reign, both her political and her religious policies. How could he combine these elements into a single, unified poem?

It is obvious that this problem is a theoretical as well as a poetical one. And William Butler Yeats suggests in his essay on Spenser that the poet had a highly theoretical mind. "He began in English poetry," Yeats also observes, "despite a temperament that delighted in sensuous beauty alone with perfect delight, that worship of Intellectual Beauty which Shelley carried to a greater subtlety and applied to the whole of life." Spenser attempted intellectual fusion of his materials by the method of allegory. The characters were allegorical characters: they could just as well represent two things as one. Thus, Artegal is a personification of justice in the moral sphere, and in the historical material which underlies Book V of *The Faerie Queene* he represents Lord Grey, Elizabeth's governor in Ireland. Thus, Duessa, in Book I, is the personification of deceit and represents Mary Queen of Scots and, for a time, even Queen Mary, daughter of Henry VIII and Katherine of Aragon. And so on with most of the other main characters.

Spenser's use of allegory is purely common-sense and practical. It is a far cry from the vital function of allegory as a literary means of expressing the inexpressible, of investigating either the spiritual or the psychological found in the work of Dante and the early court of love poets. Perhaps this will explain the thin, abstract quality of much of the poetry of *The Faerie Queene*. Spenser's poetic problem was to give body to an abstract pattern, and at times he did not achieve that body; generally his poetry in *The Faerie Queene* is either sensuous, in the pauses in the allegory, or abstraction, with relatively little unity or compression of the two.

Spenser's use of allegory was, then, the reverse of Dante's, for Dante proceeded from the body of experience to the meanings which, through the allegorical habit of mind, he found behind it. The more exactly he examined the sensible world the more minutely he filled out his meaningful pattern. But Spenser started with the organization of abstractions and meanings; he had nothing to visualize but the fiction he created. It is almost more than any poet could have expected, to make such a world sensible, human, and concrete.

INDUCTION AS POETIC METHOD
New Mexico Quarterly Review, August, 1941

In Chaucer's "Franklin's Tale" Dorigen decides she will choose suicide rather than defamation of her virtue. She reflects upon the matter in the following terms:

> "Allas," quod she, "on thee, Fortune, I pleyne,
> That unwar wrapped hast me in thy cheyne,
> Fro which t'escape woot I no socour,
> Save oonly deeth or elles dishonour;
> Oon of this two bihoveth me to chese.
> But nathelees, yet have I levere to lese
> My lif than of my body to have a shame,
> Or knowe myselven fals, or lese my name;
> And with my deth I may be quyt, ywis.
> Hath ther not many a noble wyf er this,
> And many a mayde, yslayn hirself, allas!
> Rather than with hir body doon trespas?
> (*The Canterbury Tales*, F 1355-66.)

Following this Dorigen calls to mind a great number of women who have chosen suicide rather than to allow their bodies to be defamed, listing them as illustrations of the moral principle involved.

A convenient comparison from an Elizabethan source is afforded by Hamlet's thoughts on suicide:

> To be, or not to be: that is the question:
> Whether 'tis nobler in the mind to suffer

> The slings and arrows of outrageous fortune,
> Or to take arms against a sea of troubles,
> And by opposing end them? To die: to sleep:
> No more; and by a sleep to say we end
> The heart-ache and the thousand natural shocks
> That flesh is heir to, 'tis a consummation
> Devoutly to be wish'd. To die, to sleep;
> To sleep: perchance to dream: ay, there's the rub;
> For in that sleep of death what dreams may come
> When we have shuffled off this mortal coil,
> Must give us pause . . . .
>
> (*Hamlet*, III, i, 56-68.)

Or another convenient comparison of the method of Chaucer and of Shakespeare is afforded by their treatment of the Troilus story. In the Chaucer version, Troilus answers, when in the parting scene Criseyde asks that he be true:

> To this answerede Troilus and seyde,
> "Now God, to whom ther nys no cause ywrye,
> Me glade, as wys I nevere unto Criseyde,
> Syn thilke day I saugh hire first with ye,
> Was fals, ne nevere shal til that I dye.
> At shorte wordes, wel ye may me leve:
> I kan na more, it shal be founde at preve."
>
> (*Troilus and Criseyde*, IV, 1653-9.)

In Shakespeare's version, Troilus replies to a similar request:

> Who, I? alas, it is my vice, my fault:
> Whiles others fish with craft for great opinion,
> I with great truth catch mere simplicity;
> Whilst some with cunning gild their copper crowns,

> With truth and plainness I do wear mine bare.
> Fear not my truth: the moral of my wit
> Is "plain and true;" there's all the reach of it.
> (*Troilus and Cressida*, IV, iv, 104-10.)

These passages may be compared on two important counts: first, the difference in the fullness and function of the imagery; and, second, the differences in the philosophical and psychological assumptions lying behind the uses of the imagery.

On the first point we may notice that the passages from Chaucer are relatively bare of imagery; there is only one image in the two passages, and that a non-ambitious one, in the reference to Fortune's "cheyne." Other passages occur in Chaucer with greater liberality in the use of imagery, particularly descriptive imagery of a sort which renders his close observations accurately and richly; but there remains a positive difference, even on the quantitative ground, between Chaucer's practice and the characteristic practice of Shakespeare and other Elizabethans. There is, further, a characteristic difference in function. Chaucer, in these passages, is dealing with situations which, in themselves, are of great emotional and psychological importance, but his treatment is primarily in terms of statement and of exemplary illustration.

In the first passage from Shakespeare, only slightly more than a third of the lines of the soliloquy are quoted, but they are sufficient to show the method. The two possible choices before the speaker are recognized, and as his thought pursues one or the other of the choices, the possibility of the choice comes to him clearly with the impact of images. As these imaged consequences come to mind, the speaker moves rapidly from one attitude to another in response to the thought and the image. The psychological character of the experience is rendered fully and precisely. The Troilus passage also shows a psychological interest, for it is a piece of psychological self-analysis. And Shakespeare's practice in conveying the detailed psychological character of the experience in terms of imagery distinguishes his method from Chaucer's.

II

What lies behind this shift in poetic method? Chaucer's work as a whole, of course, represents a mixed case as far as method is concerned, for he was acquainted with some early Italian Renaissance work and made use of this knowledge in the occasional psychological interest in the *Troilus* and *The Canterbury Tales*. But, as was shown in the previous chapter, medieval method most often generalized experience in poetry. The interest in the experience is directed towards the moral and theological implications of the experience. The attention is turned away from the individual, specific experience to abstract principles, which are the "explanations" of the experience and which are the source of the real interest behind the poetry. A popular practice, for example, with

Chaucer as with others, was that of *illustrating* the theme, of seeking out *exempla* of the central theme. As Renwick comments:

> The mediaeval man kept things separate, and attended to one at a time. The Griselda of the Clerk's Tale, for instance, offends the modern reader by her lack of proper pride; the Clerk's Tale, however, is not about proper pride, but about patience. So also the passivity of Emily in the Knight's Tale is someimes cited as a social document, evidence for the position of women in the Middle Ages, but the Knight's Tale is not about the relations of a young lady with two young men who are fighting for her, nor about her ideas or emotions, but about the relations of two friends who find themselves in enmity, and about the proper conduct of their quarrel.

The medieval method is prominently a deductive, illustrative one. The type of interest represented in the poetry is not personal, individual, and psychological, but is generalized, moral, and theoretical.

Residues of the same approach appear in the Renaissance period, Spenser's *Faerie Queene* being the outstanding example. Mainly, however, the method provides in Renaissance hold-overs a convenient framework which is filled with some of the immediate interest in experience characteristic of the best Renaissance practice. One such hold-over is the personification of the virtues and the vices. In an intermediate stage, represented by Skelton's *Bouge of Court*, a vice is given a personal name and is described in these terms:

Upon his breast he bear a versing-box,
  His throat was clear, and lustily could fain.
Methought his gown was all furred with fox,
  And ever he sange, *"Sith I am nothing plain . . . ."*
  To keep him from picking it was a greate pain:
He gazed on me with his goatish beard,
When I looked at him my purse was half-afeard.

In later work, such as Nashe's *Pierce Penilesse*, sins are described with even greater particularity and less suggestion of the generalized figure. Here is one paragraph from Nashe's description of greediness.

> Famine, Lent, and dessolation, sit in Onyon skind iackets before the doore of his indurance, as a *Chorus* in the Tragedy of Hospitality, to tell hunger and pouertie thers no reliefe for them there: and in the innter part of his ugly habitation stands Greedinesse, prepared to deuoure all that enter, attyred in a Capouch of written parchment, buttond downe before with Labels of wax, and lined with sheepes fles for warmenes: his Cappe furd with cats skines, after the Muscouie fashion, and all to be tasseld with Angle-hooks, in stead of Aglets, ready to catch hold of all those to whome he shewes any humbleness: for his breeches, they were made of the lists of borad cloaths, which he had by letters pattents assured him and his heyres, to the vtter ouerthrowe of Bowcases and Cushin makers, and bumbasted they were, like beerebarrels, with statute Marchants and forfeitures. But of all, his shooes were the strangest, which, being nothing els but a couple of crab shells, were toothed at the tooes with two sharp sixpennie nailes, and digd vp euery dungill they came by for gould, and snarld at the stones as he went in the street, because they were so common for men, women,

33

and children to tread vpon, and he could not deuise how to wrest an odde fine out of any of them.

With the coming of the Renaissance the center of man's interest had shifted, in philosophy and psychology as well as in literature. It shifted from the generalized, categorical explanations of experience to its particular aspects. Renwick notes in his book on Spenser:

> This separation of human functions and interests could not last for ever, and when it weakened there began the Renaissance . . . the discovery of the central inclusive facts of Life. On one hand the evasion of temperament broke down the dominion of mediaeval intellectualism, leading philosophy away from metaphysics, which exercised only logic, to ethics, which implies the co-operation with intellect of intuition and feeling; and on the other hand it removed ethics from the sole jurisdiction of dogmatic and inexpugnable ecclesiasticism, to be examined in the light of thought and experience. Men discovered that their own actions and emotions were really the most interesting subject in the world, and felt they were not receiving the serious attention they deserved.

With the Renaissance man the particular situation was at the threshold of interest. His attention began to center in the experience itself, and to proceed, whenever a principle was needed for explanation of the experience, from the experience *to* the principle—in other words, in precisely the opposite direction to the one common to the Middle Ages.

In logic and science the Renaissance man abandoned the great interest of the Middle Ages in the final or spiritual "cause" or explanation of experience. He turned more and more rapidly to the natural causes, which required observation of experience, until by the end of the seventeenth century, with Newton and the Royal Society, modern science was well under way. In the field of conduct and morals Machiavelli led the way to a new inductive positivistic approach. In drama, as Willard Farnham has pointed out, tragedy had formerly been the result of "a manifestation of man's powerlessness in an irrational world"; but with the Elizabethans, tragedy is the outcome of character, either its vices, or, as in Shakespeare's best tragedies, its excess of good characteristics.

The new logic set its foundation in sensation. Bernardinus Telesius (1508-1588) expressed the doctrine: "Sensation and appetition are modes of action of the *spiritus;* cognitive phenomena are reduced to transformations of sensation." In other words, the center of knowledge is sensation, is the particulars of experience. Campanella (1568-1639), developing Telesius' doctrine, according to Maurice de Wulf,

> lays down the thesis that all knowledge comes from sensation, and that the latter is a purely passive act which does not require the intervention of intentional species. What we call a general concept is but a weakened form or schematic *résumé* of sensation. Observation is accordingly the foundation of knowledge.

The importance of this shift in thought is indicated

by the fact that this doctrine seems but a preamble to the thought of the English empiricists and to the central problem of the philosophical thinking of the last four centuries.

III

This new inductive approach to experience demanded a new method of handling the experience for poetry. The psychological interest and the dependence upon imagery characteristic of the new practice have been demonstrated in the passages from Shakespeare quoted at the beginning of this essay. Further techniques may well be illustrated by quotations also from Shakespeare:

> Look in thy glass, and tell the face thou viewest
> Now is the time that face should form another;
> Whose fresh repair if now thou not renewest,
> Thou dost beguile the world, unless some mother.
> For where is she so fair whose unear'd womb
> Disdains the tillage of thy husbandry?
> Or who is he so fond will be the tomb
> Of his self-love, to stop posterity?
> Thou art thy mother's glass, and she in thee
> Calls back the lovely April of her prime;
> So thou through windows of thine age shalt see
> Despite of wrinkles this thy golden time.
>   But if thou live, rememb'red not to be,
>   Die single, and thine image dies with thee.
>
> (Sonnet 3.)

> Devouring Time, blunt thou the lion's paws,
> And make the earth devour her own sweet brood;
> Pluck the keen teeth from the fierce tiger's jaws,
> And burn the long-liv'd phoenix in her blood . . . .
> (Sonnet 19.)

> That time of year thou mayst in me behold
> When yellow leaves, or none, or few, do hang
> Upon those boughs which shake against the cold,
> Bare ruin'd choirs where late the sweet birds sang . . . .
> (Sonnet 73.)

Without going into a detailed analysis of these passages, it will be observed that the techniques relied upon here include a highly dramatic structure for the poem, a dependence upon metaphor and image, word play, and an adaptation of metrics to the psychological and dramatic movement of the poem. In what way were these techniques demanded by the psychology and philosophy of the Renaissance?

The first master of Renaissance poetry, and one to whom all other Renaissance poets either directly or indirectly owed a great debt, was Petrarch. And Petrarch's most famous poetry is love poetry. The world of love poetry is a psychological world; it is concerned with one person's feelings for another, and with the relationship between these individuals. The difference between the love poetry of the two periods, the Middle Ages and the Renaissance, is one of method of treatment; and the treatment accorded it by Petrarch and his followers is an illustration of the Renaissance interest in the inductive approach to the psychological experience. Francesco de Sanctis notes in his *History of Italian Literature:*

> The world of Petrarch is smaller than the world of Dante, is barely a tiny fragment of the vast Dantesque synthesis. But the small fragment has been turned into a perfect and rich thing in itself—a full, developed, analyzed world, complete and real, with every secret corner searched and characterized in its smallest details . . . . Love, set free at last from the universal things that had wrapped it round, is no longer a concept or a symbol, but is sentiment; and Petrarch, the lover, who is permanently in the centre of his own stage, depicts the story of his soul, exploited indefatigably by himself.

It is to be noted, in passing, that this psychological interest was not limited to the love-experience or to Petrarch; it was characteristic of the Renaissance, as W. Windelband notes in his *A History of Philosophy*: "The modern mind, which had taken up into itself the achievements of later antiquity and of the Middle Ages, appears from the beginning as having attained a stronger self-consciousness, as internalised, and as having penetrated deeper into its own nature, in comparison with the ancient mind."

The problem for such a poet as Petrarch, given such detailed interest in the psychological experience and such detailed analysis of it, was to find appropriate techniques for communicating this interest and analysis. This required a means of establishing an imaginative equivalent or objectification in language, so that the reader could, in the terms of the language, "re-create" the experience indicated by the poet. Then for our purposes here, the technical practices finally developed for the purpose may be justified by their ability to express the actual character of such analyzed experience; though the tendency to make this the final justification is to be guarded against; the final justification of any technical usage is an empirical one, but in relation to the product; the technical device is good or bad in a particular poem by reason of its ability or failure to aid in achieving that intelligent concentration of experience which we may expect of good poetry.

The love poetry of Petrarch derives some of its attitudes from the courtly love tradition, and in it we find the subjection of the lover to the Lady, and the figures of the lover, the Lady, and often the personification of Love. The poetry of Petrarch, however, is not simply a description of love nor even a description of the subtle psychological character of the love-experience. In his experience of love was an actual conflict, a conflict between physical desire and spiritual desire for the loved-one. The courtly love code was not his theme; rather, behind the courtly love machinery lay his basic theme, and that basic theme is a struggle within his experience.

It is obvious, then, that the general pattern of the love-experience of the Petrarchan mold provides a substance readily dramatized. In the first place, there are the conventional figures given, lover, Lady, and

Love. Each has a code of expected action, and since the Lady was usually disdainful, to Love as well as to the lover, there was conflict among the conventional figures; yet the code demanded that the characters could not escape each other, for the Lady could not rid herself of the attentions, however distasteful to her, of the lover; and the lover, though spurned, must continue his bondage to her. Thus the poet could communicate the love-experience by presenting these figures; and the result is a poem which contains a little drama. And when we extend this from the courtly love figures to others which later developed, we have the explanation of the highly dramatic structure which is found in many Renaissance poems. This was not merely a conventionalized technical device, however. As was seen, Petrarch actually felt a conflict in his experience, a conflict which became his basic theme of physical as opposed to spiritual desire. This conflict demanded a *drama*—however little it appeared in a lyric—to express conflict empirically found within the experience.

The Renaissance poets found two alternatives to the drama of characters—which might be the poem whose structure consisted of speech from the lover to the Lady, or the poem which contained both as speaking characters—but which still provided any equivalent for the dramatic character of the experience. One of those was the paradox, obviously useful by its opposition of forces in expressing a psychological experience which contained conflict, such as the conflict between a need to throw off a love which was proving painful and a need to continue the love because it seemed the central vital element of experience. The other alternative to what we might call "physical" drama was the image, especially the metaphor. The metaphor, by its identification of one thing with another, also sets up terms with a group of dramatic forces between them, though here again we must distinguish between this means of dramatizing the experience and the term more narrowly used in the sense of a scene containing personal characters. Very commonly the metaphor was, in Renaissance poetry, an extended metaphor, sometimes called a "conceit." At times it was extended even to include the entire poem, in which case the conceit became the basic structure for the poem, as in Wyatt's sonnet in which the lover is passenger and Love is pilot of a ship lost at sea because the Lady's eyes (stars) are hidden and thus no longer guide them toward the port. More commonly the metaphor, either in extended or brief form, provided a means of visualizing and dramatizing partial aspects of the experience rather than providing the basic structure for the entire poem. Thus, it is found in poems which have a drama of personal characters and in poems using a paradox as the structure for the poem. It is also found, perhaps most often in the work of such poets as Gascoigne, Ralegh, Shakespeare, and Donne, in poems whose structure is essentially expository or largely a poetry of statement. The importance of the metaphor in psychological poetry is indicated by its plurality in the later Elizabethan and the Jacobean drama, and in the poems of Donne and his followers. For the metaphor, extended or even brief, constituted an investigation of the experience as well as a dramatic equivalent for it; and the metaphor, in the hands of many Renaissance poets, included within its terms also the conceptual aspect of the experience.

This does not by any means exhaust the technical resources used by the Renaissance poet. Briefer devices, such as the pun, word play, and the correlation of metrical attention with the thought and psychological movement of the poem, particularly in conjunction with the dramatic structure of the poem, provided correspondent means of dramatizing parts of the experience, of concentrating the line with detailed perception of the qualities of the experience. The ability of these practices to perform those functions we may take as the reason for their use.

Certainly these technical devices are not to be isolated, except for purposes of analysis. Most poems used several practices in conjunction, and some poems —some of Shakespeare's sonnets and several of Donne's poems, for example—use nearly every technique in a single poem. But the Renaissance poet found, upon an empirical basis, that experience was not simple and one-directioned; rather, he found that it contained many complications of motive, thought, and feeling. The Renaissance poet did not approach the experience with generalizations which would force the experience into a simple pattern despite the complications which could inductively be found in the experience. So the dramatic structure, the paradox, the metaphor, world play, the pun, metrical devices—all became means for the Renaissance poet to achieve communication of an experience without, at least, the falsification of an approach which had generalization as its primary interest.

SUBJECTIVISM AS POETIC METHOD
New Mexico Quarterly Review, Spring, 1943

The central problem of modern (I use the term to denote the period since the Renaissance) philosophy is the epistemological one: what are the grounds of knowledge? how do we gain certain knowledge of universals from the perception of the data of experience? The ancients were not so concerned with this problem, for their philosophy of Realism gave a secure foundation for universals. The men of the Middle Ages, disturbed only faintly by Nominalism, conceived a forthright dualism by which it was thought that the mundane world had intimate correspondences with the world of truth and the spirit and that perceptions of the former gave certain knowledge of the latter. Men of the Renaissance turned inductively to the matters of experience for inquiry. Out of that interest in experience came the dependence of the modern man upon sensory data as the basis of knowledge. Hobbes, certainly one of the first thinkers clearly in the modern world, said, "Whatsoever... we conceive, has been perceived first by sense, either all at once or by parts; a man can have no thought representing anything not subject to sense."

Sensory data are not ideas, are not the universals by which we designate knowledge. The attempts of the

English Empiricists to find a sound basis for moving from the "given" sensory impressions to universals finally ended when Hume denied that there was any connection whatsoever between the two. The dominant answer proposed during the time of the English Empiricists and since—with the exception, perhaps, of the last fifty years— has been one version or another of Idealism, that is, that universal ideas are subjective, reside in the mind of the viewer and not in the object or in the world outside the mind.

It is one of the curiosities of philosophy that Idealism, when taken seriously enough to push its extremes, can logically be reduced to materialism. Kant's categories, by which it is assumed that experience is impossible to the mind unless the mind has certain ideas with which to classify the experience (and, the argument goes, we can verify that we do have experience; therefore, these ideas are true), are biological matters and thus answerable to the materialistic laws of biology. Any philosophy which places ideas innately in the mind—unless it wishes to make further assumptions—gives them this biological basis. Or if we wish to take the direction of Hegel and place an idea outside the mind—an Absolute—this idea is objective and therefore is material.

II

For poetry the importance of this shift in philosophy was tremendous. It destroyed for the public and for the poet an agreed conception of the world, a conception which, by its myths and its symbols, had provided a means of certain communication by the poet. From this time on—as in the case of Blake and of Yeats—myths were to seem strange, willful things. And symbols were to appear impulsive and private.

But more than that, the change in philosophy meant that the poet had only one material for his poetry—the material of subjective feelings and thoughts. The Romantic poets were the first to realize this, though it is implicit in the poetry of the eighteenth century as well. William Hazlitt in his *Lectures on the English Poets* said that poetry

> is strictly the language of the imagination; and the imagination is that faculty which represents objects, not as they are in themselves, but as they are moulded by other thoughts and feelings . . . . This language is not the less true to nature, because it is false in point of fact; but so much the more true and natural, if it conveys the impression which the object under the influence of passion makes on the mind.

And Wordsworth in the "Preface" said:

> The appropriate business of poetry . . ., her appropriate employment, her privilege and her *duty*, is to treat of things not as they *are*, but as they *appear*; not as they exist in themselves, but as they *seem* to exist to the *senses*, and to the *passions*.

It no longer mattered what a thing *was*, but what the subjective experience of it was. As G. M. Turnell remarks in a discussion of the poetry of LaForgue, ". . . the artist was no longer occupied with things but with his reactions to them. . . instead of the mind conforming to the real, the real is made to conform to the mind which imposes its own pattern on everything."

III

In discussing the poetic method which grew out of this philosophical situation, we must remember that we speak of a direction; for there have been a number of efforts to swim against the current, with varying degrees of insight into the problems; and now that the consequences of a purely subjective material for poetry are seen clearly, many strive away from these practices. But it is safe to say that since the time of Dryden there has not been an important poet who was not influenced by the direction we are to indicate, and, further, that there has not been one who did not in some degree work within it.

For descriptive terms we may well go to Hobbes, whose influence upon English poetry, either directly or through ideas associated with his, can hardly be overestimated. Subjective material—which is the material of poetry from Hobbes' time on—Hobbes divided into two kinds, the product of Fancy and the product of Judgment. Fancy is the ability to see connections or similarities in things. Judgment is the ability to see differences in things, of paring down the products of Fancy to those which seem valid or essential. Hobbes' attitude was that Fancy was largely irresponsible, at least at times irrational; Judgment was the responsible, rational faculty of the mind. Hobbes further thought that in poetry, as elsewhere, Fancy should go costinually subjected to the examination, if not the rule, of Judgment: for example, he opposed metaphor and at least bold figures of speech in poetry.

The dichotomy between Fancy and Judgment, often appearing in other terms, such as Imagination and Reason or Art and Science, has been with us since Hobbes used it. Recently T. S. Eliot and others have called it the "dissociation of sensibility." Yvor Winters has called it "obscurantism," or "abstractions inadequate or irrelevant to experience on the one hand, and experience on the other as far as practicable unilluminated by understanding." A recent formal statement has been that of I. A. Richards in *Science and Poetry*: "A poet today, whose integrity is equal to that of the greater poets of the past, is inevitably plagued by the problem of thought and feeling as poets have never been plagued before." And of two analogous terms, he comments: "Of verifiability and faith, I would say, if it were clear that the faith was never in anything that could possibly be verified or, conversely, that the verification was of a kind that had no relevance to the faith."

IV

Certainly Hobbes' attitude of distrust toward Fancy was dominant during the eighteenth century. Samuel Johnson, for example, understood what the Metaphysical poets were doing but objected to them because he thought their Wit or Fancy too unnatural, too bold in linking together things which obviously seemed unlike. This attitude is reflected in the texture of the poetry of the eighteenth century, for generally the figures of speech are similes rather than metaphors, calling attention solely to likenesses in objects, and those usually rather obvious likenesses, unwilling to hazard a bolder identification of things which might have some differences. Also, eighteenth-century poetry generally had comparatively few images and employed many abstract and general words; it held as a virtue, clarity and the immediate apprehension of meaning; it was often a poetry of thought in the sense that it depended heavily upon abstract thinking, showing further predilection for Judgment.

Examples of this texture may be taken from the leading classicist, Pope, and from one of the best of the early romantics. First, I quote entire Pope's "Solitude":

Happy the man, whose wish and care
A few paternal acres bound,
Content to breathe his native air
   In his own ground.

Whose herds with milk, whose fields with bread,
Whose flocks supply him with attire;
Whose trees in summer yield him shade,
    In winter fire.

Blest, who can unconcern'dly find
Hours, days, and years, slide soft away
In health of body, peace of mind,
    Quiet by day.

Sound sleep by night; study and ease
Together mix'd, sweet recreation,
And innocence, which most does please
    Without meditation.

Thus let me live, unseen, unknown;
Thus unlamented let me die;
Steal from the world, and not a stone
    Tell where I lie.

In this poem the two boldest images are the one of trees *yielding* shade and the one of stone *telling*. In neither case is the verb strained beyond immediate apprehension; in each case the metaphor is surrounded with a context which tends to limit, not to extend, the ramifications of Fancy or imaginative perception. And it will be noticed that the third and fourth stanzas, particularly, are given almost entirely in abstract terms.[*]

The next quotation is from stanzas 3-4 and 8-10 of Collins' "Ode to Evening":

---

[*] The statement is intended in a purely descriptive, not a prejudicial, sense; the place of abstract statement in English poetry is considerable and honorable, as reference to a good many fine poems will demonstrate.

Now air is hush'd, save where the weak-eyed bat
With short shrill shriek flits by on leathern wing,
    Or where the beetle winds
    His small but sullen horn,

As ofte he rises midst the twilight path,
Against the pilgrim borne in heedless hum, . . .

Then let me rove some wild and heathy scene;
Or find some ruin midst its dreary dells,
    Whose walls more awful nod
    By thy religious gleams.

Or, if chill blustering winds or driving rain
Prevent my willing feet, be mine the hut
    That, from the mountain's side,
    Views wilds and swelling floods.

And hamlets brown, and dim-discover'd spires;
And hears their simple bell; and marks o'er all
    They dewy fingers draw
    The gradual dusky veil.

Here the use of metaphor is confined almost entirely to the first stanza quoted, the reference to a *leathern* wing and to the beetle *winding* his *horn*. The latter had echoes of a classical antecedent, and the former is mainly descriptive in character. It will be found that the other images—and there are a good many— are not generally metaphorical, linking somewhat unlike things together in the manner of Fancy, but are instead descriptive. And these descriptive images are but once-removed from the abstract argument which lies immediately behind them.

The revolt against the eighteenth-century mode is commonly designated the struggle of art against science. The Romantics thought that poetry had become too abstract, too much like science. Blake raged against Newton and other scientists; one of the main problems of the Romantic critics was that of the difference between arts and science. Consequently, though much of the poetry of the nineteenth-century continued to be abstract, the business of poetry was felt to be the handling of feelings and emotions as distinct from thought. Bateson's remark about the Victorian poets can be applied to the Romantics with the reservation only that during the Victorian period the issues of the earlier period had become sharpened and more clearly realized: "The Victorians spoke two languages, reflecting the divided aims and origins of their civilization: a language of the heart, and a language of the head." And from the emphasis upon the emotional side of the dichotomy came the kind of criticism called "impressionistic," based on the notion that the aesthetic experience is a purely subjective and mainly emotional one which can be discussed by the critic only impressionistically.

Within these terms, the Romantic revolt was not a radically revolutionary movement. It continued the same dichotomy, but it threw emphasis away from Judgment to Fancy. Nor did the texture of the poetry change radically during the Romantic period. There was more regard for imagery than during the eighteenth century, but the imagery was most often descriptive and in the form of simile rather than metaphor (for example, the first half of Shelley's "To a Skylark"). Many poems have abstract language, a poetry of statement, throughout; and many others have passages essentially abstract in language (for example, the last stanzas of Shelley's "To a Skylark"). Wordsworth is not representative of all the poets of the period, but his practice indicates the general trend. The following is the opening of "Lines Composed a Few Miles above Tintern Abbey":

> Five years have past; five summers, with the length
> Of five long winters! and again I hear
> These waters, rolling from their mountain-springs
> With a soft inland murmur.—Once again
> Do I behold these steep and lofty cliffs,
> That on a wild secluded scene impress
> Thoughts of more deep seclusion; and connect
> The landscape with the quiet of the sky.
> The day is come when I again repose
> Here, under this dark sycamore, and view
> These plots of cottage-ground, these orchard-tufts,
> Which at this season, with their unripe fruits,
> Are clad in one green hue, and lose themselves
> 'Mid groves and copses.

The concreteness here, the movement away from purely abstract thought, is in terms of descriptive imagery, not the imaginative metaphor.

Now just as subjective Idealism can be reduced to materialism, so can the idealism of art be reduced to a mechanistic basis. The aesthetic experience is purely personal and subjective and a matter of emotional impressions; but, as Chrisopher Caudwell comments in *Illusion and Reality*, "ultimately the aesthetic emotion is reduced to coenaesthesia and this in turn is the excitation of certain nerves." We arrive at a purely biological basis for the aesthetic emotion.

Coleridge gives us a taste of what is to come when he divides Hobbes' faculty of Fancy into Imagination and Fancy. Under the influence of German Idealism, he holds for Imagination the ability of the Kantian category, "the living power and prime agent of all human perception, and as a repetition in the finite mind of the eternal act of creation in the infinite *I Am*." Wordsworth also describes this "innate idea" in the eighth book of "The Prelude":

> I had my face turned toward the truth, began
> With an advantage furnished by that kind
> Of prepossession, without which the soul
> Receives no knowledge that can bring forth good.
> No genuine insight ever comes to her.

Coleridge says:

> Fancy, on the contrary, has no other counters to play with but fixities and definites. The Fancy is indeed no other than a mode of memory emancipated from the order of time and space; and blended with, and modified by, that empirical phenomenon of the will, which we express by the word choice. But, equally with the ordinary memory, it must receive all its materials ready made from the law of association.

Fancy which is the main material of poetry in the new subjectivism, proceeds by the "law of association." And association has become during the last fifty years the dominant method of poetry. Yeats remarks in his introduction to *The Oxford Book of Modern Verse*, "Nature, steel-bound and stone-built in the nineteenth century, became a flux where man drowned or swam; the moment had come for some poetry to cry 'the flux is in my own mind.'" Poe (with his associational method for the construction of the poem, that is, if one would create the strongest impression, he would write of the death of a beautiful woman, and so on), the French Symbolists, Eliot, Pound, and dozens of others abandoned the logical structure for the poem. Their poems are composed of a progression of associated images.

The beginnings can be seen in Poe. Here is the first stanza of "The Sleeper":

At midnight, in the month of June,
I stand beneath the mystic moon.
An opiate vapor, dewy, dim,
Exhales from out her golden rim,
And, softly dripping, drop by drop,
Upon the quiet mountain top,
Steals drowsily and musically
Into the universal valley.
The rosemary nods upon the grave;
The lily lolls upon the wave;
Wrapping the fog about its breast,
The ruin moulders into rest;
Looking like Lehte, see! the lake

> A conscious slumber seems to take.
> And would not, for the world, awake.
> All Beauty sleeps!—and lo! where lies
> Irene, with her Destinies!

Here is almost a complete catalog of items which Poe associated with the emotion he most delighted in, an indistinct, nearly objectless grief and sadness: here are the midnight, the fog, the mountain, "universal valley," the grave, the mouldering ruin, the lake, death. All these are linked together (but apparently within the framework of an objective description of a natural scene) for their grief-provoking associations. The movement from the rosemary on the grave to the lily on the wave surely is pure association: the water has not been mentioned before, and, naturalistically speaking, it must come in as a result of that association, since the scene is apparently a "mountain top," hardly the expected place for a lake.

And here are two sections from Eliot's "The Love Song of J. Alfred Prufrock," one of Eliot's minor poems but still showing his developed method, modified later in "The Wasteland" and elsewhere mainly by an increased complexity and obscurity of association:

> Let us go, through certain half-deserted streets,
> The muttering retreats
> Of restless nights in one-night cheap hotels
> And sawdust restaurants with oyster-shells:
> Streets that follow like a tedious argument
> Of insidious intent
> To lead you to an overwhelming question . . . .

> Oh, do not ask, "What is it?"
> Let us go to make our visit....
>
> I grow old .... I grow old ....
> I shall wear the bottoms of my trousers rolled.
>
> Shall I part my hair behind? Do I dare to eat a peach?
> I shall wear white flannel trousers, and walk upon the
>   beach.
> I have heard the mermaid singing, each to each.

In the first section, given the "half-deserted streets," the association brings up the "one-night cheap hotels," "sawdust restaurants with oyster-shells," the "tedious argument of insidious intent." And the leap from the "overwhelming question" to the meager present purpose is entirely associational. In the second passage quoted, there are seven association leaps made in five lines, from growing old, to "the bottoms of my trousers rolled," to the inane question about parting the hair behind, to the equally inane question about eating a peach (made more important, within the purpose of the poem, however, by the word *dare*), to the white flannel trousers, to the beach, to the mermaids, to the singing of the mermaids "each to each," that is, excluding the speaker.

Even the Imagist poets are far removed from this practice, for their method depends upon an association, largely private to the author, between some subjective feeling and some object in the external world. Free verse became much used, too, for it did not require the intellectual organization of the standard forms; and its metrical perception is a vague one between cadences—rise and fall of sounds in the line—and subjective feelings. A single, slight example of the Imagist method is "The Skaters" by John Gould Fletcher:

> Black swallows swooping or gliding
> In a flurry of entrangled loops and curves;
> The skaters skim over the frozen river.
> And the grinding click of their skates as they
>   impinge upon the surface,
> Is like the brushing together of thin wing-tips of silver.

Here, we take it, the associations among the skaters and swallows, click of skates, wing-tips, and silver stand in Fletcher's emotion for a certain feeling; only a very similar set of associations in the reader would guarantee a similar emotional response.

There is still one step more to be indicated. Fancy, interpreted by Coleridge and most recent poets, is non-rational. As such it is subconscious in its workings, beyond control of the mind, biological and automatic. Yet in the continued opposition to Judgment or Reason, Fancy is the material of poetry. Here may be applied the argument of Kenneth Burke in his essay "Four Master Tropes" in the Autumn, 1941, issue of *The Kenyon Review*:

> For relativism sees everything in but one set of terms—and since there are endless other terms in which things could be seen, the irony of the monologue that makes everything in its image would be in this ratio: the greater

the absolutism of the statements, the greater the *subjectivity* and *relativity* in the position of the agent making the statements.

So we find the last step in the method of subjectivism is surrealism, the most absolute subjectivism because, sometimes called "automatic writing," it is the attempt to put down into words, without regard for later control or molding into form, the subconscious workings of the mind as tapped through dream or revery. The possibility of a completely surrealist method seems slight, since the subconscious does not work exclusively with words, and since translating the workings of the subconscious into words apparently demands at least some slight conscious control. Thus, almost any poet quoted as an example of a surrealist writer could reply that his method was not true surrealism. Charles Henri Ford seems to be moving rather clearly in the surrealist direction, however, and I shall quote a short poem from his book *The Overturned Lake*:

> January wraps up the wound of his arm,
> January, thieving as a boy, hides the jewel,
> sunset, bright bleeding equation.
>
> Day has written itself out, a giveaway, a poem
> that balks like a horse before the ditch of night.
>
> Tomorrow, the gash will be an eye:
> a drop of dew will travel up his cheek,
> like a tear that has changed its mind.

I cannot pretend to an adequate, to more than a very personal and wavering, exegesis of this poem. If the method is really associational, the poet has skipped several steps in almost every association, as between *sunset* and *equation*. The method seems rather to be an attempt at capturing the great leaps in subconscious association and workings.

Thus a change in philosophy has brought many changes to poetry and, if subjective Idealism be followed to its ultimate implications, has left the poet the role only of recorder of the subconscious. By no means have all poets followed the trend very thoroughly; but the conception of the Romantics that poetry is mainly concerned with emotion and feeling as opposed to thought has been almost universally held for a century, the use of the associational method is only less widespread among recent poets, and surrealism has come to be considered seriously by a large public. One may cry "Stop!" but if this discussion has truth in it, the trend is not merely an arbitrary choice on the part of the poets. A radical change in poetic method could only follow a radical change in philosophy away from subjectivism. The arguments about such a change in philosophy rest a long way outside the purposes of this essay.

II
ON CRITICAL THEORY

A READING OF THE
ROMANTIC ODES

1953

The gradual shifting of the attention of scholarly study of literature which has been going on for at least two decades has greatly altered the landscape to which we attend in the history of English poetry. Once the peaks of the great Romantics seemed gigantic and near at hand; then they diminished to very small hills as we saw overtopping them the numerous great of the Renaissance. There has ever been a tendency, which I believe Mr. Cleanth Brooks has stated most forcefully, to read the history as if the line of direct descent moved from the Renaissance in England over to the Continent with the French Symbolists and finally returned to the English language with Pound, Eliot, and many of the moderns. It is a view I cannot hold, for I think that the moderns thus mentioned are direct descendants of the Romantics instead of the Renaissance. More recently still—sometimes I think because the modern methods of study have seemed to develop instruments which need to be put alongside the poetry of all ages—there has been an effort to reread many of the Romantics. Unfortunately, I think that the result is most often to assess that poetry by the literary strategies, as Mr.

Kenneth Burke would call them, of the great Renaissance poetry, and to dismiss what is not thus subsumed into the body of strategic poetry. The result does not seem to me to do justice either to our methods or to the poetry involved.

One cannot turn from attentive reading of the Renaissance poets at their best to the whole nineteenth-century without feeling that he has turned from a green, well-tended, vegetative field to an untended desert; the beauties of the desert are real, although they are likely to be minute and startling by contrasts. Our own difficulty in this matter is that the desert extends historically into our own day and provides much of the environment of our own vision.

What I propose to do, for this brief paper, is to try to indicate the reading to which I have attained in the Romantics after chief preoccupation with Renaissance and modern poetry and after working cooperatively with students in readings when I taught the Romantic period rather recently. And I have tried to state beforehand my own inadequacies for reading this poetry.

The body of great poetry by the Romantics is probably not very extensive, being chiefly Coleridge's *Mariner,* one ode each by Wordsworth and Shelley, and four by Keats, two or three other narrative poems, and then a good-sized handful of brief poems from the entire group. For my purposes here I shall concentrate on the odes, since it seems to me that they are remarkably unified and, with the exception of the *Mariner*, the chief touchstones of these poets.

Brief quotations can serve to demonstrate something about what happened in this literary history I have mentioned. At hand I have Donne's "The Cannonization" in which I find these lines:

> Call us what you will, we are made such by love;
>   Call her one, me another flie,
> We'are Tapers too, and at our own cost die,
>   And we in us find the 'Eagle and the Dove.
>   The Phoenix riddle hath more wit
>   By us, we two being one, are it.
>   So to one neutral thing both sexes fit,
>   We die and rise the same, and prove
>   Mysterious by this love.

Then we can reflect that the Romantics had great difficulty with the love poem, that Keats yearned, apparently, for some righteous conception of physical love and did not attain it, and that the chief insight of the Romantic love poem is the emotive one of pathos, for beauty lost. And we can turn to another poem, which, like Donne's, has some notion of "oneness" in it—a poem by E. E. Cummings, one of the more skillful love poets of our time, to read:

> we're anything brighter than even the sun
> (we're everything greater
>   than books
> might mean)
> we're everything more than believe

       (with a spin
    leap
    alive we're alive)
    we're wonderful one times one

And we are beset with a frightening feeling of diminution, of lessening of intellectual and emotive power. It is this context that we must keep in mind in reading the Romantics. Something had happened between the Renaissance and them to cause a great diminution in the ability with which the poet could bite and chew. We can try to account for this diminution in many ways, but I shan't try it here. We can also speak most kindly and say that the needs and interests of men had changed in history; this would be, surely, a lie in our teeth. The lessening can be indicated, I think, by the following: the great theme of the Renaissance—the almost exclusive theme of the most ambitious works—is the epistemological one, the theory of knowledge, the problem of knowledge. With various subspecies of the theme—such as the ethical problem of right action in private and public affairs, or the problem of man's relationships with God—once can span almost the entire poetry of the Renaissance. The theme of the Romantic odes, I think, is much narrower—it is the aesthetic one, or chiefly the problem of the imagintion. Further, it is the problem of the imagination treated under the supposition that the imagination is irrational. Coleridge's are not the only poems of this period which use irrational procedures; I believe that the basic structure of each of the great odes is associational, that the characteristic structure of the Pound and Eliot poem is in these poems, too.

The first poem to consider is Wordsworth's great "Ode to Intimations of Immortality." Mr. Brooks has a great deal to aid us in our effort to understand the poem. It is as if he took quite seriously the three-line prologue:

> The Child is father to the Man:
> And I could wish my days to be
> Bound each to each by natural piety.

Despite the difficulty of those three lines, they are probably more understandable than the poem itself. One can only wonder, at the start, why the usual procedures of the man fathering the child and of days being linked by time are being reversed, and seek the answer in the poem. And there we find three motifs trying to exist more or less side-by-side, surely not at all fused into one theme.

The first motif is found in the considerable imagery of light. As Mr. Brooks points out, we do not find in the poem a simple relationship of light contrasted with darkness, morning and day with night; rather, there are two kinds of light. One kind of light is associated with birth: "The sunshine is a glorious birth," "Trailing clouds of glory do we come from God, who is our home," "the fountainlight of all our day," "a master-light of all our seeing," that light which makes the child an "Eye among the blind." The other light is the "light of common day" into which we die. This latter light is probably that which informs Nature, which the poem gives a bountiful power of its own: "Earth fills her lap with pleasures of her own. Yearnings she hath in her own natural kind."

The second motif is that of the dream, also indicated in such terms as "glory" and "vision": "That there hath past away a glory from the earth," "Whither is fled, the visionary gleam: Where is it now, the glory and the dream?" Other images for this state are: "That, deaf and silent, read'st the eternal deep, Haunted for ever by the eternal mind," "those first affections, those shadowy recollections, Which, be they what they may, Are yet the fountain-light of all our day, Are yet a master-light of all our seeing," "moments in the being Of the eternal Silence: truths that wake To perish never." These two motifs have strange reversals or ironies, similar to those of the prologue. I am not sure that Mr. Brooks is justified in calling them paradoxes, however. It is true that reality and unreality, learning and forgetting, can change places; but it is difficult to feel that these tensions in perception are ever subsumed in one fusion. The statement seems to be that Nature has a great quality of light, perhaps we can say even of truth and vision; the soul of man, placed on earth, brings to Nature a somewhat alien quality—it, too, has light, but a light which is more visionary, more glorious, than the light of Nature, which gradually imprisons man and his vision. His own glorious vision gradually diminishes until man is not certain of its quality or truth: he can only call it a dream and wonder where it now resides: "Where is it now, the glory and the dream?" This recalls the last words of Keats's "Ode to a Nightingale," "Do I wake or sleep?"—that is, what is reality, the imaginative act or a "light of common day"?

Thus we come to the third motif of the poem: It seems that Wordsworth's poem cannot assert the full significance of the imaginative power or visionary dream, which is knowable, if at all, only to the child, that is, innately and instinctively; man, who finds that there has "past away a glory from the earth," has fallen into Nature, as it were, and cannot "bring back the hour Of splendor in the grass, of glory in the flower." Yet his position is doubly difficult because Nature, which can be immediately apprehended, participates in some level in the great light and has a kindly movement which enmeshes yet nourishes man. Man, because of his natural heart, finds much there: solace, a primal sympathy, the philosophic mind, a slight echo of the imagination. The imaginative act is not fully possible; but in Nature and, presumably, in the recollection of his own feelings, man has a partial basis for the use of his faculties. This position, if it can be asserted from the poem, is not so strange, if we think of much Christian imagery of the fall from grace; yet Wordsworth has given it a non-Christian statement and feeling which is not capable of fusing the motifs into a single thematic apprehension.

The Ode, in a far-fetched comparison, has a greater control of its associations and movements than has Eliot's *Wasteland*, although a strategy not too distant from that poem; it does not realize thematic unity but comes closer than does the Eliot poem; and I think that by its narrow improvement in strategy and in thematic statement—and also for some fine passages of verse which Eliot's practice hardly equals—it is that much the greater poem. Like the Eliot poem, it is partly wonderful for fragmentary phrasings, some of which I have quoted.

I must confess that "Ode to the West Wind" is one of the few poems by Shelley for which I have any sympathy. It is a vastly imperfect poem, imperfect by its lack of true imaginative vigor: for although the poem indicates a desire for self-immolation in the forces of nature, the reason seems anything but sacrificial, indeed, seems quite personal and selfish—that is, that the poet is world-weary and in pain and pleads that his words be scattered fruitfully in the vast imaginative breath of nature. The poem is much easier to understand than any of the other odes being considered. The basic apprehension of the poem is that destruction is in the hands, to borrow the words of Edwin Arlington Robinson, of "laws That have creation in their keeping." The imaginative act, then, is to subject oneself to that great force which is at once destructive and creative. The conception is not unfamiliar to us; indeed, it has been said a good many times since Shelley and is similar to Emerson's doctrine of the oversoul. One may have simple faith in this immolation of the self, as indicated by the last line: "If Winter comes, can Spring be far behind?" I presume that this says, we can have faith that, if we dissolve ourselves, we shall also automatically partake of birth, as well.

I shall not go into any more detailed reading of the poem, but I should like to pause over a few aspects of the verse. First, the poem is again fragmentary. Such lines as "Thou, from whose unseen presence the leaves dead, Are driven" show a great power with verse methods, but they are only occasional. Second, the poem seems remarkably modern: it recalls the central insight of he surrealists, who believe that immolation, even more, degradation, is essential to insight; it recalls the desire for self-destruction to the forces of nature found in such writers as D. H. Lawrence and Hart Crane. Finally, I want to contrast such Shelley lines as "Scatter, as from an unextinguished hearth Ashes and sparks, my words among mankind!" with the greater vigor and feeling of Crane's lines from "Praise for an Urn": "Scatter these well-meant idioms Into the smoky spring that fills The suburbs, where they will be lost. They are no trophies of the sun." And to contrast the simple, narrow faith of the last line of Shelley's poem, "If Winter comes, can Spring be far behind?" with the much more complex faith indicated in the last line of Crane's "Voyages II": "The seal's wide spindrift gaze toward paradise." "Ode to the West Wind" is a poem of considerable power, particularly in fragments; it names an imaginative act from which it largely withdraws; and it is a weak statement of the theme in comparison with the energetic treatment of the same theme in such a poet as Hart Crane.

Moving to Keats is a considerable relief. But the transition is easy. Shelley said of the west wind, "The tumult of thy mighty harmonies Will take from both a deep, autumnal tone, Sweet though in sadness." It is a feeling toward the problem of the imagination, not a close thematic treatment of the problem, which we will most richly find in the Keats odes; and feeling is richly and precisely stated within the essentially scenic strategy of his language, and the feeling, at its best, is true and powerful.

Keats has the dubious honor of being the historic poet about whom we know most concerning the process of his thinking and creative activity. I am aware that some of the problems of his verse can seem to be solved by what we know outside the verse. For example, the famous problem of the "Beauty is truth, truth beauty" statement. We know that Keats had achieved a statement that, for him, whatever the emotions strongly assert, was truth; thus, by an attack upon the Grecian urn statement with this knowledge, we may try to interpret the statement as meaning something close to tautology; beauty, that is, strong emotion, is equivalent to truth. Mr. T. S. Eliot has helped us by his insight that Keats's verse was never quite able to reach the maturity of thought which he achieved in his letters. The trouble is that the words have great disparity and they are, as Mr. Allen Tate feels about one of the statements in "Ode to a Nightingale," a little like asserting that A=B when we find that the assigned values of A & B are respectively 1 and 3.

The problem of this urn statement has been variously debated. Mr. Burke makes out an interesting dialectical arrangement for it; Mr. Brooks would say that we don't have to put it to the test of truth falsity since we can provide it the forgiveness of a dramatic context in which it is really the assertion of a character, the urn, and is not a thematic position of a poem. The trouble with these accounts, as I have already said, is that they are the ingenuities of Mr. Burke and Mr. Brooks and are not the ingenuities of the poet Keats.

My own reading of the "Ode on a Grecian Urn" would coincide closely with what I presume Mr. Tate's to be. His argument runs something like this: He quotes Robert Bridges as saying, "Keats's art is primarily objective and pictorial, and whatever other qualities it has are as it were added on to things as perceived." The essential problem, then is, what does Keats add on to things as perceived? And Mr. Tate replies, "This affirmation of life through death is the element that Keats adds on to things as perceived." But this life-in-death is presented pictorially and statically, not under the order and responsibility of time. My own phrasing would be that Keats presents the essential paradox of the imaginative act, that is, its ability to arrest time in a moment of vision, but the vision is, by its arresting, a static vision, that is, a dead vision.

Of this poem we might say what Mr. Tate says of the "Ode to a Nightingale," that it is "an emblem of one limit of our experience: the impossibility of synthesizing, in the order of experience, the antinomy of the ideal and the real." Keats can point to the problem of imagination, but he cannot handle it thematically. Another fine poem of similar kind, I wish to remark in passing, is the poem called "Medusa" by Louise Bogan. Miss Bogan stops on the problem about where Keats would have been if he had not written the last stanza of his "Ode on a Grecian Urn": my own thought is that he might well have stopped there, for the final stanza does not complete any acceptable insight.

In its method, "Ode to a Nightingale" is more modern—we recognize the dense associational structure.

The problem is posed again, more clearly than in the urn poem; although the answer is not here, either, the poem moves more carefully and humanly into the problem and is a greater poem, I should judge, by a considerable degree. The management of stanzaic and verse structure is of the first order, except for the third stanza, which shows no way of comprehending mundane experience: and the detail is significant. The movement of the poem, you will recall, is, first, a projection of the poet into the song of the bird, indeed, into an imaginative, shadowy, unreal land where song must live (not the nature of Wordsworth, certainly); after a brief moment of self-pity that the poet must live in a more mundane world, this imaginative world is further projected and is then rounded out with the desire for dissolution, since only death seems to have the possibility of attaining that land; this is followed by the assertion, which remains assertion, that song is immortal, that the real bird which sings and which we know to be mortal is really immortal, and then, finally, the awakening from the vision to the question "Do I wake or sleep?" The poet cannot attain a symbolism through which he may know the common and the ideal reality in a single imaginative act. Like the poem on the urn, discounting its last stanza, the nightingale ode wonderfully prefigures the problem but uses for the problem only some rather vague notions that life-death-love are somehow one. Indeed, the only answer Keats has, as I have indicated, is this vague notion; but he greatly achieves not only a statement of the problem but also an aura of important feeling in response.

"Ode to Psyche" seems to me too filled with rather meaningless detail, but the feeling at the end, in the face of what Keats left as the unanswerable problem, is very fine:

> Who, breeding flowers, will never breed the same:
> And there shall be for thee all soft delight
>   That shadowy thought can win,
> A bright torch, and a casement ope at night,
>   To let the warm Love in!

Nearly the final word of Keats on the problem is "Ode on Melancholy." It is almost a frank admission of inability to penetrate the problem, but it is a rich tinkering with the feelings he found appropriate. They are the feelings also found, less precisely stated, in the Wordsworth and Shelley odes:

> Ay, in the very temple of Delight
>   Veil'd Melancholy has her sovran shrine.

The "Ode on Melancholy" has both the auditory energy and the pomposity that Keats picked up from his last great teacher, Milton, but I think that its virtues are those we are nowadays likely to overloook: the sort of striking of a pose that in the face of the unknowable one might still valiantly wish to be "among her cloudy trophies hung."

DEFOE AND THE ART OF FICTION
Western Humanities Review, Spring, 1950

The literary critics of our time believe that they are prepared—probably better than the critics of any other time—to come to terms with a poem. But these critics have only recently turned to fiction and have done so with less assurance. The assurance is less, I believe, partly because of the newness of the concern but more because of the apparent complexity of the problem. A novel, for example, is commonly long, and to deal with it closely, rather than impressionistically, would seem to require a lengthy discussion; it is also commonly made up of many shifting relationships among characters and situations.

The novel is spectacular: it is the newest of the great literary forms and only a little more than two centuries old. It has risen rapidly to complete dominance, and the presses spew forth many more than a thousand tomes each year.

I propose that in the problem of building a fruitful criticism of the novel a particularly helpful step would be to examine the novel at its historical beginning. For, contrary to poetry and the theater, whose origins are outside our history, the novel is a growth of our own well documented culture. And I have chosen to begin briefly with Daniel Defoe. I am quite aware that we could dispute for hours concerning what piece of writing to call the first novel *per se* and also that many would think Defoe not a novelist at all. Yet the frequent claim for Richardson and *Pamela* is surely placed too late, since twenty years before, Defoe had written full-bloom fiction of novel length and constructed something in addition to a story. And whatever we may call the narratives before Defoe's, we recognize that a new treatment of narrative is to be found in Defoe's work.

I

A glance at Defoe, the man, will help us see what we find in the art form of the novel. Defoe, the man, survived seventy years one of the most vigorous lives known to biographers. His vigor he greatly needed, for his seventy years were beset with as many setbacks as successes. Pilloried, several times imprisoned, harried most of his life by creditors, known as a man with fertile schemes most of which failed, attacked by nearly everyone who could find a voice, left during many of his last months with little contact with his family and, probably, the defection of his oldest son—these are part of a most remarkable record of difficulties. Vigor and energy, then, are the strongest impressions one first gets of the man Defoe.

These impressions are to be followed by ever greater ones—amazement at the multitudinous activities in which he engaged with marked success. In our time we are accustomed to rather rigid definition of roles —and important reputations are usually made within single roles. But Defoe performed many. He was not chameleon. He lived in a time such that he has an important role in many histories—as economist, adviser to governments, secret service agent and spy, merchant and trader, reporter and journalist, commentator on all affairs from manners to matters of state, essayist and opinion-maker, writer of stories and novels. The novels came late in Defoe's life, and the biographical problem, so far as the novels are concerned, is to place that writing in relationship with the other activities of Defoe.

Defoe's career was a single career, although, it is true, a ragged career. He did not have the strength of purpose or the settled direction of a Milton, who could interrupt his career as a poet to become a great political essayist and Latin Secretary, and then return when this was done to reach the great goals he had set for himself many years earlier. But Milton and Marvell, Fielding and Sterne, and many others in our modern culture, which has no safe home for the artist, demonstrate that accomplishment in other fields can be joined with great accomplishment in art. Defoe's is remarkable not for the fact of diversity of accomplishment, but for the extremity of that diversity.

The career of a Milton or another literary artist, however, hardly offers the appropriate parallel insight into the life of Defoe. Rather, he was more like

Robinson Crusoe—and like many another isolated individual of the pioneer sort. Like the pioneer, he ventured constantly and had to make his own bed out of what he had at hand, and then lie in it. Defore was not, in fact, a tremendously isolated individual, but after the success of *Robinson Crusoe* it is revealing that Defoe claimed the story to be essentially, if allegorically, his own story.

Defoe was isolated and something of the lonely pioneer in ways which he only dimly saw or acknowledged. For at least one generation before him, during his own lifetime, and for two or three generations after him, England was going through one of the great modern revolutions. Much less bloody than the revolutions to come in other countries, this revolution was to see established in England the dominance of the middle class and its culture. Defoe preeminently was middle class, and probably no man, in the diversity of changes which such a revolution would dictate, had more than Defoe to do with furthering that revolution and with leading it to self-consciousness in his own clear, if non-systematic, thinking.

Defoe had reason to think that his career was something like Crusoe's. In all the bickerings, contests, difficulties of his life, he could not clearly see the large contest embodied in his efforts. It was to pioneer a new world. He could not envisage it; he did not have vision or spiritual strength or even a coarse poetic fancy; his sustenance came from the thin hind teat. Rather, he battled vigorously and importantly under the lifted flags of a new class striding forward. These flags were Dissent, Trade, and Adventure.

Each of these may be considered briefly. Dissent had long been joined with the other ideas of the rising bourgeoisie—with the individual conscience, with democracy, with an economy of individual aggression and capital. Defoe had these in the center of his concern. Robinson Crusoe was the third son in a middle class family; Moll Flanders was the underprivileged and unprotected woman who so much concerned the author. Each was solitary, as indeed was Defoe much of the time. Each could "get ahead" financially by his wits and rise and fall according to his guesses and his application of what providence put before him. Each was a living democrat, the underdog made important but not given the vanity of class, race, or nationality. Crusoe particularly, although a dissenter thrown among Papists, found that many Papists were more Christian than the Protestants; that the hated Spanish frequently bred up better men than many an Englishman. Crusoe despised the Orient but mainly for economic reasons; those poor people did not enjoy the civilizing and cosmopolitan influence of Trade such as Europe enjoyed.

To Defoe, Adventure and Trade must have been much the same thing. To the readers of his day the adventures of Moll must have been more breath-taking than they are to the reader today, for her adventures had only one pattern—that of the unprotected strumpet who could control the economy of nearly every action she made, who was wise in the knowledge of goods and money and could buy and sell, even herself, at a good bargain. Her bargains are indeed breath-taking and constitute the dozens of crises in her life.

But Trade, as Defoe argued so well, led to international commerce, and international commerce was a physical adventure, truly, in his time. Crusoe had the itching feet and the restlessness we recognize in the capitalist ever since, and he launched himself upon the sea both as tradesman and adventurer; without the trade there had been little adventure, and the adventure came with the commerce of the day— the international rivalries, the contact with savages in all parts of the world who were to be civilized by the blessings of European culture whose center, as it touched them, was exacting Trade.

II

Thus in the hands of Defoe the novel was launched as the great art form contributed to literature by the middle class. When Defoe turned to fiction, he had a purpose. He was not the first to write fiction; indeed, in the preface to Moll Flanders he fears that his story will be neglected in a world "so taken up of late with novels and romances," or, as we would probably call them, memoirs, tales, narratives. Perhaps this is only a gesture from Defoe, for the narrative of a life was tremendously popular in his day and he made use of a form whose readers were apparently omniverous, as they are today. But although he made use of a form much written, he added the first and central ingredient which distinguishes the art of fiction from any other telling of tales—and that is theme, the notion that story is a means of projecting an idea, not as conceptual and abstract, but as dramatic in movement of character and situation.

Defoe made the narrative thematic and thus made the basis for an art of fiction. But his contribution was much more than this—he used the great theme, almost the only important theme, of modern fiction.

One can argue this theme either from the position of the bourgeoisie or from the novels themselves.

The middle class had a particular view of man to project. The view incorporated man as individual conscience. Man was then isolated and alone, in his essence, even in his relationship with his God. And society was a collection of such individual consciences. They met in a common arena in which the most important problem was economic. One could not satisfy his wants entirely by himself; even Crusoe could not do that. So, man must satisfy them through trade, the process by which he endeavored to satisfy his needs and wants through giving and taking with others; he who was better than his fellows at taking than at giving was better off in the process. Through trade man could have his cake and eat it, too; that is, he could remain essentially alone and committed to the least, but at the same time he could enjoy the satisfaction of his needs possible only in a diverse society. Man's isolation, the quality and degree of his commitment to society, the moral choice involved in balancing between anarchism and too much involvement—these produced the fundamental characters and the basic theme for the art of fiction to our day.

Defoe had all these central to his novels. With the history of a subsequent literature now long behind us, we talk of it in terms which Defoe could not have thought of, but useful terms in indicating the direction of Defoe's thinking. Norman Nicholson in a manuscript soon to be published upon the novels of H. G. Wells speaks of the great revolt of Rousseau's

> cult of the Natural Man and the Noble Savage, whose obvious Utopia was a South Sea Island, deserted or inhabited only by primitive tribes. The myth for Rosseau's dream was supplied by the last man from whom you might have expected it; the practical-minded, matter-of-fact, nonconformist Englishman, Daniel Defoe. Robinson Crusoe offers nearly all the requirements of a Rosseau Utopia—solitude, the sea, an island where life is reduced to the elementals. It offers the struggle with nature, closeness to the soil, closeness also to animals, and lastly, in Man Friday, the Savage himself—not entirely noble, but potentially so. The reduction of society to a unit of one, and the absence of women . . . were all escapes from the complications of civilized life. But Robinson Crusoe offered more than this. It offered Crusoe's piety and protestantism,

thereby making the book acceptable to many who would never have allowed themselves to approve of the naked primitive. Moreover, by a final touch of irony, Defoe combined his story of escape with the very virtue preached in the world from which he was escaping, and Crusoe became a hero of individualism, the economic man, champion of hard work, puritanism, enterprise and Self-Help.

Subsequent history gives us another advantage over Defoe. The middle class has worked out its destiny sufficiently that now we are quite aware of the tensions, ironies, difficulties in its view of man. Oddly enough, and I count this one quality of the greatness of Defoe's best fiction, Defoe was so honest to the thinking of his characters and their way of life that those tensions are present in his work. Defoe sketched the way of life at its begining; we can look at it with much experience as it possibly nears its end or faces considerable change. Defoe, of course, would not have recognized all the potentialities of these tensions, and we have a situation fairly common in literature, the ability to read a work with more subtlety and richness than could the author himself. In this case the subtleties and richnesses are not betrayals of the work but, instead, a testimony to the ability of the writer to get a way of life into his work.

Norman Nicholson's comments quoted above indicate one such irony in Robinson Crusoe—that Crusoe prefigured the Natural Man escaped from the damage of society but, still, prefiguring also the essential qualities of that society from which he had escaped.

Defoe, I am sure, intended no irony; he thought that Natural man and Economic man were the same man. Yet he did not in the novel betray the potential difficulties. Crusoe, quite honestly, is tied to a strange but common wrack; when he is home for two days he is restless to be gone, and when he is gone he is restless to be home again; and he cannot understand, however much he prays to be rid of it, this compulsion of his, which is, perhaps, the assumed and unexplained compulsion of the middle class. Further, Crusoe knows that he would have starved, probably not even able to live as a savage, without the providence of the wrecked ship to rifle, with its interesting store of Occidental artifacts. When he finds another man, he is joyous and no longer alone, although with that man he can act the part both of master and of helper. Crusoe's life on the island was no more idyllic than his life was elsewhere; the adventure of the isolated man was technically successful but in more important ways unsuccessful. And when the island finally was shaped presumably to the needs of man, that is, to provide the advantage of primitivism tempered with civilization, neither Crusoe nor anyone else wanted to remain there long.

More subtly psychological are the tensions for Moll Flanders. John Peale Bishop outlined many of them aptly in an essay entitled "Moll Flanders' Way."

> Moll Flanders is a professional thief, and is no more honest in the Shakespearean sense of the word than in ours. And

yet there is no quality by which she so profoundly impresses us as by her honesty. She does not deceive herself; she deceives us only in so far as we want to be deceived. Her hypocrisy is a concession to the society in which she found herself in the England of the seventeenth century. It is perhaps also a concession to existence.

And further,

> . . . with the rise of the middle class what is left is . . . the disparity between what is willed and what is done. There is scarcely a heroine of the novel, from Moll Flanders on, who is not in need of a great deal of extenuation. . . . It is precisely the greatness of the novel that it has been able to do this: that, in circumstances so small that they have lost the possibility of tragedy, it has been able to find tragic possibilities not in what was done, but in the failure of accomplishment, that, working with a minor scale, it has yet been able to measure simultaneously the meanness of action and the essential greatness of the human soul.

III

In addition to those claims, there is at least one other claim to be made for a critical study of Defoe's use of the novel. This claim concerns a technical matter, but surely the central technical problem in fiction. That central problem is what I choose to call, for want of a better term, commitment to the imaginative act in fiction. It involves the commitment of the author to the notion that what he has to say of a way of life, that his theme, can be stated and realized not in abstractions, not directly from the writer at all, as in the writing of opinion and the essay, but can be completely realized in dramatic situation and scene. There is more than one way of achieving this "commitment to the imaginative act in fiction," but the one which is most fetching to us nowadays—I think partly because it goes whole hog and makes the commitment without reservation and makes possible the greatest subtlety of perception—is the achievement of dramatic situation and scene and character in which the author, as in a play, is not present except as creator of the total construct. The key to this commitment is, of course, definition of point of view whereby the viewing of the situation, the *statement* of situation, is an integral part of the situation, not outside it.

This commitment was made by many of the early novelists but was not made again by many until the practice of Flaubert. At times the commitment was achieved through the device of letters. In the case of Defoe the device grew out of the memoirs and, as he calls them, the "novels and romances" of his day—the first person narrator. We recognize that this is not so subtle as the device of Sterne later, or the third person limited point of view so much used today, or, for that matter, the first person narrator as minor character or combined with other devices, in Conrad. We recognize at once that Defoe used something ready at hand, and that he is not half so subtle as we can now read him. For after the clear fall from grace of the bourgeois way of life, as Bishop said,

That day in whose dawn it had been a very joy to be alive grew so dark that even the very hope of happiness disappeared. . . . It was in the midst of this disastrous triumph, that the novelists began to grow self-conscious. The old easy assurance . . . was gone. With Flaubert all innocence is lost, he must know what he is doing, as he places each word, he is condemned, like Adam after the Fall, to sweat and unremitting toil, and like Eve he can bring his conceptions to birth only after long and excruciating labor. Henry James explores the techniques of his chosen craft, with a conscience as delicate as though he were probing a course of conduct by which he would be forever saved or damned.

But we recognize that Defoe did make the necessary commitment and made the technical discovery to the art of fiction. Moll Flanders may speak a bit mannishly and as though with the voice of Defoe, but she remains a woman; the novel is made of her actions and decisions and thoughts but also, importantly, of her perception of those actions and decisions and thoughts. Defoe may, after the fact, have claimed Crusoe as an allegorical projection of himself, but Crusoe is a true imaginative projection; for the eyes which view the action of the novel are those of Crusoe and not those directly of Defoe. And Defoe mastered the point of view to a great extent, as is indicated by the selection of detail which is perceived by the narrator. The detail does tend to glut the market; yet each is significant to the eye of the perceiver, who also knows what details to skip, when to speed through many days in a single sentence, and when to devote pages to a moment.

I suppose that Defoe was little concerned consciously with the critical preoccupations which concern us today as we attempt a body of important critical insight into the art of fiction. Indeed, as Bishop noted, he seemed to accept the novel as if it were ready made and not with any awareness that he was a creator of the form; yet we can hardly identify any novel, as we think of it after Defoe, before his writing. But he was a man of uncommon common sense and rather uncritical activity; the novel was, indeed, ready made for him when we consider the common sense development necessary to the memoir and narrative if the form would satisfy Defoe's needs. And this development included, if this essay is close to being right, the four essentials to the art of fiction as practiced since: first, the development of thematic narrative; second, the central theme of modern fiction, that of man alone in society and preoccupied with his relationship to that society; third, the use of the moral choice as the common dramatic tension in fiction; and fourth, the commitment to fiction as an imaginative act, including a successful treatment of the central problem of point of view. We may further honor his insight in fastening upon the novel as a form of literature, since it is adapted so intimately to the middle class reader as well as to the middle class writer. Unlike the drama, for example, it is perhaps the form of literature most appealing to the individual reader; it is indeed, the form made for the individual reader, who sits in isolation with the book in his hands and may take it up or put it down as he wishes, as free as a true individualist; the individualist reading the novel is himself an embodiment of the central theme of the novels he reads.

In all these respects Defoe's common sense inaugurated a great literary form. A study of his practice can do much to help us achieve a self-conscious understanding and criticism of the art of fiction.

AN ESSAY IN THE THEORY OF TRADITIONAL METRICS
Talisman, 7, 1955

The poetic age just passed—self congratulatory and a bit smug about its own efforts—has had a most interesting situation with regard to the theory of metrics. I judge from the practice of the poetry produced, and from the scattered references I have seen by poets and critics with regard to metrical theories presumably explaining or justifying the work.

Most comments seem informed by that vice of would-be criticism—impressionism, that is, pronouncements without a full consideration given to basic theory; and suffering, as well, by a considerable ignorance of traditional practice. Despite our self-congratulation upon the supposed "experimentation" of our period of literature, we have probably contributed extremely little to the theory of metrics; and our age has probably been no more experimental with regard to such theory than many another age.

The two considerable exceptions to our paucity of significant comment on metrical theory are the comments by Yvor Winters in various passages in *In Defense of Reason* and in a recent essay on "The Audible Reading of Poetry" and the chapter on metrics in *Understanding Poetry* by Cleanth Brooks and Robert Penn Warren. My own indebtedness to those comments will be clear to the informed as I attempt, here, a brief essay in basic metrical theory.

Rhythm

We recognize that a *sine qua non* of the arts is what we call "rhythm"—repeated elements of color, line, sound, or texture, depending upon the particular art. In the case of two of the arts, music and poetry, rhythm is chiefly in the repeated organization of sound.

The first question we need to ask ourselves is this: Why do we have rhythm in the arts? What functions are performed by rhythm?

The most common answer to this question—including particularly the answer in our own period, when an effort at answer has been made at all—is some version of the notion that rhythm is innate in the universe and that the art object "naturally" partcipates in this structure of the universe, seemingly without the will or choice of the artist.

I do not care in this brief space to try to debate philosophies about the nature and structure of the universe. But our own practice, in which we have quite capably indicated an ability to write poems which don't have any significant rhythm, ought to demonstrate to us that the notion is somehow faulty. For the artist, at least, the premium, if he has sense, must be upon his conscious endeavor; the art medium is under his control, insofar as he is able, so that he can achieve the communication of which he is capable. To think otherwise is to make him something other than the true "maker" of art objects.

Surely it is clear that, whether or not there is rhythm, say, in the stars, rhythm placed in the poem, or any other art object, is placed there by the artist. And he does so because rhythm has basic (those *sine qua non*) functions to perform in his effort at the communicative object.

These functions are probably several, but I can dwell here only over the two which seem to me paramount and particularly important to basic theory.

First of all, rhythm is an *organization* of sensory material; in the case of poetry, which I shall use henceforward in the essay, rhythm is an organization of sound. It is the achievement of a *pattern*. And I think much in modern epistemology would go along with the notion that the achievement of a *pattern* or *organization* is the achievement of a *meaning*. At least if I may be permitted to liberalize use of the word *meaning* just a little from its more common confinement within the abstruse, my point is that rhythm is the perception of a meaning. It is the basic pattern, meaning, perceived and achieved in the poem.

Second, rhythm is a particularized patterning in any one poem, of sound, and hence is a management of sense data as these data impinge upon the reader and listener. It becomes a means of control of sensory awarenesses communicated in the poem.

Thus, rhythm performs, at a most elemental level in a poem—nearly intuitive since conceptual "meanings" are not usually brought by it into consciousness—the very first, basic, double-faced functions of communicating a perception of "pattern" or "meaning" *and* of condensing, managing, controlling the sense data of the sounds of the words.

ACHIEVEMENT OF RHYTHM IN POETRY

Rhythm is achieved in the poem by the arranged and repetitive patterns of the sounds of the syllables and words. Various methods of achieving rhythm will attend to particular aspects of the sounds—duration of the sound in time, as spoken; accent of syllables as spoken, these two being the most common and nearly the only ones used. Not often used are such aspects of the sound as tone, pitch, depth or lightness of vowel, type of consonant, etc., however aware one may be of these aspects of the sound. In other words, the pattern is established by certain repetitions of a selected aspect or group of aspects of the sound.

In an effort at basic theory, we must attempt to achieve meaningful categories. In the achievement of rhythm in poetry, the two fundamental ones are these: Rhythm is achieved either through the use of a metrical "system" for management of rhythm, or a nonmetrical "system." In the former case, of metre, we mean that the poet has used one of the recognized formal systems; in the latter case, we mean that the poet has achieved a rhythm but without use of one of those formal systems.

METRICAL SYSTEMS

In the history of occidental poetry, four metrical systems have appeared.

1. *Quantitative metre.* Used chiefly in ancient Greek and Roman poetry, the quantitative system achieves rhythm by an arrangement of *duration* of syllables into patterns of short and long (with the various combinations of bi-syllabic and tri-syllabic units or "feet" and these, in turn, into groups to form the verse or line). Elaborate rules were deduced to indicate length of syllables in problematical cases.

2. *Accentual metre.* Used chiefly in Old English and much Middle English verse, the accentual system achieves rhythm by an arrangement of accented or stressed syllables. Most popular rhythm within the metre was apparently the use of four accented syllables to the verse or line. Commonly this organization was elaborated with an additional factor, the caesura breaking the line into two parts with two accents on each side of the pause; further elaboration was the use of alliteration of certain of the accented syllables. Under this metre, the number of unaccented syllables could vary considerably. Presumably the verse was often chanted to the accompaniment of a stringed in-

strument and the accented syllables would fall upon the rhythmic beat of the accompaniment. Thus the varied number of unaccented syllables would be hurried over or dwelt over according to their number between the rhythmic, accented beat.

3. *Syllabic metre.* Used chiefly by modern French poetry, in a language with very little accentual stress, syllabic metre is a counting of number of syllables within a verse.

4. *Accentual-syllabic metre.* Since the Renaissance, the accentual-syllabic metre has been the chief traditional metre of English poetry—and also used in the poetry of many other languages, such as German, Spanish, Italian. It is the arrangement of sounds in patterns of unaccented and accented syllables, and like the quantitative system uses the method of various combinations of bi-syllabic and tri-syllabic feet together in a verse or line. Indeed, because of its similarity in this respect with quantitative metre, we have had the rather unfortunate situation of using terms borrowed from quantitative metre. Commonly we speak of long and short syllables (according to quantitative nomenclature) when we mean unaccented and accented syllables; we borrow the name of our feet, such as the iamb, dactyl, etc., from the quantitative metre. Special care must be exercised to prevent easy confusion about our terminology because of this borrowing.

Many poets and critics today, as well as readers of

poetry, are not aware that all four of these metrical systems have been used in English. Thus, there has been some confusion in reading and description. The practice of the Renaissance resulted in the nearly total abandonment of the accentual metre and almost the total adoption of the accentual-syllabic metre in English. However, accentual metre has been used in modern times in some early two-stress metres of W. H. Auden and may, by some apparently confused theory by Gerald Manley Hopkins, have had its influence upon that poet's experiments. Further, some modern efforts at free verse seem wavering between the accentual metre and a true free verse. Quantitative metre was much argued and used in the early English Renaissance, and one may recall the concern of Gabriel Harvey, Sir Philip Sidney, and critics of "bastard rhyming" (apparently confused with an accentual-syllabic metre which commonly used rhyme) over this matter. In the Renaissance the song-writers were the most notable users of quantitative metre in English, including Thomas Campion. In more recent times, Robert Bridges wrote a number of poems in quantitative metre. Syllabic metre has also been used in modern times—by Robert Bridges, his daughter, Elizabeth Daryush, and Marianne Moore. Bridges' use of these various metres qualifies him, surely, as the outstanding "experimenter" of the last half-century, not the Pounds, Eliots, Cummingses, and others who "sprung" various forms of accentual-syllabic metre (such as blank verse) or wrote poems in free verse.

Free Verse

Poems written in non-metrical achievements of rhythm are free verse. Because of the confused thinking on metrical problems in modern times, free verse is often difficult to distinguish, since an author may at times be seeming to write a metrical line, or one which employs considerable freedom in varying such a line, and then in the same poem, perhaps, write a line which is not metrical at all. A line, however, which achieves a rhythm *without* use of one of the formalized patterns of one of the metrical systems (or an explicable variant of such a pattern) must be considered free verse.

The theory of free verse has never been adequately set down. One sees reference to "cadence," "rising and lowering" of sounds, etc., as explanations of this non-metrical rhythm. But none of these seems very adequate to the problem of descriptive theory.

So far as I am able to detect, free verse is normally written by one or another of two theories.

The first of these is the employment of a loose accentual system. At times, such verse may be analyzed as being really metrical, according to the accentual metre. But so often it would appear that the poet has not been conscious of the similarity or has employed such marked variants that one cannot feel that the accentual metre has been used; instead, a loose, rather than very formalized, patterning of accents has apparently been in his mind.

Yvor Winters, in *In Defense of Reason,* has gone farthest to describe much free verse in the terms of accentual metre, and he makes an outstanding case for his argument. The difficulty seems to me, first, that the poets are so inconsistent that the accentual formality is largely a useful analogy but not used in the practice with any consistency, and, second, that much free verse does not use a patterning of accents at all in the composition of the verse. But Winters' comments are most enlightening and helpful in reading what is probably the best free verse composition—as seen in some of the poems by William Carlos Williams, Wallace Stevens, and a few others.

The second theory lying behind much free verse (and, I should judge, *most* free verse published, quite often of indifferent or worse quality) seems to be what I call syntactical theory. A basic problem in writing poetry is to determine the *verse,* the line. By any of the traditional metres, the length of a line is "given" by the theory of the metre; in accentual-syllabic metre, for example, if one is writing iambic pentameter, the line has, by definition, ten syllables, and once ten syllables are written, the next line must be started. But in a non-metrical composition, the line length is not so exactly given. If the free verse is written by a loose accentual pattern, then the verse will be organized around a variation from two to three (very common in this verse) accents, or it may use four accents as a sort of norm. But in this second theory for much free verse, the only determinant for the line length seems to be a dividing of the words into syntactical units—phrases, sometimes single words, commonly clauses and sentences. A completion of a bit of "sense," according to many poets who write such verse, will be the determinant to start a new line.

Limitations of Free Verse

Poets of the last half century have commonly congratulated themselves on freeing themselves from traditional metrics. They have felt that by so doing they have escaped "limitations" of metre and launched themselves bravely upon the greater possibilities of freedom. However, by now their practice as well as their theory can be seen to be at fault. Not that free verse isn't reasonably resourceful, and many fine poems, even great poems, may be written in free verse. But they are almost certainly to be minor poems, for the resources of the versification available to the use of the poet are, by number or variety of effectiveness, simply less than those of traditional metres, particularly in English of the accentual-syllabic metre. The argument, indeed, runs exactly contrary to the theory they have adopted. Again, Winters' *In Defense of Reason* provides the brilliant argument in this theory, and I can only paraphrase distantly my own comprehension of the theory. But without an exact pattern as the basic organization of the line, the poet cannot provide the greatest precision to his employment of syllables, perceptible nuances of variation, precision of control of reading of the line. For these great values in versification—for the poet who has the ability and has learned to use them—a metrical system appears very nearly mandatory; free verse cannot, at least, provide the opportunities of the metre. Further, "variation" as a usable tool of the poet is hardly available to the writer of free verse; where the basic theory of the line is variation itself, then management of a variation against a basic pattern is simply not possible. Only rather gross perceptions of change in movement (as between speed and slowness of a line, for example) remain possible in free verse. In most capable hands, this still becomes a great instrument, but not, surely, of the greatest. It is upon this theory (and comparison with fine practice of traditional metres), for example, that we can maintain that such a significant poet as T. S. Eliot, who only rarely makes consistent use of a traditional metre, has a rather poor, even gross, ear; his verse cannot have the subtleties of rhythmic accomplishment, whatever its other subtleties, that have been attained by a good many poets in the tradition.

Resources of the Traditional Metre

Practically speaking, the resources of the traditional metre seem innumerable. When one considers the *variety* of patterns available, one knows that no one poet is likely to exhaust a large proportion of them. In the choice of the iambic metre alone, one thinks of the possible choice among lines of single feet or double feet, on up through the trimeter, tetrameter, and even longer lines; then the choice of various stanza and poem arrangements, rhymed or unrhymed. The variety is tremendous! And the poet has before him probably all that he can possibly use.

But a more important way of looking at the resources of the traditional metre is not that of the variety of forms alone, but of the variety within the single form. One who would take, for example, blank verse and compare the uses of it among Marlowe, Shakespeare, Webster, Milton, Landor, Stevens—the great ability of such a complex and great instrument can tax the care of the greatest poet.

But even more is the ability of the traditional metre to record, if the poet is able to rise to the occasion, the nearly infinite perceptible nuances of emotion and thought. The basic theory is that probably no two syllables—certainly very few—have exactly the same accents; further, the accent given to one syllable in one context will be slightly changed in another context, under the influence of the differing movement of thought and the surrounding syllables. Therefore, the basic pattern or "theory" of the line, say, the iambic pentameter, is an expected pattern set up between the writer and the reader; the exact syllables used in any one line do not realize completely the "theory" in the sense that every second syllable is of exactly the same stress as all its fellows or that every uneven numbered syllable is exactly the same in its lack of stress. Actually, then, the line moves toward the "theory" of the line, individual lines varying considerably in their realization of that theory; the spoken stress pattern and the theoretical stress pattern are each, in a sense, a commentary one upon the other. And that commentary seems to have nearly infinite variation of possibility, each variation immediately perceptible to the reader, despite the fact that normally the line is read without conceptualizing, bringing into words, the commentary achieved by the variation. Where the pattern is agreed, the variations from the pattern are perceptible, can be given almost agreed-upon nuances of feeling, and constitute resources as great or as little as the ability of the poet; in theory, the resources are there for the greatest of poets, but the little poet will find himself running short of ability to use them.

Thus variation from the theoretical stress pattern of an accentual-syllabic metre is not a negative thing; it is not, as one finds in manuals for poets, something to be inserted now and then to keep the verse from becoming monotonous. It is, instead, an inevitable, necessary matter, because of the tremendous variety of accent in our language; and it is, further, a reservoir of positive resources, to be used by the poet according to the ability to which he has attained in his versification.

In the discussion above of the functions of rhythm in poetry, I stressed the double-faced ability of rhythm as a means of achieving basic "pattern" or meaning in the organization of the sound and as a means of controlling the auditory sense awarenesses communicated in the poem. In the case of the traditional metrical system, we see this double ability at its keenest, for the patterning has been chosen with exactness (and not the sloppiness of *most* non-metrical composition) and the pattern is exactly determinable between poet and reader; further, the sense data of the sounds have the immediately perceptible nuances of variation from the theoretical pattern, thus enriching the awareness of the minutiae of sense data. And what we nowadays talk about so much as "sensibility" of a poet is exactly to be studied in this aspect of his versification.

Other Resources of Traditional Metrics

A brief essay must always be aware of its coming end. But I should not like to close this effort in basic theory without pointing to the analogous argument with regard to other common aspects of traditional metrics—the verse, the stanza, rhyme, patterns for complete poems (such as the sonnet). Indeed, versification is composition *in verse*, that is, in lines determined by the poet and not, as in prose, in lines set up by the exigencies of the type space, varying from one printed version to the other. At the start, then, we have the subtlety of an order which, in a figurative sense, looks both ways. A verse, a line of poetry, is both a unit in itself (or else the line would not be so separated and printed as such) and a part of a larger unit. Similarly with rhyme, the stanza, the individual units (such as the octave and sestet of the sonnet) within the poem which has a predetermined pattern throughout its length. Like the individual accents within the verse itself, we have that tremendously resourceful and challenging beauty of the language in knowing an aspect of "completion" within the unit and yet an awareness of an on-going quality. This balancing between the two constitutes an essential part of the complexity of the poem—as the most subtle, complex use of the language, normally. Indeed, in structure, it constitutes the complex, subtle relationship among two or more things, that we expect the poem to constitute in its complex, subtle, determinable relationship among thought and emotion and sensory awareness.

Thus, to indicate a particular example, a poet who is careless about placing a preposition or simple conjunction at the end of a line (in a place normally stressed by metre but also doubly stressed because of its ending of another "unit," the verse) is very readily convicted of carelessness, indeed! Yet the ability is there for that rare occasion (one can find a few examples in Shakespeare) in which such placement of a preposition might be exact exercise of position for special emphasis or subtlety of meaning. Similarly with a stanza. The "sense" of a stanza is that it is a complete unit and normally is a period-stop; that is, at minimum a sentence-meaning ends with its end. One of the interesting problems of composition is, indeed, to achieve that exact conjoining of structure with meaning, so that no excess word, syllable, is there, nor any distortion of the language to indicate that the meaning was not co-terminous with the structure of the language. Yet, the stanza is also a part of a larger unit; and at times the use of a run-on of an incomplete meaning, an incompleted sentence, to another stanza may be exactly communicative of a feeling or meaning that enlarges the poem, or achieves it more exactly than by another practice. But carelessness in this respect, the run-on of lines or stanzas just to achieve insignificant effects, a self-assumed "versatility," violence of feeling which is not supported by other aspects of the poem—such carelessnesses are recorded there for all to see!

By a man's deeds shall we know him. By a poet's deeds in the choices he exercises in his composition shall we know him to be a good poet or a bad one. Indeed, the poet fully documents the record for us!

III

ESSAYS ON ENGLISH LITERATURE

JOHN SKELTON: THE STRUCTURE OF THE POEM
Philological Quarterly, January, 1953

In the work of John Skelton appears the first important Renaissance break with the medieval tradition in poetry. His work covers almost every type of verse practiced in his day, including the morality play; but he proceeded from acceptance of the medieval tradition, through varying stages of revolt against that tradition, to a new form which he devised. This type was highly individualistic, however, in the sense that it did not have much "carry-over value." Though he finally broke with the medieval method, Skelton's experiment did not, as did Wyatt's, discover the method which was used so effectively by the great Elizabethan and Jacobean poets.

Skelton's two elegies—"On the Death of the Noble Prince, King Edward the Fourth" and "Upon the Dolorous Death and Much Lamentable Chance of the Most Honourable Earl of Northumberland"—and his three prayers—"To the Father of Heaven," "To the Second Person," and "To the Holy Ghost"—are clearly in the fifteenth-century literary manner, the manner of Lydgate. They belong to what Nelson calls "the tradition which conceived of literature to be a means of propagating virtue."[1] The theme of the first elegy is that of the Fall-of-Princes:

> Where is now my conquest and my victory?
>   Where is my riches and my royal array?
> Where be my coursers and my horses high?
>   Where is my mirth, my solace, and my play?
> As vanity, to nought all is withered away.[2]

The theme is old and is not at all re-vitalized in this poem. It has the same lack of imagery as in Lydgate and Hawes. Though the second elegy has a different theme, an argument against the commons who killed Northumberland and a recital of the earl's virtues, it may be characterized in the same fashion. Only a touch of the later Skelton is present, as in the word play of

> Yet shamefully they slew him: that shame may them befall!

and the confused image

> the commoners under a cloak,
> Which kindled the wild fire that made all this smoke.

The prayers have a characteristic medieval rhetoric of abstractions:

> O Radiant Luminary of light interminable,
>   Celestial Father, potential God of might,
> Of heaven and earth O Lord incomparable,
>   Of all perfections the Essential most perfite!

---

[1] William Nelson, *John Skelton, Laureate* (New York, 1939), p. 142.
[2] *The Complete Poems of John Skelton, Laureate*, edited by Philip Henderson (London, 1931), pp. 2-3. All quotations from Skelton are from this edition.

> O Maker of mankind, that forméd day and night,
> Whose power imperial comprehendeth every place!

Skelton's first major attempt marks his first unmistakable move away from the medieval tradition. In the large, *The Bouge of Court* is a typical fifteenth-century allegory. It has the

> same astrological introduction, the insistence upon the necessity of "covert Terms," and the usual assumption of modesty: the poet then falls asleep and his dream becomes the substance of the poem: he wakes up at a critical moment in the action and writes his "little book," for which he makes a conventional apology.[3]

In addition, the characters of the poem, with the exception of one, are personifications such as might be found in late medieval allegory. They include Drede (the dreamer himself), Dame Saucepere, Danger, Bon Aventure, Favell, Suspect, Disdain, Riot, Dissimuler, and Deceit.

But the poem is not completely abstract in its conception. It is first of all definitely localized:

> At Harwich port slumb'ring as I lay
> In mine hostes house, called Powers Key.

More important yet, the descriptions of the personified characters are a mixture of medieval abstraction and of touches of reality. For example, in this description of Disdain,

---

[3] *Ibid.*, p. xxviii.

> He bit his lip, he lookéd passing coy;
>   His face was belimmed as bees had him stung:
> It was no time with him to jape nor toy!
>   Envy had wasted his liver and his lung,
>   Hatred by the heart so had him wrung
> That he looked pale as ashes to my sight:
> Disdain, I ween, this comerous crab is hight.

only the fourth and fifth lines seem to belong to medieval description; such expressions as "His face was belimmed as bees had him stung," "pale as ashes," and "comerous crab" set before us a distinct and physical person. This quality of the poem has its climax, moreover, in the description of Harvey Hafter, a real person with a real name among abstractions:

> Upon his breast he bear a versing-box,
>   His throat was clear, and lustily could fain.
> Methought his gown was all furred with fox,
>   And ever he sang, *"Sith I Am Nothing Plain . . ."*
> To keep him from picking it was a greate pain:
> He gazed on me with his goatish beard,
> When I looked at him my purse was half-afeard.

John M. Berdan speaks of this last line as a "triumph of suggestiveness."[4] The characterization of Harvey Hafter does not stop here, however; it continues through the medium of his own speech to Drede, one stanza of which is:

> *Princes of youth* can ye sing by rote?
>   *Or shall I sail with you?* afellowship assay?

---

[4] John M. Berdan, *Early Tudor Poetry, 1485-1547* (New York, 1931), p. 97.

> For on the book I cannot sing a note.
>   Would to God it would please you some day
>   A ballad book before me for to lay,
>   And learn me to sing *re mi fa sol!*
>   And, when I fail, bob me on the noll.

It is evident from this poem, then, that at the time he wrote it Skelton was not yet prepared to break completely with the medieval tradition. He had not yet, we may suppose, invented a structure for the poem which would be compatible with the direct way in which he approached experience and to the realistic materials which he wished to place in his poem. His answer to the problem at this time was to borrow an old shell and fill it with new drink.

The same method is also evident in Skelton's morality play, *Magnificence*. He borrowed the structure of a literary type well-known in his day but used for ecclesiastical and moral purposes. His characters all have abstract names. There is the typical abstract argument:

> Liberty. What, Liberty to Measure then would ye bind?
> Measure. What else? for otherwise it were against kind:
>   If Liberty should leap and run where he list
>   It were no virtue, it were a thing unbless'd.

But the play is filled with much specific material. Occasionally an image, instead of abstract terms, is used to describe the characters, as in this comment upon the taking of the assumed name, Sure Surveyance, by the character Counterfeit Countenance:

> Surveyance! where ye survey
> Thrift has lost her coffer-key!

or this comment upon Cloaked Collusion:

> By Cock's heart, he looketh high!
> He hawketh, methink, for a butterfly.

There is a specific reference to King Louis XII. As Henderson comments, although Skelton's purpose "is distinctly moral, . . . he is chiefly concerned with showing that the wages of imprudent spending, through certain unnamed evil advisers, will be, for a certain unnamed rich prince, adversity and poverty. The case at issue is not so much universal as particular—although, of course, it can be interpreted universally—and the play contains much indirect satire of Wolsey's influence on the young Henry VIII."[5]

A further step from the medieval method is apparent in the first of Skelton's major satires, *Speak, Parrot*. At first thought it would seem that the poem is similar to the medieval type of the bestiary, since a bird is the main character. But in this poem the parrot is not at all approached as were the beasts in the *Physiologi*, with an attempt to find some allegorical significance to the animal's habits or physical character. Rather, here the parrot is realized as the brightly-colored bird who is captured in distant places and brought off in a cage to be a plaything for idle women:

---
[5]Henderson, p. xxvii.

My name is Parrot, a bird of Paradise,
  By nature devised of a wondrous kind,
Daintily dieted with divers delicate spice
  Till Euphrates, that flood, driveth me into Ind,
  Where men of that countrie by fortune me find
And send me to greate ladyes of estate:
Then Parrot must have an almond or a date.

A cage curiously carven, with a silver pin,
  Properly painted, to be my coverture;
A mirror of glass, that I may toot therein:
  These, maidens full meekly with many a divers flower,
  Freshly they dress, and make sweet my bower,
With "Speak, Parrot, I pray you." Full curtesly they say
"Parrot is a goodly bird, a pretty popinjay!"

With my beake bent, my little wanton eye,
  My feathers fresh as is the emerald green, . . .
  I am a minion to wait upon a queen:
"My proper Parrot, my little pretty fool!"
With ladies I learn, and go with them to school.

Also, this parrot can speak Latin, Hebrew, Arabic, Chaldean, Greek, Spanish, French, Dutch, English, and Portuguese; and like the parrot Skelton garbles his smatterings of words and phrases from these languages. It is this near-confusion of language which has attracted the most attention from scholars, though the purpose of the indirection of statement is frankly admitted:

> For in this process Parrot nothing hath surmised,
>   No matter pretended, nor nothing enterprised,
> But that *metaphora, allegoria* with all,
> Shall be his protection, his paves, and his wall.

Underneath the confusion of language two principal attacks are readily apparent, one against the study of Greek, and the other, more violent, against Wolsey.

What is more interesting for our purposes here is the method involved. It certainly is not medieval, for no indirect preparation, no dream setting or allegorical structure, is provided. The poem starts with the description of the parrot, quoted above, continues the description for a number of stanzas, and then proceeds to the statements by the parrot. The parrot provides, then, the single structural element of the poem: about the facts that the parrot lives in places of court intrigue and that he can speak are gathered the satirical matters of the poem. And the principle by which the satirical matters are gathered is simply one of accumulation: the parrot speaks of matters which the author wishes to satirize, and at the time he wishes to satirize them. This is attested not only by the fact that there are two principal objects of satire, as noted above, but also by the fact that the poem has several envoys, each of them dated and "constituting a series of fortnightly reports on the current activities of Cardinal Wolsey."[6] And the parrot remains the only connecting link among these accretions, whether in terms of time or of matter.

The complete break with the medieval manner is apparent in *Colin Clout*. "Here the dream-structure is abandoned in favor of a single dramatic ego; per-

---
[6]Nelson, p. 135.

sonification and allegory change to direct statement; and the rime-royal is abandoned in favor of the Skeltonical verse."[7] There is no attempt at narrative to link together the various satirical matters of the poem. The structural element, bringing together into one poem such various matters, is provided by the figure of Colin Clout:

> Thus I, Colin Clout,
> As I go about,
> And wand'ring as I walk
> I hear the people talk.
>
> Take me as I intend,
> For loth I am to offend
> In this that I have penn'd:
> I tell you as men say.

As the parrot is used in *Speak, Parrot,* so here also the structural element, the "single dramatic ego" of Colin Clout, is used to link not only various materials —which include attacks upon church corruption, the confusion of temporal and spiritual powers of the Church, the lack of learning and the laziness of many priests, and Wolsey's attempt at advancement—but also parts composed at different times.[8] This is apparent also in the third major satire, *Why Come Ye not to Court?* In that poem, only a little more than a quarter of the way through the complete work, appear the lines:

---
[7]Berdan, p. 179.
[8]*Ibid.*, pp. 195-198, gives indications that *Colin Clout* was circulated in fragments and thus must have been composed piecemeal.

> Thus will I conclude my style,
> And fall to rest a while,
> And so to rest a while.

Thus the poem must have ended at this point once, to be taken up again as new instances of corruption came to Skelton's attention.

The structural relationship among these matters within the poem can be only slight. This is particularly true of *Why Come Ye not to Court?* which does not have a parrot or a Colin Clout to provide some semblance of unity. Combining such various matters at various times in the same poem, Skelton returned often to the same attack, securing intensification and a well-rounded picture by repetition and by the addition of many new examples. As Berdan comments of *Why Come Ye not to Court?*, "The natural result is that the poem is powerful only in detail. As a whole it has the incoherence of anger."[9]

This use of repetition, or parallelism, as it might be called, appears not only in the large units of these poems but also in smaller units. It is a striking characteristic of those poems by Skelton which are out of the medieval tradition; and the same structure, as Nelson notes,[10] is just as strikingly absent from the poems composed in rime-royal. An example is this from *Colin Clout*:

---
[9] *Ibid.*, p. 193.
[10] Nelson, p. 87.

> Farewell benignitie,
> Farewell simplicitie,
> Farewell humilitie,
> Farewell good charitie!

Another is from *The Tunning of Elinor Rumming*:

> Another set of sluts:
> Some brought walnuts,
> Some apples, some pears,
> Some brought their clipping shears,
> Some brought this and that,
> Some brought I wot n'ere what;
> Some brought their husband's hat,
> Some puddings and links,
> Some tripes that stinks.

In these poems, then, Skelton has arrived at a method which is definitely not medieval. The writing is direct, not indirect; there is no allegorical covering, but instead an attempt to provide structure through the dramatic figure of a bird or a man who repeats what he hears. Above all, Skelton has thrown over the psychological and philosophical principles which underlie the medieval method. He does not approach experiences with preconceptions; experience is not intellectualized into categorical compartments. Instead he seems to be trying "to get the facts." His own program for church and civil reform is only slightly emphasized compared with his insistence upon the evils which exist. He is gathering data for a program, for a philosophy of action. The poems exhibit a sort of inductive thinking.

In terms of verse structure, we may, for the sake of convenience, term his method "accumulative." He gathers data not once but time after time to cover the same point again and again. "Over and over again he repeats the same things, devoid of all logical form and construction—although these pieces may be said to have certain concentric[11] movement of their own—round and round the same point he goes, always coming back to where he started from."[12] And this accumulative method is apparent not only in terms of materials but also in terms of the structure of the verse from line to line, as has been pointed out.

The same method of accumulation is characteristic of Skelton's best non-satirical work. It is especially evident in *The Tunning of Elinor Rumming*, an extreme example of a direct, non-intellectualized approach to sordid elements of experience. The poem is composed of scenes and portraits—almost photographic in their fidelity to fact—of women found at a tavern. And the scenes and portraits are left at the level of description: at the end the poet has merely written enough:

> For my fingers itch,
> I have written too mich
> Of this mad mumming

---

[11]Ten Brink, as Arthur Koelbing points out ("Barclay and Skelton," *The Cambridge History of English Literature* [Cambridge, 1909], iii, 84) called Skelton's method "concentric."
[12]Henderson, p. xxix.

> Of Elinor Rumming!
> Thus endeth the geste
> Of this worthy feast.

At the same time, repetition and accumulation form the dominant verse-structure throughout the poem. One example has already been quoted. Of the same sort, but here used in conversation, is:

> He calleth me his whiting,
> His mulling and his miting,
> His nobbes and his coney,
> His sweeting and his honey,
> With "Bass, my pretty bonny,
> Thou are worth goods and money!"

Broad, indefinite metaphors and similes are often used in the portraits. They cannot be put together, as images, to make a clear picture, for the analogies are drawn from so many realms of experience. They function, then, as momentary impressions of detail, the complete portrait being achieved through the accumulation of many such images. The following, to give an example, are less than a fourth of the lines devoted to the portrait of Elinor Rumming:

> With clothes upon her head
> That weigh a sow of lead,
> Writhen in wondrous wise
> After the Saracen's guise,
> With a whim-wham
> Knit with a trim-tram
> Upon her brain-pan;
> Like an Egyptian

>   Cappéd about.
>   When she goeth out
>   Herself for to shew,
>   She driveth down the dew
>   With a pair of heeles
>   As broad as two wheeles;
>   She hobbles as a gose
>   With her blanket hose,
>   Her shoon smeared with tallow,
>   Greaséd upon dirt
>   That bawdeth her skirt.

Philip Sparrow is something of a special case, because for the first of its two parts Skelton has again gone to a convention to secure a structure for his poem. In this case, the convention, as Ian Gordon has pointed out, is the Services for the Dead of the Roman Church.[13] Gordon lists all the forms of the Services for the Dead and comments:

> Skelton uses all these forms except that of Matins, and *Philip Sparow* is remarkable in the way it uses first the Vespers in the Office for the Dead, then without indication or warning becomes the medieval Mass of the Birds . . . ; again without warning shifts into the Absolution over the Tomb; and then with a few lines on the coming on of night returns to the close of Vespers in the Office. After a section on the composition of a Latin epitaph . . . we find ourselves at the *Commendatio*—commendations, not of the soul of Philip Sparrow, but, with an obvious play on the double meaning of the word, on the beauty of the girl who was supposed to have recited part one.[14]

---

[13]Ian A. Gordon, "Skelton's 'Philip Sparrow' and the Roman Service-Book," *Modern Language Review*, xxix (1934), 389-396.
[14]*Ibid.*, p. 390.

Within this structure Skelton's method of accumulation of detail and perception is apparent, particularly in the second part, where he proceeds from one aspect of Joanna's beauty to another. The following is his comment upon her wart (perhaps a mole) upon her cheek:

> And when I perceived
> Her wart and conceived,
> It cannot be denay'd
> But it was well conveyed
> And set so womanly,
> And nothing wantonly,
> But right conveniently,
> And full congruently,
> As Nature could devise,
> In most goodly wise!
> Who so list behold,
> It maketh lovers bold
> To her to sue for grace,
> Her favour to purchase;
> The scar upon her chin,
> Enhached on her fair skin,
> Whiter than the swan,
> It would make any man
> To forget deadly sin
> Her favour to win!

Within the first part, also, the same verse-structure is used. A Latin phrase from the Services for the Dead introduces each new movement, and within each appear such passages as:

> Sometime he would gasp
> When he saw a wasp;
> A fly, or a gnat,
> He would fly at that;
> And prettily he would pant
> When he saw an ant!
> Lord, how he would pry
> After a butterfly!
> Lord, how he would hop
> After the gressop!
> And when I said, "Phip, Phip!"
> Then he would leap and skip,
> And take me by the lip.

And:

> O cat of churlish kind,
> The fiend was in thy mind
> When thou my bird untwined!
> I would thou hadst been blind!
> The léopards savage,
> The lions in their rage
> Might catch thee in their paws,
> And gnaw thee in their jaws!
> The serpents of Libany
> Might sting thee venomously!
> The dragons with their tongues
> Might poison thy liver and lungs!
> The manticors of the mountains
> Might feed them on thy brains!

But it is to be noted that in addition to his accumulative method Skelton in this poem makes use of his convention in a way not characteristic of his other poems in which a convention is found. Here the

Services for the Dead are not merely framework, as is the dream-framework of *The Bouge of Court*. The Services are integrated into the poem and act as an undercurrent of commentary on Joanna's sorrow and lamentation. Commenting on this usage, Gordon says, "The formulae of the various Services are introduced, but they are unchanged and perhaps not always even ridiculed. Instead they give a mock-serious background to the lament for Philip that is at any time liable to lose its mockery."[15] It is this management of tone between humor and pathos, between burlesque and sentimentality, which is one of the important achievements of *Philip Sparrow;* and the use of the convention as a functional device in managing the tone represents a further step in Skelton's handling of structural elements in his poetry.

And just as in this poem there is a functional use of the framework, so also there is a functional modification of his characteristic accumulation. In one of her first laments, Joanna says:

> When I remember again
> How my Philip was slain,
> Never half the pain
> Was between you twain,
> Pyramus and Thisbe,
> As then befell to me:
> I wept and I wailed,
> The tears down hailed,

---
[15]*Ibid.*, p. 396.

> But nothing it availed
> To call Philip again,
> Whom Gib, our cat, hath slain.

Here the repetitive pattern for the verses is familiar. But it is not so straightforward as before; there is a balance of tone which we found extended throughout the poem by means of the undercurrent of commentary through the parody of the Services for the Dead. The first seven lines quoted seem all of one attitude, a genuine lamentation for the death of the sparrow. But the object of the lamentation is merely a pet bird; a single attitude of such pathos toward such an object would seem sentimental. So against the attitude is balanced one of mockery of the lamentation itself, expressed in this passage by the exaggeration of the metaphor *hailed* in the eighth line and by the near-humor involved in the name of the cat, in the implied situation, and in the exaggerated heroism of the words *hath slain* of the last line. Similar balancings of attitudes are found throughout Joanna's part of the poem. There is straightforward grief in some of the descriptions, as that of the bird crawling beneath the girl's night clothes:

> And on me it would leap
> When I was asleep
> And his feathers shake,
> Wherewith he would make
> Me often for to wake,
> And for to take him in
> Upon my naked skin.

> God wot, we thought no sin:
> What though he crept so low?
> It was no hurt, I trow,
> He did nothing, perde,
> But sit upon my knee!
> Philip, though he were nice,
> In him it was no vice!
> Philip might be bold
> And do what he wold:
> Philip would seek and take
> All the fleas black
> That he could there espy
> With his wanton eye.

Or, after a recollection that with a knowldege of magic she might be able to bring Philip alive again, Joanna thinks of the time she tried to stitch Philip's likeness in a sampler:

> But when I was sewing his beak,
> Methought my sparrow did speak,
> And opened his pretty bill,
> Saying, "Maid, ye are in will
> Again me for to kill!
> Ye prick me in the head!" . . .
> My needle and thread
> I threw away for dread.

Finally, this accumulative method is the foundation of Skelton's best lyrics. Occasionally, there is a certain reverse process, a general statement followed by the realistic image; the organization is apparent in this quotation from *Upon a Dead Man's Head*:

> It is general
> To be mortal:
> I have well espied
> No man may hide him
> From Death hollow-eyed,
> With sinews witheréd,
> With bones shiveréd,
> With his worm-eaten maw,
> And his ghastly jaw
> Gasping aside,
> Naked of hide,
> Neither flesh nor fell.

Obviously even here the interest is not primarily upon the general statement but upon the actual effect of mortality.

At times appears the accumulation of detail towards a general statement, as in the last three stanzas of *Knowledge, Acquaintance, Resort, Favour with Grace*:

> Remorse have I of your most goodlihood,
>   Of your behavior courteous and benign,
> Of your bounty and of your womanhood,
>   Which maketh my heart oft to leap and spring,
>   And to remember many a pretty thing:
> But absence, alas, with trembling fear and dread
> Abasheth me, albeit I have no need.
>
> You I assure, absence is my foe,
>   My deadly woe, my painful heaviness;
> And if ye list to know the cause why so
>   Open mine heart, behold my mind express:
>   I would ye could! then should ye see, mistress,

> How there nis thing that I covet so fain
> To embrace you in mine armes twain.
> Nothing earthly to me more desirous
> > Than to behold your beauteous countenance:
> But, hateful Absence, to me so envious,
> > Though thou withdraw me from her by long distance,
> > Yet shall she never out of my remembrance:
> For I have gravéd her within the secret wall
> Of my true heart, to love her best of all!

These two poems are also basically "occasional." The former is addressed to a woman who sent the poet a death's hand " for a token," and the letter is addressed by the lover to the loved-one. In each case the realistic, accumulative method is at times confused, in the first poem by moralizings upon mortality, and in the second by the intrusion of a medieval personification of Absence. In Skelton's best lyrics, however, there is not this confusion. In a number of them, such as *Lullaby, Lullaby, like a Child; The Ancient Acquaintance, Madam, between Us Twain;* and *Mannerly Margery Milk and Ale,* the poem has a narrative basis. But the interest is not merely in the narrative. The first-named poem is a song, and the music for it has come down to us; it has the quality of statement and the repeated refrain common to the song tradition. In the others appears a greater attempt to get at the details of the narrative situation and of the characterization, with Skelton's favorite method of providing detail:

> What dream'st thou, drunkard, drowsy pate?
> > Thy lust and liking is from thee gone;
> Thou blinkard blowboll, thou wakest too late,
> > Behold thou liest, luggard, alone!
> > Well may thou sigh, well may thou groan,
> To deal with her so cowardly:
> Ywis, pole hatchet, she bleared thin eye.

At their best, then, Skelton's lyrics have dropped the generalization from a place of prime importance. In its place appears an interest in getting the details of characterization and of the experience. These details are expressed, not through a close analysis of the elements or through means of an extended metaphor, but through almost a riot of images which seem to have little connection or coordination but each of which expresses some facet of the experience; and by the accumulation of such facets a rounded, full communication of the experience is occasionally attained. Skelton's method produces at its best, in the lyric, such a poem as "To Mistress Margaret Hussey" from *The Garland of Laurel*:

> Merry Margaret,
> > As midsummer flower,
> Gentle as falcon
> Or hawk of the tower:
> With solace and gladness,
> With mirth and no madness,
> All good and no badness;
> > So joyously,
> > So maidenly,
> > So womanly

        Her demeaning
        In everything,
        Far, far passing
        That I can indite,
        Or suffice to write

Of Merry Margaret
        As midsummer flower,
Gentle as falcon
Or hawk of the tower.
        As patient and still
And as full of good will
As fair Isaphill,
Coliander,
Sweet pomander,
Good Cassander,
Steadfast of thought,
Well made, well wrought,
Far may be sought
Ere that he can find
So courteous, so kind
As Merry Margaret
        This midsummer flower,
Gentle as falcon
Or hawk of the tower.

THE PENTAMETER LINES IN SKELTON AND WYATT
Modern Philology, August, 1950

The first problem confronting the student of Renaissance metrics in England is that of reading the iambic pentameter line as it began to be written in the early sixteenth century. Discussion of the problem usually centers upon the characteristics of Wyatt's early work, but similar phenomena occur in Skelton's poems.

The usual conception of Wyatt's work, as Chambers points out in disagreeing with the opinion, is that the early poems were "prentice-work, in which Wyatt was fumbling his way to a comprehension of the pentameter, with the help of a text of Chaucer perverted by oblivion of the Chaucerian inflections."[1] Behind this conception is the assumption that Wyatt—as well as Skelton—in the early years of his practice did not know what a pentameter line was, could not write one with consciousness of what he was doing, and only gradually gained comprehension of the line.

Stated in such terms, the conception is surely false. Good pentameters were written by Skelton, and by Wyatt in his early verse; they are also found in the

---

[1] E. K. Chambers, *Sir Thomas Wyatt and some collected studies* (London, 1933), p. 121.

English poetry of Thomas More. The following stanza from *The bouge of court* is unmistakably after the pentameter pattern:

> In autumpne, whan the sonne *in Virgine*
>   By radyante hete enryped hath our corne;
> Whan Luna, full of mutabylyte,
>   As emperes the dyademe hath worne
>   Of our pole artyke, smylynge halfe in scorne
> At our foly and our vnstedfastnesse;
> The tyme whan Mars to were hym dyde dres.[2]

The first five lines are the pentameter—the first four exactly so, and the fifth by the very normal 1–2′–3–4′ grading of emphasis of the opening four syllables. In the sixth line the allowance of trochaic substitution for the second foot indicates the basic pentameter pattern for the line; it is also possible that the third word was pronounced *folý* and the line quite regularly pentameter. The only considerable difficulty is with the last line. In quoting the passage, John M. Berdan had considered this line to have ten syllables. This I cannot detect according to modern pronunciation; it is quite possible, however, that the position of *e* in *dyde* between dentals might indicate a two-syllable pronunciation. The passage well indicates, then, the problems which confront the reader of such verse —verse which is mainly iambic pentameter but which has disconcerting variations from the normal pattern.

The last two lines specifically illustrate the most im-

---

[2] John M. Berdan, *Early Tudor Poetry, 1485-1547* (New York, 1931), p. 163.

portant question which must be answered before the precise nature of the metrical practice in this work can be determined. That question concerns pronunciation, including the vexing problems of accentuation and of syllabification. Is it possible that Skelton read the sixth line as normal pentameter? If so, he accented *foly* upon the second syllable. Is it possible that he read the last line with ten syllables? If so, he must have pronounced one of the final *e*'s in the line. But there are three words containing a final *e—tyme, were, dyde;* and if one final *e* is to be pronounced to make a ten-syllable line, which word is to be bi-syllabic? The difficulty with Frederick M. Padelford's suggestion that the final *e* may be pronounced in this verse[3] is thus seen to be that it cannot be reduced to any consistency.

Furthermore, there is the difficulty that, if Wyatt and Skelton knew this "secret" to Chaucer's versification, it would seem most probable that the Elizabethans and Dryden should have known it also. It is doubtful, even if Wyatt and other poets of his time pronounced the final *e* in some cases, that they could have rationalized Chaucer's practice. The Chaucer texts which the early sixteenth-century readers had did not contain all the final *e*'s that our modern texts supply. See A. K. Foxwell, *A Study of Sir Thomas Wyatt's poems* (London, 1911), for convenient quotations

---

[3]Frederick Morgan Padleford, "The scansion of Wyatt's early sonnets," *SP*, XX (1923), 148.

from the Richard Pynson edition of 1526. There is, of course, the possibility that the ending *e* might occasionally have been sounded in Wyatt's time without its employment to rationalize Chaucer's metrics; but it would seem doubtful that the ending was pronounced at all.[4]

Nor can Padleford's suggestion that the *es* ending is to be pronounced be reduced to consistency. In the following line from Wyatt, such a pronunciation will make a pentameter line:

> To fa/sshion faith / to word/es mu/table
> [Rondeau 6, 1. 12].[5]

But, in the following line, the ending *es* is evidently not to be pronounced:

> Of for/ced sighes / and trus/ty fere/fulnes
> [Sonnet 14, 1. 8].

An interesting analogy is provided by the ending *ed* in the line just quoted. Throughout the practice of most English poets the convention has been recognized that the ending is sometimes pronounced as an additional syllable, sometimes not; and this is obviously common in Tudor poetry.

Thus, if one were to apply the pronunciation of the final *e* or the final *es* in either Skelton's or Wyatt's verse with any consistency, as many lines which are

---

[4]However, Jakob Schipper in *A history of English versification* (Oxford, 1910), p. 163, reads some lines from both Wyatt and Surrey with the final *e* pronounced.

[5]Wyatt is quoted from *The poems of Sir Thomas Wiat*, ed. A. K. Foxwell (London, 1914).

now read as pentameter would drop from the classification as would be made regular.[6]

In one respect, however, Skelton and Wyatt seem to have applied a syllabification and accentuation which varies considerably from the modern. These concern words derived from French. There appears no historical justification for a Romance pronunciation in English of the early sixteenth century. Skeat says that, by 1400, French was no longer used in England as a spoken language outside the law courts, where either Latin or Anglo-French was used down to the year 1730.[7] Wyatt and Skelton seem normally to have employed English pronunciation of words borrowed from French:

> With quak/ing plea/sur more / than ons / or twise
>   [Wyatt, Sonnet 20, l. 4].

> I was / content / thy ser/vaunt to / remayn
>   [Wyatt, Sonnet 8, l. 5].

> Whose beau/ty, ho/nour, good/ly port
>   [Skelton, *The bouge of court*].[8]

> That ye / shall stand / in fa/vour and / in grace
>   [Skelton, *The bouge of court*].[9]

---

[6] Interesting confirmation of the opinion that the final *e* was not generally pronounced in Skelton's and Wyatt's time is provided by the song music which has descended to us. Berdan, p. 165, notes that according to the pronunciation indicated by the music for Skelton's "Manerly Margery Milk and Ale," "it can be stated positively that the final *e* was in no instance pronounced." John Murry Gibbon, in chap. iii. pp. 25-37, of *Melody and the lyric from Chaucer to the Cavaliers* (London, 1930), quotes several songs, with music, from the time of Henry VIII; and in no case does the music indicate the syllabification of a final *e*.
[7] W. W. Skeat, *A primer of English etymology* (Oxford, 1924), p. 6.
[8] *The complete poems of John Skelton*, ed. Philip Henderson (London, 1931), p. 41; cited hereafter as "Henderson."
[9] *Ibid.*, p. 42.

Yet there was undoubtedly a division in their practice, for they commonly used a Romance pronunciation for words derived from the French when those words appear at the end of the line. This practice is not limited to Skelton and Wyatt, however. In quotations which Berdan gives[10] from Caxton, Barclay, and Hawes, there are the following rhyme words: *eloquence, presence; britaigne, fountaigne, slayne; pleasaunce, suffesaunce; heryng, thing; sentencyous, pytous; invencyon, translacyon, ymaginacyon; dalour, langoure; doublenes, unhappines, doubtles; apparayle, male.* Similar rhymes are found in the work of the Scots poets of the time. And much later than Skelton and Wyatt, similar rhymes appear in the miscellanies; in *A gorgeous gallery of gallant inventions*, for example, are found such rhymes as *stable, comparable* and *passion, occasion*, the meter indicating that these last words should be stressed *occásión* and *pássión*. In Skelton there are such rhymes as *space, menace; counsell, hell*.[12] And in Wyatt there are such lines as:

> Yet this trúst I háve of fúll great áperáunce
> [Sonnet 9, 1. 9].

> That thérewithál be dóne the récompénce
> [Sonnet 9, 1. 12].

---

[10]Berdan, pp. 55-56, 147.
[11]*A gorgeous gallery of gallant inventions*, ed. Hyder Edward Rollins (Cambridge, 1926), pp. 53, 58.
[12]Henderson, pp. 44, 46.

Yet, though we grant a Romance pronunciation wherever it is needed in the work of Skelton and Wyatt, it is to be noted that such pronunciation only partially affects the problem of syllabification; it is, however, of aid in the accentuation of many lines.

With these preliminary questions answered, the next problem concerns definition of the precise character of the metrics found in Skelton and Wyatt. In a trial reading of the 126 lines(one of which was completely French and thus not included in the listing below) of the introduction to *The bouge of court*, 66 lines, or more than half, were found to be ten-syllable lines easily read as iambic pentameter with its normal variations of trochaic substitution at the beginning of the line or immediately following the caesura. Of these 66 lines, only 3 required a French accentuation of any words in the lines, 3 were read with the syllabification of a final *es*, only 4 contained a trochaic substitution after the caesura, and the final *e* was not pronounced at all. Twenty-eight lines had eleven syllables, a fairly common variation of the pentameter line; some examples are:

> His héad may be hárd, but féeble ís his bráin.
>
> She cást an áncor, and thére she láy at róad.
>
> Amóng all óthers I pút mysélf in préss.

Thirteen lines were also unmistakably after the pentameter pattern but had only nine syllables; some examples are:

> That 1 ne wíst whát to dó was bést.
>
> At Hárwich pórt slúmb'ring ás I láy.[13]

Thus 109, or more than 86 per cent, of the lines are iambic pentameter or common variations of the pattern. The remaining 16 lines were divided as follows: 7 lines containing ten syllables and five unmistakable accents, but not in the iambic pattern; 1 line with twelve syllables in the iambic pattern; 3 lines of twelve syllables but with five accents; and 5 lines of classified as "broken-back" line (or the four-beat doggerel); some examples are:

> What thóugh our cháffer / be néver so déar.[14]
>
> Wherebý I réde / their renówn and their fáme.[15]

The metrical character of Wyatt's early work is very similar. A trial reading was made of Rondeaux 1, 2, 5, 6, 7, and 8 and of Sonnets 1-21. Rondeaux 3, 4, and 9 and Sonnet 22 were not included because they were evidently intended to be tetrameter or the broken-back line of four marked accents divided in the middle by a heavy caesura. Sonnets 23-32 were excluded because they appear to be later work than most of the poems included in the reading and are quite close to pentameter regularity.

Excluding the refrains from the rondeaux, 372 lines were analyzed. More than half—208—of the lines

---

[13]*Ibid.*, p. 40.   [14]*Ibid.*, p. 41.   [15]*Ibid.*, p. 39.

could be read as iambic pentameter, allowing common inversions in accent. The ending *es* was used only once, and the ending *e* not at all. Of the remaining lines, 60 were found to contain ten syllables, but none of these was metrical in an iambic pattern. A somewhat smaller number of lines—56—contained eleven syllables. Many of these lines were metrical, with the variation of an extra unstressed syllable in one of the feet, as in the following example:

> That áre / with mé, / when fáyn / I would bé alóne
> [Sonnet 11, 1. 10].[16]

Twenty nine-syllable lines were found. In some of these, Wyatt evidently intended the pause at the caesura to compensate for a missing unaccented syllable; in others an unaccented syllable was left out for what seems a conscious desire to secure a "hovering"[17] effect by placing two accented syllables together, as in this line:

---

[16] I think that "I would" was contracted to "I'd" in speaking, and that this line is pentameter.

[17] The practice of using the pause at the caesura as compensation for a lacking unstressed syllable has been recognized by students of versification. The usage referred to here is merely an extension of that practice to other positions in the line. The position of two accented syllables together requires a certain compensating pause between the two syllables, which partially takes the place of the missing syllable. This practice, particularly when used frequently within the line, has also been called "sprung rhythm." When occurring in isolated cases, the practice, without strictly being a spondee, produces a spondaic effect. The practice has been used by poets other than Wyatt, as will be shown by these two lines from Yeats's "After long silence":

"Speech after long silence; it is right . . .
Upon the supreme theme of Art and Song. . . ."

> Unkynd / tóng! / right íll / hast thóu / me réndred.
> [Sonnet 11, l. 3].[18]

Sixteen lines were octosyllabic; of the 16, 13 were metrically regular tetrameters. Nine of these occur in Rondeau 2, a poem in which Wyatt started out with ten-syllable lines, then in the second stanza shifted to octosyllabics. The consistency within the individual stanzas would indicate, however, that Wyatt was conscious of the difference between the two. Finally, 13 lines contained twelve syllables. Most of these were metrically sound Alexandrines, but some others apparently had only five accents, the lines being conceived as variations upon the pentameter. The problem presented by such lines may be illustrated by the following:

> I fléy / above the wýnde, / yet cán / I nót / arríse
> [Sonnet 12, l. 3].

This line could easily be rationalized as a line of six iambic feet; but, since it occurs among a group of iambic pentameters and since it has five main accents, as marked, it is evidently to be read with five principal stresses. The line is thus a variation of the normal pattern, not written after a new pattern; one

---

[18] This example may have been intended as a ten-syllable line, with *red* of the last word as unaccented syllable. One rhyme word is *honoured*, which would indicate perhaps a weak-syllable rhyme between the two; but the other two rhymes in the octet are *aferd* and *towerd*, which would indicate, perhaps, that the two words *rendred* and *honoured* were slurred. The practice suggests the medieval rhyming of unaccented syllables, but the presence of the two other rhyme words indicates, certainly, a mixed usage or slurring.

foot is a foot of four syllables instead of the normal two; perhaps the effort is to achieve a metrical adjustment, through a "rushing" effect within that foot, to the meaning or image of flying "above the wynde." The explanation is tenuous, of course, and, I should judge, a very unusual one to be called upon in reading Wyatt's verse; yet I have proposed it thus seriously, for the moment, to illustrate further problems confronted in Wyatt's early metrical practice, especially.

A final observation on the metrics of these poems is that, if the verse is read not so much in an attempt to force the lines into strict iambic pattern, but more as prose is read, the poems will not present the rhythmical problem which at first seems to appear.[19] For example, we may take Wyatt's Sonnet 11, one of the "rough" sonnets:

> Bicause I have the still kept fro lyes and blame:
> And to my power alwaies have I the honoured;
> Unkynd tong! right ill hast thou me rendred;
> For suche desert to do me wrek and shame.
> In nede of succor most when that I ame,
> To aske reward, then standest thou like oon aferd:
> Alway moost cold, and if thou speke towerd,
> It is as in dreme, unperfaict and lame.
> And ye salt teres, again my will eche night
> That are with me, when fayn I would be alone:

---

[19]This is, of course, a subjective judgment; but perhaps it will not seem so much if the reader will consider the poems to present much the same rhythmical problem as the poetry of the Anglo-Saxons, of *Piers Plowman*, of the prose of the King James Version, and of modern free verse. As will be seen below, the association is of some importance, for the accentual rhythms of Old English verse still affected the metrics of the poetry immediately preceding Skelton's and Wyatt's.

> Then are ye gone when I should make my mone.
> And you, so reddy sighes to make me shright,
> Then are ye slake when that ye shulde owtestert,
> And onely my loke declareth my hert.

In this sonnet, six lines—4, 5, 9, 11, and 13—are easily read as metrical pentameters. Line 7 presents little difficulty, for we need only allow the accent to fall on the second syllable of *towerd*, an accent indicated by the rhyme, to read it as pentameter. And all the other lines except 8 and 14, have each five distinct accents. Thus the rhythmical pattern of all but two lines is quite similar if we allow the practice of using a greater or lesser number of syllables, or amount of time, between accents—what is normally called "sprung rhythm."[20] Lines 8 and 14 each have four distinct accents; these two lines seem to move in the direction of fifteenth-century poetry, a line divided by a heavy caesura and having two strong accents on each side of the caesura. The entire poem, then, does not present excessive difficulty if the lines are read naturally with normal accentuation—except in the case of *towérd*, as noted, and the probable case of *alwaíes*. Only two lines do not have a basic rhythm of five accents, and those two have the rhythm of much fifteenth-century verse.

The discussion up to this point would seem to in-

---

[20] Yvor Winters ("The sixteenth century lyric in England. Part I," *Poetry*, LIII [February, 1939], 265), says that sprung rhythm appears in Wyatt's sonnets and, more particularly, a "juxtaposition of accented syllables by . . . the dropping of an unaccented syllable from between the two accented."

dicate that the character of Skelton's long line and of Wyatt's early metrics has been misstated. In an endeavor to put the problem more appropriately, as a result of that discussion, we may make the following statements with reasonable assurance: (1) Wyatt did not "discover" the iambic pentameter line; it was in use by Skelton. (2) In a major portion of their work both Wyatt and Skelton seem to have had in mind a five-stress line as the normal pattern. (3) The "roughness" of much of Skelton's and of Wyatt's early metrics has been exaggerated.

At the same time, there appear in this verse many more variations from the normal pattern than are commonly used in the modern practice of metrics. It is this fact that disturbs the modern student of Skelton and Wyatt. The problem which confronts him is this: Why, when both Skelton and Wyatt knew the iambic pentameter pattern and based a large portion of their verse upon a five-stress line, did they allow so many variations from the pattern, variations which even, on occasion, destroy the pattern?

The following suggestions are offered as possible explanations of the metrical method involved in this verse. The first two, if found acceptable, would tend to limit the problem even more than the discussion above by explaining individual practices without providing an insight into the complete problem presented by the metrical practice. The last suggestion is by far the most inclusive.

1. The first suggestion is that perhaps we are to read more of the lines as pentameter than we currently do. There is some indication that both syllabification and accentuation were either wrenched or at the time naturally so pronounced that some of the lines which we now find "rough" were read as regular pentameters. Justification of this suggestion rests on two grounds: (a) The language in the early sixteenth century was somewhat unstable and this instability seems to have affected the syllabification of words. An example is the verbal ending *eth*. In the following lines the *eth* is surely to be pronounced:

> All thát / he wéar/eth ít / is bór/rowed wáre.[21]
>
> Thy shérpe / repúlse, / that príck/eth áy / so sóre
> [Wyatt, Sonnet 7, l. 6].

In the following line appear both practices, unless one should allow three syllables in the second foot:

> Who ríd/eth on hér, / he néed/eth nót / to cáre.[22]

Yet in the following lines the *eth* seems not to have been pronounced:

> Now háve / at áll / that líeth / upón / the boárd.[23]
>
> Who déaleth / with shréws / hath néed / to
> lóok / abóut.[24]
>
> And sóm / becáuse / the líght / doeth théim / offénd
> [Wyatt, Sonnett 10, l. 3].

[21] Henderson, p. 55.
[22] *Ibid.*, p. 53.
[23] *Ibid.*, p. 52.
[24] *Ibid.*, p. 56.

In Wyatt's Epigram 6 the *eth* was certainly pronounced, or there would be no rhymes for most of the lines:

> Ryght true it is: and said full yore agoo:
> "Take hede of him that by thy back the claweth";
> For none is wourse than is a frendely ffoo:
> Though they seme good: all thing that thee deliteth:
> Yet knowe it well, that in thy bosom crepeth;
> For many a man such fier oft kyndeleth,
> That with the base his berd syngeth.

But in the epigrams Wyatt has started to elide the vowel:

> The sonne retornth that was under the clowde
>   [Epigram 10, 1. 2].
>
> Sayth thebrew moder: "O child unhappye
>   [Epigram 16, 1. 3].
>
> Gaynward the sonne that showth her welthi pryd
>   [Epigram 20, 1. 4].[25]

(*b*) In addition to the argument upon the basis of the instability of the language, there is evidence that Skelton and Wyatt, as well as many other authors of the sixteenth century, did occasionally employ a wrenched accent. The clearest examples of this practice are the Romance pronunciations as discussed above where we found that such pronunciations must certainly have been used by a number of poets. One among many decisive examples is No. 2 of Wyatt's Miscellaneous Poems:

---

[25] These lines are possible four-stress lines, but this would not be an argument against considering the *eth* as not pronounced.

> O restfull place; reneewer of my smart:
> O laboors salve: encreasing my sorowe:
> O bodyes ease: O troobler of my hart;
> Peaser of mynde: of myne unquyet fo:
> Refuge of payene: rememberer of my wo:
> Of care coomefort: where I dispayer my part;
> The place of slepe: wherin I doo but wake.
> Bysprent with teares, my bedde I thee forsake.

Here the pentameter pattern is clearly dominant in every line except the second. But, inasmuch as every line but the second is patterned carefully upon the pentameter movement and inasmuch as each line seems to be carefully constructed in a similar way (a marked caesura at the end of each second foot is particularly noticeable), it may be considered probable that Wyatt wrenched, or at least leveled, the accent on the last word and read the line thus:

> O lá/boors sálve: / encréas/ing mý / sórowe.

2. The second suggestion refers particularly to Wyatt and is developed from a comment by Chambers upon Wyatt's early work:

> The measure of indebtedness [in the translations] varies from very close translation to the loosest of paraphrases. This division of Wyatt's work furnishes something of a puzzle. Much of it, especially in the sonnets, is stiff and difficult to scan; and even when full allowance has been made, both for Romance accentuation and for textual corruption, many lines can only be regarded as simply unmetrical.[26] The con-

---

[26] This term is acceptable only if Chambers refers to the iambic pentameter line. As we shall see in discussing the tradition of metrics which Wyatt inheritetd, the lines may not be precisely called "unmetrical."

trast with the finished *technique* of the balettes is very striking. Attempts have been made to explain these derivative poems as prentice-work, in which Wyatt was fumbling his way to a comprehension of the pentameter, with the help of a text of Chaucer perverted by oblivion of Chaucerian inflections. I cannot say that I find them plausible. No doubt Wyatt read Chaucer, and no doubt the true Chaucerian line had long been lost and the versions current in the sixteenth century lent themselves to misinterpretation. But Wyatt, in the balettes, shows himself as finished a craftsman with the pentameter as with any other measures. Clearly he understood it when they were written, and there is no reason for ascribing a priority in time to the sonnets and their congeners. . . . I cannot, of course, prove that some more awkward sonnets were not early. But it is noticeable, I think, that the awkwardness is at its height in those which most closely follow their originals. And my impression is that these ought to be regarded as mere exercises in translation or adaptation, roughly jotted down in whatever broken rhythms came readiest to hand, and intended perhaps for subsequent polishing at some time of leisure which never presented itself.[27]

It is hardly possible to believe, as Chambers suggests, that the translations were hurried work intended for later revision. Such revisions were made, but the translations were not fitted closely to the iambic pentameter line. Besides, if they had been hurried work, they probably would not have been circulated so widely as they appear to have been. And, finally, Wyatt was admired by his contemporaries as the person who introduced Continental literature and forms into England; so his readers must have considered the "roughness" to have been justified for some reason.

---

[27]Chambers, pp. 121-22.

But is is possible to believe, perhaps, that Wyatt, with some of his translations, considered his most important task in translation to be that of presenting a close rendering of the matter of the poem. Many of his versions are close versions; Wyatt was very much interested in the paradox or conceit in the poems that he was translating. Interested so much, then, in the content of the poem, he perhaps considered a polished metrics to be a secondary consideration and thus was content to leave many metrical irregularities. This opinion would, at least partially, account for the fact that the sonnets which are translations are the most irregular sonnets, metrically speaking, and for the presence of a "rough" sonnet—No. 26, a translation—among the group of metrically adequate sonnets, and Epigrams 22 and 26, also translations, among the "smooth" poems surrounding them.

3. The third suggestion concerns the metrical tradition which Skelton and Wyatt inherited. That tradition maintained a sharp distinction between lyrical and nonlyrical poetry. The former had been, particularly the songs, metrically successful during the fifteenth century. The serious verse, such as that of Lydgate, Hawes, and Barclay, generally employed a longer line, which was ponderous and cumbersome metrically. As C. S. Lewis points out in a very fine essay on fifteenth-century metrics:

> We often speak carelessly as if "metre" in general were bad in this period; but we are usually thinking only of the lines

which we try to read as decasyllabic. The octosyllabics even of Lydgate are good enough; so are the carols and other lyrics, and so, in its way, is the loose ballad metre of *Camelyn* and *Beryn*.[28]

The longer line, which we have called the "broken-back" line and which Lewis calls the "heroic" line of the fifteenth century, is characterized by Lewis as "a long line divided by a sharp medial break into two half-lines, each half-line containing not less than two or more than three stresses and most half-lines hovering between two and three stresses, in a manner analogous to the Anglo-Saxon types D and E."[29]

Now it is clear, as has been seen, that Skelton and Wyatt have in mind an iambic pentameter as the basic pattern for a large portion of their verse. At the same time, the metrical tradition which they inherited for serious verse did not include the iambic pentameter as a particularly common metrical type—however much the iambic foot in other measures was used in more lyrical verse. In fact, the tradition for this verse dictated no strict pattern, since many variations were allowed in the broken-back line of the fifteenth century, including little stricture upon the number of unaccented syllables and even a considerable variation in the number of stressed syllables in a line; thus the tradition, if it dictated anything, dictated a carelessness a b o u t metrical pattern, a variable metrical

---

[28] C. S. Lewis, "The fifteenth century heroic line," *Essays and studies by members of the English Association*, XXIV (1938), 28.
[29] *Ibid.*, p. 33.

scheme. So far as the tradition affected the poet, there was no compulsion toward a fixed form, and the poet could move from one pattern to another with comparative ease.[30]

There are lines in Skelton which cannot be resolved into five stresses and which seem definitely akin to the broken-back line:

> What thóugh our cháffer / be néver so déar.
>
> In a thróne which fár / clearer did shíne.[31]
>
> Of póetes óld, / which fǘll cráftily.
>
> Wherebý I réde / their renówn and their fáme.[32]

In the third line quoted above the double accentuation mark has been used to indicate secondary stress. The broken-back line commonly varied from two main

---

[30] I hope it is clear that I have tried to state this situation most cautiously and conservatively within the terms of the discussion previously applied to the problems. Actually, I believe that what we have is the existence side by side of two metrical traditions. The songs of the fifteenth century commonly continued the accentual-syllabic metrical system, known and useful to Chaucer. But the long line of the century was primarily adapted from earlier poetry, other than that of Chaucer, and was thus primarily in the accentual metrical system. Skelton and Wyatt inherited two metrical systems of arranging the poetic line. Certainly, Skelton—as evidenced by the "Skeltonics" of the short line—and possibly Wyatt felt no great qualms in mixing, upon impressionistic or whatever grounds, the two traditions in one composition. It would be likely that they so read Chaucer. And they were performing a job of adapting the long line, again, to the accentual-syllabic system. Wyatt, perhaps because of the Continental practice with a precise metrics and surely because of his own ability to detect the value of the commitment, made the complete transfer to the accentual-syllabic metrics. His practice was found useful to later poets and led to the use of the accentual-syllabic metrics as the chief metrical system from then to very recent times.

Confirmation of certain arguments in the text comes later in the century from Gascoigne, who in his *Certain notes* insisted that words in poetry should not be pronounced contrary to common use and who also advised that a poet should hold, throughout a poem, the "measure" with which the poem was begun.

stresses to two main stresses and one secondary stress on each side of the medial pause.

In Wyatt occur similar lines. The clearest examples appear at the ends of poems, where they seem to give a rushing, decisive effect, a sense of denouement. In addition, the four examples quoted below have a proverbial quality which might indicate that Wyatt associated the old metrics with a certain homely, proverbial wisdom and relied upon the metrics of such lines, as well as upon the meaning, to convey the right tone of decision for ending the particular poem. The examples are:

> For góode is the líff, / énding fáithfully
> [Sonnet 2, 1. 14].

> And wýlde for to hóld: / though Í sëme táme
> [Sonnet 3, 1. 14].

> [Plóweth in wáter / and só]weth in the sánd
> [Sonnet 8, 1. 14].[33]

> And thé rewárd / lítle trúst for éver
> [Sonnet 9, 1. 14].

In addition, Wyatt has among his sonnets obviously patterned after a five-stress line, one, No. 22, which is not five-stress at all; nor is the poem iambic pentameter. A majority of the lines are clearly broken-back in pattern:

---
[31]Henderson, p. 41.
[32]*Ibid.*, p. 39.
[33]This line might be read as a five-stress line, though not strict iambic. The brackets are a part of the Foxwell text of the poem.

> I abíde and abíde / and bétter abíde ...
> And éver my ládye / to mé dothe sáye,
> "Let me alóne / and I will provýde.
> I abíde and abíde / and tárrye the týde ..."
> Thüs do I abíde / I wótt allwáye,
> Nóther obtáyning / nor yét deníed.
> Àye mé! / this lóng abídyng
> Sémithe to mé / as whó sayethe
> A prólongíng / öf a díeng déthe,
> Ór a refúsing / öf a desýred thíng.
> Möch wáre it béttre / fór to bë pláyne,
> Then to sáye abíde / and yét shall nöt obtáyne.

Skelton's tetrameters present the same problems.[34] Here, for example, is a stanza from "Against Garnesche":

> My time, I trow, I should be lese
> To write to thee of tragedies,
> It is not meet for such a knave.
> But now my process for to save,
> Inordinate pride will have a fall.
> Presumptuous pride is all thine hope:
> God guard thee, Garnesche, from the rope!
> Stop a tid, and be well ware
> Ye be not caught in an hempen snare.
> Harken thereto, ye Harvy Hafter,
> Pride goeth before and shame cometh after.[35]

The first seven lines are clearly good tetrameters, metrically speaking; and the slight variation of an extra very weak syllable in lines 5 and 6 is common in

---

[34] It is to be noticed, however, that Wyatt's tetrameters, even the early ones, do not present the "roughness" of his work in the five-stress line.
[35] Henderson, p. 136.

verse. The eighth line has the common variation of omitting the first unaccented syllable; the ninth has an extra syllable; and the last line has six syllables carrying considerable stress. Such variations—which we should be careful not to overstate, since the last line, too, can be rationalized as a variant, if an unusual variant, of the iambic tetrameter—are just as surprising to the modern reader as a stanza of broken-back lines in the middle of a poem predominantly using a five-stress line:

> Malicious tongues, though they have no bones,
> Are sharper than swords, sturdier than stones.
> Sharper than razors that shave and cut throatis.
> More stinging than scorpions that stang Pharsotis.[36]

In trying to explain such metrical practice, one cannot say that Skelton and Wyatt could not write iambic lines, for they wrote many of them; in a number of poems the large proportion of the lines are, without question, iambic. But the main point of the discussion here is that Skelton and Wyatt were in the tradition of literary poetry when they did compose "rough" lines and thus that they would have felt no compulsion, other than that of their own ear and their own intentions, to make the lines fit a single pattern. But, under the influence of the metrical practice of Petrach and his follows, Wyatt must have experienced a pull in the direction of accepting a fairly exact pattern for

---

[36]*Ibid.*, pp. 140-41.

the normal measure of the line. In his later work he did make that acceptance.

The suggestion that Skelton and Wyatt need not have felt any compulsion toward a strict metrical pattern has interesting confirmation in the practice of poets who followed Wyatt. In *Tottel's miscellany,* for instance, the common meter is iambic. Tottel's editor very largely revised Wyatt's poems to conform with the meter. But there are many lines in the miscellany which present much the same problems of analysis as do many of Skelton's and Wyatt's five-stress lines. In No. 129,[37] a poem by Nicholas Grimald, who is thought by some to have been the editor of the miscellany and who was certainly a pedestrian poet, there are the following lines:

> So plaines Prometh, his womb to time to faile.
>
> Daphne, in groue, clad with bark of baytree.
>
> I mought say with myself, she will be meek.

Each of these lines may, of course, be read as iambic pentameter; but to do so would be completely to ignore common speech accent, a condition paralleled by many lines in Wyatt's early poems or in Skelton's use of the five-stress line. Likewise, in poem 187 appears the following line:

> In great pleasure liue I in heauiness.

---

[37] References are to *Tottel's miscellany (1557-1587)*, ed. Hyder Edward Rollins (Cambridge, 1928).

To read this line as strict iambic pentameter requires a Romance pronunciation of *pleasure* and a heavier stress on *I* than on *liue*, though *liue I* can be rationalized by the "hovering" effect that it achieves on those two words.

A rapid search among a few poems in the miscellany yields the following lines which present similar problems:

No. 201 (poulter's measure):
  Ah wofull man (quod he) fallen is thy lot to mone.

No. 241:
  Suffreth her play tyll on his backe lepeth she.

No. 253:
  No raunsome can stay the home hastyng hart.
  And sithe thou hast cut the liues line in twaine.

No. 259:
  That may myne hert with death or life stere.

No. 260:
  With golde and purple that nature hath drest.

A gorgeous gallery of gallant inventions, a miscellany published in 1578, more than twenty years after Tottel's, contains verse which presents very similar problems. Particularly striking are similar problems of rhyme and Romance accent, as well as of metrical pattern. On page 53, lines 15 and 16 are:

  Then say that who of fayth is holden stable:
  There may be to him none els bee comparable.

A set of rhyme lines of the sonnet, "A true description of Love," on page 58, are:

> Aske what loue is? it is a passion ...
> With talke at large, for hope to graze vpon,
> It is short ioy, long sought, and soone gon ...
> A great fier bred of small occasion.

The rhyme requires that *occasion* and *passion* be stressed *occásión* and *pássión*, usages very similar to lines in Wyatt's early sonnets. Indeed, this stressing of those two words, and similar words, seems to have been standard in literary pronunciations until about 1595. Further, unless the final *e* in *soone* is pronounced, in the third line quoted, two accents are thrown together, a condition similar to that of many lines in Wyatt and Skelton.

To take another example, in the *Shepheardes calendar* Spenser apparently tried to adapt his versification to the station of the rustic people who appeared in the eclogues. According to E. K.'s preface, he was also trying to achieve a manner like that of the "ancients." The result is that in certain sections of the *Calendar* we have an early Elizabethan attempt to write, so far as vocabulary and metrics are concerned, in the older tradition of English verse, the same tradition which Skelton and Wyatt inherited. The following speech by Thenot in the February eclogue (ll. 9-24) is metrically very similar to some of Skelton's and Wyatt's poems:

> Lewdly complainest thou laesie ladde,
> Of Winters wracke, for making thee sadde.
> Must not the world went in his common course
> From good to badd, and from badde to worse,
> From worse vnto that is worst of all,
> And then returne to his former fall?
> Who will not suffer the stormy time,
> Where will he liue tyll the lusty prime?
> Selfe haue I worne out thrise threttie yeares,
> Some in much ioy, many in many teares:
> Yet neuer complained of cold nor heate,
> Of sommers flame, nor of Winters threat:
> Ne euer was to Fortune foeman,
> But gently tooke, that vngently came,
> And euer my flocke was my chiefe care,
> Winter or Sommer they mought well fare.

The line in this passage seems normally to have four accents, with perhaps a suggestion of five accents in a few lines. But the pattern is quite loose: apparently, the accents may fall in almost any position, either immediately together or separated by more than one syllable. In the last two words of the next-to-last line quoted, it will be noticed that two accents are thrown together, a practice to be found frequently in the work of Skelton and in Wyatt's sonnets.

The parallel between Spenser, on the one hand, and Skelton and Wyatt, on the other, is by no means, of course, a complete one. By Spenser's time the iambic pattern—indeed, largely through Wyatt's efforts—had been well established. In many of the eclogues of the *Calendar* iambic pentameter is used. So in Spenser's work there is a conscious mixture of traditions, a greater choice than perhaps can be allowed Skelton or the early Wyatt. And the similarity in practice between the passage from Spenser and some of Skelton's and Wyatt's work throws significant light upon metrical problems confronting the early Renaissance poets. In writing as they did, Skelton and Wyatt were not being slipshod or unmetrical. Unlike the condition at Spenser's time, the iambic pentameter was not firmly established; rather, the metrical practice which preceded Skelton and Wyatt dictated, if anything, a very loose metrical structure. So Skelton and the young Wyatt were following a tradition of metrics, though in a different manner from that of Spenser; Skelton and Wyatt moved toward a full acceptance of the iambic pattern, whereas Spenser, in the eclogues, moved away from the iambic toward the o l d e r tradition for immediate purposes in those poems.[38]

---

[38] Pollard and Berdan also rely upon the metrical tradition to explain the metrical practice of the early sixteenth century. Says Pollard: "The modern reader who expects to find all the lines of a stanza of equal metrical length, or of different lengths arranged in a fixed order, may look askance at the suggestion that Barclay normally uses lines of four accents, but mixes with them (especially towards the beginning of his poem) others of a slower movement with five. Yet this is what Barclay found when he read Chaucer, as he must have done, in the editions of Caxton, Pynson, or Wynkyn de Worde, and I believe that he accepted these alterations as a beauty, and one which should be imitated" (quoted by Berdan, p. 51). Berdan says of the pentameter line: "In actual practice, however, this theoretical regularity was modified by opposing tendencies. Of these, undoubtedly the most important was the old national system of versification, according to which poems were still composed in the fifteenth century. The numerous manuscripts of the *Vision of Piers Plowman* attested the popularity of the type. But there, versification is based upon stress, and the exact number of syllables to a foot is unimportant. To the ear trained in such a system, therefore, an occasional extra syllable in the line was a matter of indifference. There was thus a strong tendency to scan the line by the number of accents, rather than by the number of syllables" (*ibid.*, p. 146).

IV

ON CONTEMPORARY LITERATURE

HART CRANE

University of Kansas City Review, Winter, 1949
Writers of Our Years, ed. A. M. I. Fiskin, 1950

I am one who looks upon the career of Hart Crane with bitterness. And I submit that it is difficult for a poet to write even today, nearly seventeen years after his suicide, about a poet who is so much an object-lesson in all that we think and do. Indeed, I would gladly go so far as does Yvor Winters and extend the comment; for Crane is not only an object-lesson for the poet today but also for Professor X, for the professor of English and American history and literature.

Crane's history is so commonly known that I need recapitulate it very briefly here. He was born nearly fifty years ago, on July 21, 1899, in a small Ohio town. From a pioneer heritage of trekking from New England to the Western Reserve country and then of moving from the farm to business, Crane's father became a wealthy candy manufacturer in Cleveland. When Hart Crane was seventeen, his mother and father separated; the youth, who had already started to write poetry, sided with his mother. An ambivalent attitude toward his father—rejecting the commercialism of the parent at the same time desiring recognition from him—was apparently only an initial and perhaps precipitating agent for the many ambivalences which plagued Hart Crane throughout his life. Always he alternated between hate for his father and a desire to please him; between trying to adjust to a commercial culture and rejecting adjustment to the standards of his society; between periods of exaltation and depression. The alternations gradually became more frequent as his life continued; they were stimulated by the problems of homosexuality and by his drunkenness and sexual excess. When it appeared that his most ambitious poem was largely a failure and he was unwilling or could not return to certain earlier and more successful modes of writing, he surely became manic depressive. After a year in Mexico, on April 27, 1932, as Crane was returning to New York, he threw himself into the sea.

Self-destruction ended the greatest poetic talent ever seen in America. It is a pitiful story which has affected all who have been interested in recent American poetry. Unfortunately, it is a story which has not brought a great deal of reflection upon its meanings. Crane has become, for a few, the poet who most brilliantly worked—as Crane himself occasionally thought—in a direction opposed to what was thought the world-weariness and negativism of T. S. Eliot. But as it turned out, Crane was the one most worldweary and most negative, and Eliot has survived to a Nobel prize.

Crane's suicide was in 1932, the year, it is to be remembered, at the bottom of the depression. Immediately he was considered to be martyr to America's social and economic follies; shortly his name was on the lips of those who had thought they could not understand his poetry before. Since that time the legend of his martyrdom and the attention brought to his verse have made him what might be called the poet's poet of our day; his influence has been second only to that of Eliot.

In one respect, I believe Crane's influence has been greater than that of Eliot. And that is that probably several times as many poems have been written about Crane as about Eliot. John Williams and I once started an anthology of these poems which we had thought of publishing for the fiftieth anniversary of Crane's birth. I am not certain that the collection has any considerable poetic power, and surely it is more enlightening about the attitudes of poets toward their craft than it is about Crane. These poets have put Crane in the center of almost every imaginable response to the craft of poetry and the position of the poet in our culture: there are many English poets represented as well as American, they run the gamut from the Freudian interpretation of a poem by Brewster Ghiselin to the directly Marxist of David Wolff. There is not space to quote from the several dozen examples, but two of the best, to my mind, are by Richard Esler and Yvor Winters. The last stanza of Esler's "At the Grave of Hart Crane" is

> There is for me no word beyond the Word,
> For him no fear beyond a futile fear;
> And I was driven to forget the spring
> And walk in the lost strict fabric of the year.

And the last stanza of Winters' "Orpheus: In Memory of Hart Crane" is

> Yet the fingers on the lyre
> Spread like an avenging fire.
> Crying loud, the immortal tongue,
> From the empty body wrung,
> Broken in the bloody dream,
> Sang unmeaning down the stream.

Certainly the poems about Hart Crane serve to demonstrate that Crane could mean different things to the poets who honored either his career as poet or his career as martyr. At first the career as martyr was of dominant interest. Crane was the latest example of the homeless modern poet, the poet who lived in a culture which could not sustain him either as writer of poetry or as person of sensitivity. It was not a new story. Probably no poet in England or America had felt at home in his culture since the time of Dryden. Various types of homelessness had been characteristic of poets before; bohemianism, sensational living, sexual and other perversion, all had been common for nearly two centuries. Bitterness, sporadic and unsystematic revolutionism, even prophecy and oracularism had been characteristic of many. And, in the extremes, had been the madness of Crabbe, Blake,

Clare, and the second James Thomson; there had been the effort to seek unconsciousness of pain in Coleridge, Poe, and others, and the greater effort to interrupt the continuity of modern experience of chaos, in such people as Rimbaud, D. H. Lawrence, and the developing surrealists; and there was the suicide of Vachel Lindsay and Crane's friend Harry Crosby, and the kind of "cultural suicide" of Rimbaud. Pain, homelessness, chaos were the common heritage of modern poets, and Crane suffered from the heritage more than most.

Insofar as anything so abstract and divorced from individual responsibility can be thought to blame—a culture, I suppose, can be blamed for its heritage. But the culture does not dictate the response to it; it may demand or exhort a response, but it cannot dictate the response completely. What is more remarkable than the failures of poets in the last century and a half is the number of great successes. Crane himself added a few pieces to this body of achievement. Indeed, if the culture is to be blamed, it is to be blamed not so much for the kind of isolation and pain forced upon the poet as for the kind of ideas it handed him for his use. Crane, then, is the most spectacular example of a double-edged fault which has affected poetry for many generations: on the one side is the fault of a society, itself so shoddy and chaotic that it cannot justly nourish its artistic talent, and hardly any better its scientific and inventive talent;

and on the other side is the fault of a group of shoddy ideas about poetry and art which the modern poet inherits and which are probably more difficult to throw off than the shackles of a famishing society. I am well aware that the two are intimately connected, but perhaps the division can be permitted here, for the moment, for what value it may have in this discussion.

And Crane was killed with a two-edged ax: one edge was honed sharp by the materialistic culture in which he was born, and the other edge was honed sharp by the ideas of Poe and Emerson and Whitman and Pound and Eliot; swinging the ax was Crane himself, and he used the two-edged ax to cut himself down.

II

I should like, now, to detail some of those ideas and their effect upon Crane's verse, and, finally, to devote some space to Crane's most successful poetry.

Crane was a brilliant example of the kind of poet so desired by the Romantics—the untutored youth who could speak great poetry. He was one of the least educated of modern poets; he quit high school after three years and, although he reported that his father had set aside money for his college work, he never used it. He had started writing poetry when he was thirteen, was publishing in the advanced journals of his day when he was seventeen and eighteen, at twenty-three he had thought of his largest conception, the idea for *The Bridge*, and he never matured to any large extent after that age. After he completed *The Bridge*, overwhelmed with a sense of its failures, it appears that he regressed to even more youthful ideas, and he committed suicide when thirty-two.

Untutored and youthful as he was, it must not be thought that Crane was a man unaware of the philosophic currents of his day. Indeed, it appears that he knew nearly all of them, and as a writer of prose he was quite conscious of these philosophic directions. And it is not to be thought that if he had had more education he would have been a better poet; this is an idle speculation, and it is quite possible to think that the schools, never noted for their fostering of genius, could have done him more harm than good. But, being untutored and youthful and striving to develop a point of view of his own, he in fact sampled the ideas current in the poetry and criticism of his day and gave them all a try in his thinking and in his poetry. In his poetry and in his life it is quite possible to chart most of the important influences upon poetry during the time of its publicized renaissance.

Crane, like Pound and Eliot before him, started out under an attachment to the immediately preceding poetry he knew—that of the late Romantics, Swinburne, Wilde, and the Pre-Raphaelites. Its attention upon an aural pattern and upon decorative image is evident in Crane's first published poem, "C 33":

> He has woven rose-vines
> About the empty heart of night,
> And vented his long mellowed wines
> Of dreaming on the desert white
> With searing sophistry.
> And he tented with far truths he would form
> The transient bosoms from the thorny tree.

But, like those older men, he quickly found his verse quite appalling. At the time, he was in New York—eighteen years old—and learning something of the exciting developments there; he was reading Marlowe, Donne, Rimbaud, Laforgue; but he was also reading with more immediate effect, the work of Melville, Whitman, Sherwood Anderson. Two of his early prose pieces were appreciations of Anderson. Advanced literature was dividing rather clearly into two groups: one we might call the sophisticate, which collected to its arms the metaphysical poets of the seventeenth century, the French Symbolists, and had as its leaders such writers as Joyce, Pound, and Eliot, with such magazines as *The Little Review* and *Others* as its publications; the other was that which felt itself as indigenous and traced its ansectry to Emerson, Whitman, Melville, and had as its leaders such people as Dreiser, Anderson, Sandburg, Masters, Lindsay and, at a critical level, those who sought an American myth, such as Waldo Frank and Gorham Munson, two who remained among Crane's closest literary friends; its magazines were *Seven Arts*, *Masses*, and *Pagany*, to which Crane shortly contributed.

Crane never clearly fell into either group. When arguments among them were forced upon him, he temporarily lost a friend or made a statement he later regretted; but of all the poets of his time he most attempted and achieved a synthesis of the two. His own practice and thinking demonstrate that the two were not essentially far apart in their dictates for the method to be used by the poet.

Let us take the American tradition, as we may call it, first. Poe has had a remarkable influence upon modern poetry, but mainly indirectly through a subterranean passage of the practice of the French Symbolists; there he most affected Pound and Eliot. Crane, too, was thus affected, but he is perhaps the only important modern American poet who read Poe directly as progenitor. It is difficult, however, to trace this influence exactly. Crane immediately recognized the faults of Poe's impressionism and his poor verse texture; but he apparently liked the rhythms and, with this as one reason among many, never did like the free verse of the Pound-Eliot practice. In Poe he found a fascination with the sea, which became Crane's greatest symbol, and such correlate images as the Isle, Belle Isle. There are a few other direct contacts between Poe's work and Crane's, notably in the evocation of Poe's image in "The Tunnel" section of *The Bridge* and in one or two parallel passages.

But the influence of Emerson and Whitman was more direct. In these two Crane found justification for being the innocent and untutored and child-like; Crane was almost the living embodiment of the Emerson and Whitman idea of the poet. Yvor Winters has ably argued, in his essay on Crane, the essence of the Emersonian doctrines, and I need only paraphrase the argument here. Emerson has said, "No man need be perplexed in his speculations. Let him do and say what strictly belongs to him, and though very ignorant of books, his nature shall not yield him any intellectual obstructions and doubts." He recommended "abandonment to the nature of things"; he said "that only in our easy, simple spontaneous action we are strong, and by contenting ourselves with obedience we become divine." Thus the counsel was surrender to the changing flow of experience and to impressionism and even to unconsciousness. Emerson—as well as others—lies behind the doctrine of automatic writing.

Crane was early attracted to Sherwood Anderson because he thought Anderson was so close to the undirected experience of men and women in the small towns; he once asked Munson, as early as 1919, if the success of Dreiser, Anderson, and Frost had not been achieved "more through natural unconsciousness than with a mind thoroughly logical or propagandistic." He all through his life felt that his primary job was to explore the emotions, his own emotions, as completely as possible. The poetry of John Donne stood for him as "a dark, musky, brooding, speculative vintage, at once sensual and spiritual, and singing rather the beauty of experience than innocence." Whitman, Anderson, and Emerson would have shown, then, the beauty of innocence.

In a strict sense, there is no difference—to use Crane's terms—between "sensual and spiritual." The godhood, the over-soul, is in each of us; by obedience to the inner impulse and insight only can we become divine. This doctrine naturally gathered to it a great many ideas which appealed to Crane. First was the attitude of contempt for the bourgeoisie and the feeling that the artist has the role of bringing new insight to them; an interesting experience of this kind is a passage from a letter in which Crane writes of Isadora Duncan's visit to Cleveland:

You, as well as some of my local friends, must share in my excitement at seeing Isadora Duncan dance on Sunday night. She gave the same program (all Tschaikowsky) that she gave in Moscow for the Soviet celebration and, I think, you saw it in New York recently. It was glorious beyond words, and sad beyond words too, from the rude and careless reception she got here. It was like a wave of life, a flaming gale that passed over the heads of the nine thousand in the audience without evoking response other than silence and some maddening cat-calls. After the first movement of the "Pathetique" she came to the fore of the stage, her hands extended. Silence—

the most awful silence! I started clapping furiously until she dissappeared behind the draperies. At least one tiny sound should follow her from all that audience. She continued through the performance with utter indifference for the audience and with such intensity of gesture and such plastique grace as I have never seen although the music was sometimes almost drowned out by the noises from the hall. I felt like rushing to the stage, but I was stimulated almost beyond the power to walk straight. When it was all over she came to the fore-stage again in the little red dress that had so shocked Boston, as she stated, and among other things told the people to go home and take from the bookshelf the works of Walt Whitman and turn to the section called "Calamus." Ninety-nine percent of them had never heard of Whitman, of course, but that was part of the beauty of her gesture. Glorious to see her there with her right breast and nipple quite exposed, telling the audience that the truth was not pretty, that it was really indecent, and telling them (boobs!) about Beethoven, Tschaikowsky, and Scriabine.

Another appealing idea was that the American tradition involved some kind of robustness and earthiness; Crane once said that the refiners of poetry were Williams, Moore, Stevens, but that the robust talent lay with Masters, Lindsay, and Sandburg. Crane was also much affected by the doctrine of searching for new sensations, indicated by Emerson and voiced so loudly by Whitman: in writing to Allen Tate about Eliot, Crane said early in his career: "I would like to leave a few of his negations behind me, risk the realm of the obvious more, in quest of new sensations, humours." This doctrine quickly gets a mystic glow which Crane recognized. The poet might be, as in

Shelley's phrase, an unacknowledged legislator to the world; he created new conceptions; by following the dictates of association and the metaphor he led to new, if illogical, insights; art, in this doctrine, is the search for new insight and for beauty. And, by a simple extension of the doctrine into the chaos of modern society, the poet quickly assumes a prophetic role—as did Emerson and Whitman: the man of letters in the twentieth century is a pioneer on new frontiers, seeking the mystically new; as in Crane's original conception of *The Bridge*, the poet might perform the prophetic role of erecting a bridge between the modern man's past and his future, showing him the mystical meanings behind the apparent chaos of his present. He could apprehend, as Whitman tried, the spirit of America. He continually dreamed and conquered new forms of life. The poet could lead the people to see that the meaning of present existence was linked with a past and with a glorious future. And, as one step along the way, the poet could, as Crane said in an essay on modern poetry, "absorb the machine, *i.e.*, acclimatize it as naturally and casually as trees, cattle, galleons, castles, and all other human associations in the past." His own effort in this direction—attempted also by Sandburg, Stephen Spender, and others—is indicated by the much-anthologized passage from "Cape Hatteras" beginning "The nasal whine of power whips a new universe." "It involves," Crane said, interestingly enough, along with traditional qualifications of the poet, "an extraordinary capacity for surrender, at least temporarily, to the sensations of urban life." This is Emerson almost by the word!

From this "American" tradition, Crane could have it both ways: he once quoted in an essay on Anderson a passage from one of Anderson's letters which read, "I am in truth mighty little interested in any discussions of art or life, or what a man's place in the scheme of things may be. It has to be done, I suppose, but after all there is the fact of life. Its story wants telling and singing. That's what·I want—the tale and the song of it." And, on the other hand, Crane could have the privilege of Whitman's role of the prophet. Surely only in the Emersonian doctrine of surrender to flux could it be thought that these roles could be bound together. Crane, of all the "robust" followers of the doctrine, was the one who took it seriously and tested it with his great talent. He found that the prophecy arrived at was faulty, and the failure of *The Bridge* was a contributing factor to his death.

We may now turn to what we are for the moment calling the sophisticate tradition. Instead of the role of the Isadora Duncan bringing culture to a people, the poet here has the role of the clown. This role is an old insight—it is found throughout nineteenth-century poetry, in Eliot's Prufrock and in others of his characters; Pound's career has been largely that of the clown. Crane's fullest statement of this is in his poem "Chaplinesque." It is a difficult poem, but the "we" of the poem, Crane once explained, includes Chaplin and the poet; the kitten represents the waifs whom Chaplin, the clown, would give succor:

> We make our meek adjustments,
> Contented with such random consolations
> As the wind deposits
> In slithered and too ample pockets.
>
> For we can still love the world, who find
> A famished kitten on the step, and know
> Recesses for it from the fury of the street,
> Or warm torn elbow coverts.
>
> We will sidestep, and to the final smirk
> Dally the doom of that inevitable thumb
> That slowly chafes its puckered index toward us,
> Facing the dull squint with what innocence
> And what surprise!
>
> And yet these fine collapses are not lies
> More than the pirouettes of any pliant cane;
> Our obsequies are, in a way, no enterprise.
> We can evade you, and all else but the heart:
> What blame to us if the heart live on.
>
> The game enforces smirks; but we have seen
> The moon in lonely alleys make
> A grail of laughter of an empty ash can,
> And through all sound of gaiety and quest
> Have heard a kitten in the wilderness.

Like the famous figures of the Tramp in American literature, the figure of the clown in our sophisticated literature—and of the court minstrel in an older literature—is that of the naïf, the person too innocent and innately pure to comprehend the forces which work upon him, or to stop traveling the endless road which he believes will end in fulfillment of desire and the capture of beauty.

Crane immediately recognized that this greater sophistication provided subtleties and possibilities the robustness of the "Americans" could not provide. Pound had once said that Whitman was the poet who broke the wood on which Pound would do the carving. At one level this involved a quality of language. Pound had revolutionized the language of poetry and provided a new diction, a denser diction than for any English poetry at least since Blake. And Crane appreciated the possibilities of this language. He once wrote to Tate that he was working "hard for a more perfect lucidity" of language. By that he meant—as in the doctrine of Eliot—that the word would be used with several layers of meaning; each layer could be peeled away to divulge another as lucid as the one before.

As a result of this practice and the criticism of Eliot and of Richards, among others, Crane developed a theory to justify his own handling of elliptical expressions. He called it the "logic of metaphor." The starting point seems to have been in Crane's use of the word *mirror*. For him, an image was a mirror; it flashed back to the poet and to the reader his own emotion and feeling; it flashed back reality. In an early poem, "Legend," he wrote:

> As silent as a mirror is believed
> Realities plunge in silence by
> . . . .
>
> Until the bright logic is won
> Unwhispering as a mirror
> Is believed.
>
> Then, drop by caustic drop, a perfect cry
> Shall string some constant harmony,—
> Relentless caper for all those who step
> The legend of their youth into the noon.

But the mirror-image is more than mirror, as he later discovered; it leads into reality, it *explores* reality. This conception is more dynamic than that, say, of MacLeish, who said

> For all the history of grief
> An empty doorway and a maple leaf.

MacLeish had the mirror-image conception, but not the conception of the image as means of leading into reality and exploring it. Following Eliot and Richards, Crane justified the associated metaphor on the basis of "pseudo-statement," that is, that poetry need not stand the test of examination with traditional logic. Instead, there is another kind of "truth," a truth non-scientifically determined, which is stated and explored in the immediate apprehension of the combinations of the metaphor. Crane thus absorbed the dominant attitude of poetry of his time—that poetic truth is different from scientific truth, yet valuable for its difference; that the poet is not a man of thought but a man who has techniques, through the metaphor and other devices, of exploring and communicating precise or vague emotion; the better the metaphor, the more precise the mirror of emotion.

The fallacies of this position have been well indicated by Yvor Winters: a language which is primarily connotative in intent gradually loses its power; the use of language with connotative intent and with ignorance of denotative intent is the use of one crutch instead of two; a poem depending upon the "logic of metaphor" is a poem without a subject or content. The difficulty is indicated even in one of Crane's remarks. In his essay on modern poetry, Crane said, "When Blake wrote that 'a tear is an intellectual thing, And a sigh is the sword of the Angel King'—he was not in any logical conflict with the principles of the Newtonian Universe." Blake, fortunately, understood this better than did Crane; he knew that his ideas were in conflict with Newtonian science and he, in fact, thought that Newton was a creature of the devil.

On one important principle, the "sophisticated" school of Pound and Eliot completely joined hands with the "American" school, and that is the principle of organic form. Crane seemed at times to see the difficulties of the principle, for he often spoke of the necessity of the poet to give form to the chaotic experience of modern industrial life. But the impact of the principle was too strong on a man who tried almost all ideas, particularly an idea which permeated the writing of the most powerful and even divergent influences of his day. When Crane was working on *The Bridge* and finding it hard going to whip the conception, in which he had largely given up faith, into its final form, one of the sections remaining to be done was "The River." He wrote to friends that it would not "spill" out its "organic form (there is always just *one*)." He had come to be able to write only under the pressure of a new conception and in a highly excited emotional state; the poem had to come shaped from his original insight or he found it nearly impossible to get it down at all. Indeed, while he was finishing up *The Bridge*, he wrote to Munson: "God knows, some kind of substantial synthesis of opinion is needed before I can feel confident in writing about anything but my shoestrings . . . These Godless days! I wonder if you suffer as much as I do. At least you have the education and training to hold the scalpel." Note the need that the form be presented to him; his doctrine of organic form required that form be given to him with the conception, or he could not attain form.

A number of curious ideas flow logically from the doctrine of organic form, and Crane, I believe, knew them all. The doctrine simply says that the job of the poet is to *discover* the form of an experience; the poet is a *discoverer*, not a *maker*. To Crane and Eliot and many others, modern life was chaotic, lacking spiritual or other direction. Thus, the form of experience, and of poetry also, must have those characteristics; this explains, for example, the romantic irony, the twists and shocks, in much of Eliot's early practice. The doctrine is one whereby the poet may surrender to his material, not manage it. If one is mystical in the Emersonian sense, he need not worry about this surrender, for the apparent chaos of flux is only apparent chaos; the presence of the over-soul in the flux makes it directional. As Winters has pointed out, such people as Emerson, Whitman, and Eliot had certain reserves, of character or habit or whatever, which prevented complete exploration of the doctrine of surrender; only Pound, apparently, and Hart Crane had, at times, the sensibility and the power to do so. Crane could surrender. As early as the fall of 1922 he wrote some friends: "I want to keep saying 'Yes' to everything and never be beaten a moment." And his biographer Brom Weber (to whose work I am indebted for quotations from "C 33" and for the many quotations from letters used in this essay) points out that all the spiritual strains of his life, despite their pain, combined to make him consider the flux of events as the expression of forces more powerful and true than himself, and therefore to be welcomed rather than rejected. Indeed, he borrowed three further doctrines from the general theory. One was that only in the experience of artistic endeavor (or in unconsciousness) could one escape the surrender or participate in it selflessly. Another was that the surrender was most valuable when there was most immersion in feeling; like Thomas Wolfe, Crane believed in the efficacy of strong sensation, from drunkenness to whatever else. And the third, which links up with the long tradition of pain and isolation I have already indicated for the poet in western culture, was that through immersion in pain came the greatest understanding and spiritual insight. Shelley had expressed it innocuously and innocently when he said, "Our sincerest laughter with some pain is fraught; Our sweetest songs are those that tell of saddest thought." Only a Rimbaud or a Crane, who thought that he was Rimbaud's heir, could take the idea completely seriously and live it.

Under the doctrine, then, pain was necessary to insight. "The Tunnel" section of *The Bridge* evokes the figure of Poe and his pain and the long history of exploring degradation as a means of getting at the essential and simple knowledge. This interest in degradation had dominated much literature for a century. Again, Crane felt that a certain amount of confusion was necessary in experience before the artist could bring it into form. And finally, the ultimate conclusion of the direction is indicated by an event in Crane's life in 1930. A friend had suggested to Crane that he should submit to psychoanalysis to see if that could help his psychological state. Crane refused, and he did so on grounds—perfectly sound grounds, under an extension from the doctrine of organic form—that he couldn't be sure disorder wasn't responsible for his past achievements and that his talent for new achievements wouldn't be destroyed by greater order in his own life!

The case of Hart Crane is surely that of the greatest poetic talent ever born in America, not fostered or provided a true home in the culture into which he was born, and bred upon a group of ideas which he inherited from Poe, Emerson, Whitman, the French Symbolists, Pound, Eliot (and also from the men who shaped the thoughts of those men)—a group of ideas which Crane had the great ability to explore fully as no other among them, except possibly Pound, had the talent to explore. What is the result? Pound is now in a mental institution, and Crane destroyed himself. I prefer to think that among all the forces upon Crane, the forces of these ideas were sufficient to destroy him.

III

I want now to try to assess what residue is left from Crane's career. The full book of his work is not large, and most of the work in it must be scattered to dust. The doctrines he used would produce poetry almost by miracle; but Crane was at times a mystic and himself a miracle, as with genius, and at times the miracle of important composition happened to him.

First of all, there is the great verbal magic of his lines. Mainly they make only fragments. To try to list all of them would be an arduous and not significant task. But I wish to use only a few phrases to indicate the great "logic of metaphor" he could command; meantime, these lines and the methods behind them will prepare us for a better reading of the full poems I shall consider.

Some of the best of these lines are those dealing with mystical experience. By definition, I suppose, the mystical experience is not amenable to usual logical expression; only the metaphor will do it adequately. In one of his early poems, "Possessions," Crane concluded:

> The pure possession, the inclusive cloud
> Whose heart is fire shall come,—the white wind raze
> All but bright stones wherein our smiling plays.

This is, I believe, a true metaphysical metaphor; that is, it progresses intellectually as well as sensibly. The experience of possession is here mystical, the possession of the apprehension of truth; in that experience is the heart of fire in the midst of an inclusive cloud; the wind, which surely comes by association from the cloud and the breath which feeds the fire, is white with purity; yet even such purity can raze, can raze all consciousness of another possession, a worldly possession of goods, shall we say; but it cannot raze the essential thing, "the bright stones wherein our smiling plays." Here the imaginative leap is great. The stones are bright, I suppose, spiritually, analogous to the white wind; they are stones because stones are the most permanent things known to man's senses and the most indestructible; in this permanence are plays or delights, and our smiling has a home, as perhaps in heaven.

Another is much more brief, from the poem "Recitative," in which Crane surely comes close to capturing the experience of time as a unity which Whitman and Eliot so endeavor to attain. It is a specious effort, perhaps; at least the confusion of time is very much like the confusion of subject which lies at the heart of Eliot's connotative handling of language; but here is Crane's effort to put it into a metaphor:

> In alternating bells have you not heard
> All hours clapped dense into a single stride?

I shall not pause over it except to remark the word *dense;* if the perception of time as unity is possible, it must be dense, for it combines past, present, and future into one.

One of the most remarked metaphors in all modern poetry occurs in two lines from the last section of *The Bridge.* The words are addressed to The Bridge as symbol which unites many things which we shall examine more closely below.

> O Thou steeled Cognizance whose leap commits
> The agile precincts of the lark's return.

I have many times participated in parlor games of argument concerning this metaphor. Is it metaphysical, with intellectual development, or is it merely operative at the sensory level? It is obviously sensory; we are supposed to see the bridge leaping through the air, which is the precincts of the lark's return. However, I am now convinced that it is intellectual, too. The bridge, by a species of expansion of a physical fact which delighted Crane so much, is a steeled cognizance (only a disciple of pantheism could, of course, believe that steel has cognizance) which in its leap across space does a great deal. First of all, the leap *commits*; it is statement and action; and it commits "the agile precincts of the lark's return." Once I would have thought this pure sensory derangement, as in the French Symbolists and their followers, for precincts cannot be agile; but the words attribute to the precincts a characteristic of the lark, which certainly can be agile. This, again, rests upon a particular mode of belief: the air and the earth, which are the precincts of the lark's return, are agile, alive, cognizant, possibly as much so as the bridge; but the aliveness has a direction, for they are not the precincts of the lark's flight or adventure, but of the lark's return, as if he were returning to his nest and home. I do not like to place the reading of these lines upon such a personal basis; but the "logic of metaphor" is so undemonstrable, at times, that one is left only with asserting the reading to which, at that moment, he has attained. Unfortunately, it remains assertion.

The number of Crane's poems which seem completely successful is quite small. His method, as with that of most modern poets, was not conducive to writing a rounded, completed poem but rather to the composition of brilliant passages; particularly is this true of one who strained the theories and the language so strongly, discontent with both used more tamely. Winters greatly admires only two: "Repose of rivers" and "Voyages II." Tate has called "Praise for an Urn" the greatest elegy written in America. I shall comment on this core of three poems admired by such distinguished critics, plus a few others.

"Praise for an Urn" is an admirable poem which, as I return to it again and again over the years, seems to me to work less and less successfully. The early parts of it, particularly, I now find vague and soft. I believe that it is not nearly so good an elegy as Edwin Arlington Robinson's "For a Dead Lady." In fact, "Praise for an Urn" is in part not so much an elegy as a critical comment on modern life, and I think that its last stanza, a fragment, makes a fine statement of a certain predicament in modern life:

> Scatter these well-meant idioms
> Into the smoky spring that fills
> The suburbs, where they will be lost.
> They are no trophies of the sun.

The poem combines, at a fairly high order, I think, awareness of the character of our cities, our suburbs, and our mechanized civiliziation with a fine apprehension of the romantic emotion of loss with which they may quite properly be viewed.

A very great statement of this loss, but more urgently and spiritually considered, is in "Voyages V." The opening of the poem is marred by verbal pyrotechnics and lack of control of the language, but this section, again a fragment, seems to me altogether admirable:

>   For we
> Are overtaken. Now no cry, no sword
> Can fasten or deflect this tidal wedge,
> Slow tyranny of moonlight, moonlight loved
> And changed . . . "There's
>
> Nothing like this in the world," you say,
> Knowing I cannot touch your hand and look
> Too, into that godless cleft of sky
> Where nothing turns but dead sands flashing.
>
> "—And never to quite understand!" No,
> In all the argosy of your bright hair I dreamed
> Nothing so flagless as this piracy.

I submit that this is a very special kind of piracy; the spiritual loss is greater, surely, than in Eliot's "The

Hollow Men." (It is, by the way, a poem which is an echo of Poe's "The Sleeper.")

"Voyages VI" is also greatly to be admired. I can understand a refusal to like it, for it is one of the poems in which Crane is trying his best to grasp the image of true knowledge and belief, the source of permanence. Without a feeling for romantic pantheism, the poem is largely verbal trick. I shall not quote it but invite a reading of the catalog—which remains catalog, largely, I am afraid—of the images Crane uses for the idea of permanence.

For those who have read Winters' story "The Brink of Darkness," I think there will be recognition of the reason he has so admired Crane's "Repose of Rivers." The poem is the exploration of a problem similar to that of the story: the terror of the doctrine of surrender, the terror which lies at the heart of full acceptance of the Emerson, Whitman, Eliot notion of letting the experience shape itself. The Winters story and the Crane poem are the only two thorough examinations of the problem which I know in story or poem. "Repose of Rivers" is to be examined at leisure throughout the entire poem, for it is one of the few pieces by Crane which is great composition throughout its entirety.

Similarly do I agree with Winters concerning "Voyages II." I believe that it would be difficult to find any modern poem other than this one which would receive so great an unanimity of agreement upon its greatness among critics of various perspectives. Insofar as Eliot's *The Wasteland* has a subject, I believe that "Voyages II" has a similar subject. It is concerned with the basis for knowledge and faith, in other words with the descent through the wasteland to purgation, even death, to attain some permanence. It is thus upon the theme which most of the serious poets of the last fifty years have attempted at one time or another, and it is surely one of the greatest poems written on the theme.

I have left only a few paragraphs for a consideration of *The Bridge*. I suppose one might say that there have been three efforts, in recent times, to write major poems in English. One is Pound's *Cantos*, another is Eliot's *The Wasteland*, and the third is Crane's *The Bridge*. Perhaps there are others, but I do not recall them at the moment. One should note that the effort of this kind by William Carlos Williams, *Patterson*, is partially completed.

Without a great deal more study, I should not like to hazard a guess concerning the comparative value of the three efforts. Pound's, as a matter of fact, is not completed, although we do not expect him to give us, in the last seventeen cantos, much work different from that he has given us in the first eighty-three. But certain it is that all three poems are very faulty poems. *The Cantos* and *The Wasteland* are very much alike in that their structure is the speaking voice of the Pound-Eliot conception of the cultured gentleman, like Coleridge, who reads widely and who has little faculty other than that of letting the unconscious and conscious mind work on the reading and regurgitate it in an associational pattern. Crane's at least was not like that, although I think his failure may have been greater.

The Bridge was conceived early as one of Crane's efforts at the role of the prophetic Whitman. He would write a poem which would explain the essential and ongoing spirit of America to the American people. But he could not do it with the shoddy nuances and sloppy feelings of a Sandburg talking about wheat in the Midwest or Chicago as hogbutcher of the world. He needed a tougher, denser language, and that involved a symbol; he even wanted a myth, and thereby lay one of his troubles. I do not know that anyone has demonstrated how myths arise (perhaps the rising young critics of myth will do it for us), but I am quite certain that a myth is not created by the assertion of one poet's will to myth. So the bridge remains a symbol, not a myth, of American development. And also it does not achieve, as Crane hoped, a mystical apprehension of an American spirit; it is doubtful if there is any such spirit, but if there were, it would hardly be apprehended by considering only a few selected facts of American history.

The bridge is a symbol of Crane's effort to suggest a way of uniting the American past with its destined future and thus to show the meaning of its present.

The bridge, of course, is Brooklyn Bridge, considered one of the mechanical beauties of our culture. Crane discovered, after he had left it, that he had lived in the room occupied by the cripple who had supervised the construction of the bridge, and Crane even projected a biography of this little-known engineer. The bridge is a physical fact, joining two shores. With the species of expansion upon a physical fact, which I have remarked above as particularly delightful to Crane, the bridge becomes extended as a symbol of material progress, the spanning of any two shores, however extensive. And then it moves to become a spiritual symbol, a link between cultures, between ideas, perhaps between God and man. In addition, the bridge, at the physical level, becomes other things. At times in the poem it becomes a ship, at times a world on which man stands, at other times a woman, and also, because of its cables, a harp. The bridge shall vault not only East River but also a continent, two seas, Europe and Cathay, the West and the East, matter and spirit.

The fault of the symbol is fairly obvious: it is too mechanical and will not take the whole weight of dense meaning put upon it. Crane early recognized this. A considerable time before its completion, Crane wrote to friends that he was finding the theme and project more and more absurd. Yet he determined to finish it, largely out of honor and out of the debt he felt to Otto Kahn for the money Kahn had given him for completion of the work. He determined to make it a brilliant, a great, failure, and this he did.

The extent of the success and of the failure will take considerably more examination. Still greatly to be admired, I think, are the verbal ability and also the tentative insights provided by the last section, although that section, upon which the final thrust of the poem depends, is largely a failure and even works, as Brom Weber has indicated, at cross-purposes to the original idea of the poem. Of this final section "Atlantis," from "O Thou steeled Cognizance" to the end of the poem, I can only assert that even Eliot and Pound cannot write so well without a subject.

Another much-quoted section is "The Tunnel," in which the dread of modern life is reported so well; but it remains essentially brilliant reporting, unless one take the attitude presented by Brewster Ghiselin that, under a Freudian interpretation of Crane, the tunnel is Crane's mistaken but self-imposed psychological need to degrade himself and then a failure to face the degradation. Tate's comment seems to me extremely pertinent: the "Cape Hatteras" section uses the airplane as symbol of man's growth and spiritual development, but in "The Tunnel" section the subway is used for the opposite symbol. Tate wonders why the two can't be interchanged; the mechanical nature of the symbols and their impressionistic character are thus quite clear.

It is my impression that the other sections of *The*

Bridge are not so generally known and anthologized as "The Tunnel" and part of "Atlantis." However, there is much great poetry in several of them, too much to be noted in detail here. "Proem" is certainly important language, and I would agree fully with others that "The River" section has, at its close, the finest poetry in *The Bridge* and some of the best Crane ever wrote.

In the much belabored passage called "The Dance" Winters and others have paused to note that in a decisive moment, when Crane would establish in the verse the mystical union with Pocahontas as also a union with the American earth, he says, "Lie to us,—dance us back the tribal morn!" It is worth remarking, because here we have another evidence of Crane's thinking similar to that of many of his fellow-writers. As in much of D. H. Lawrence, and as in such Eliot lines as "I should have been a pair of ragged claws scuttling across the floors of silent seas," there is an indication of the death-wish, the wish, at least, to give up consciousness to the unconscious life.

IV

Tate has remarked that the ideas Crane held asked of nature that it have perfection, and that they asked of the poet that he have intensity. This is a wise insight. Crane certainly had intensity, most among the writers of our time; nature was probably imperfect. Crane lived certain theories fully and, in a sense, rode them to his own destruction. Out of the intensity of experience and of language he left some very brilliant fragments and a few full passages of great poetry. It is idle to speculate what he would have been like—what he would have done— with other ideas; I believe he recognized as well as anyone that they were the source of what accomplishment he had attained and also that they were destroying him. We have left the contemplation of the life and of the poetry, so spectacularly full of pain and bitterness, once for Crane and always for the onlooker. I hope that this essay will help the onlooker to a feeling of a double-edged tragedy in the pain. It is the feeling with which I would read that much remarked and very great line with which I close; Crane knew, I believe, that the arrows were shot by others but also by himself, and that they were not merely physical. The line is

> I could not pick the arrows from my side.

THE SAGE OF PALO ALTO
Rocky Mountain Review, Spring-Summer, 1940

Yvor Winters was born in Chicago in 1900, received his A.B. and A.M. from the University of Colorado and his Ph.D. from Stanford, and is now professor of English in the latter university. Though he is now but a little less than forty years old, he has distinguished himself, in his later poetry, as one of our most serious and intelligent poets, has fathered a group of poets first gathered about his little magazine, *Gyroscope,* and easily ranks among our four or five most stimulating and most penetrating critics.

It is with the criticism that we are primarily concerned in this essay, but it will not be amiss to notice one or two other matters about Mr. Winters. One of them is that he carries his own critical judgments over into his creative work, and, reciprocally, his critical judgments have often grown out of his working experience. An example is his attitude toward free verse: Winters' first poetry was experimental work in free verse; it is an experimentation with, and an investigation of, the technical possibilities of free verse, as is shown in *Primitivism and Decadence,* more self-conscious and critical than that of other writers of free verse, including Pound; and when Winters found the free verse technique essentially limited, he turned elsewhere for the techniques of his later poetry.

A second matter of interest about Winters is that he is disliked in many poetry camps. The fact is significant in that it throws light upon our poets and critics and upon Winters himself. For the truth is that our poetry, and especially our criticism, is today dominated by various cliques. One sometimes suspects that Winters himself is not absolutely above this tendency when he puts such a high opinion on his group of Gyroscope poets and when he occasionally lets his critical theories over-rule his empirical judgment of a poem; but that he has such a little of this tendency is a great relief in an age when it is so blatant among others. Fundamentally, Winters holds to his resolve and to his opinions without quarter to any reputation. He has one of the most prized of Western virtues, the determination to "stick by his guns."

Winters' criticism is, in one sense, no more than well under way: his last work, for example, announced two more projects of work. So this is no time to attempt a summary of his criticism. But while we are waiting for his third book, we may consider for a moment his fundamental position and some misconceptions his reviewers have had concerning his work, and may strive to call more attention to his stimulating, but too much neglected, books.

The reviewers have falsified Winters' work by looking only at what they have sometimes called his conservative, moral, and humanist position. There are many, including the present writer, who cannot see their way clear to the acceptance of the attitude outlined by those reviewers. But to stop at that point is to abrogate the function of the critic. For Winters' fundamental critical theories are as applicable, as good basic criticism should be, to one position as to another. Indeed, though Winters does not fear to state explicitly his judgments of specific literary works and of individual authors, he nowhere thrusts forward his own position on social or other specialized philosophical and esthetic problems. The present writer would, in fact, feel hard pressed to state Winters' position upon crucial problems of our times; that position may be what the reviewers believe it to be, but Winters' critical work is obviously to be criticized on the basis of social ideas only if and when another position would find his critical theories false to the literary problem or when Winters, if he ever does, makes an issue of his social ideas. His work to date, however, has remained remarkably close to considerations of the technical literary problem.

One matter that has thrown the reviewers off the track—through their own misinterpretation, however—has been Winters' concern with the "moral" obligation of the writer to the "moral" element of the particular work. But Winters apparently uses the term *moral* in a sense which we might describe, though with some falsification, as similar to the psychologists' concept of *attitude*. It is the integration (if the author attains integration) of response by the author to the literary situation. As such it emphasizes the dramatic character of the work, the writer as *dramatis persona,* an element which, though many writers do not seem to be aware of it, is an absolute ingredient of composition (*composition* is here used as a pun, meaning both the act of writing and the finished piece). In fact, Winters is much concerned with arguing for and illustrating the validity of using this element of art as one basis for criticism. And it would seem to this writer that this concern should be as pleasing to the Marxist, for example, as to any.

Moral, in Winters' terminology, then, stresses the writer as *man,* as social and moral man as well as, if he can be conceived by any one but the casuist for pure poetry, professional (nothing-else-but) writer. The writer has an obligation, a necessity, in fact, if he is to write well, to write as a full-bodied man, as a man of responsibility in possession of his faculties; this position is also implied in Coleridge's famous definition of imagination as "the balance or reconciliation of opposite or discordant qualities;" for to be sentimental is to be less than the full-bodied man. And Winters maintains that this "moral" element of a work is one of the subjects of criticism. It is a critical principle which the Left has attempted to establish for some time, though the left critics, when not muddled, have carried it too far or have used it in an entirely specialized and thus, in Winters' sense of the term, "immoral" manner.

Winters is also, and perhaps primarily, concerned with the "moral" value of particular literary techniques, with the value of those techniques for the objectification of the "moral" experience in the particular literary work. This matter, with a wealth of illustration and argument, occupies the longest and most valuable portions of his first critical book, *Primitivism and Decadence* (Arrow Editions, 1937). Analyzing recent American experimental poetry, Winters finds that the techniques used in that poetry are, in reality, essentially limited techniques, that they are valuable in objectifying only a limited range of experience, and that they often tend toward diffuse and uncontrolled ("immoral") writing. He argues that the acceptance of a stricter form allows the poet opportunity for more freedom and precision than does the acceptance of a loose structure. His comments upon metrics of both the experimental and the traditional poetry are especially valuable.

Winters' second book of criticism, *Maule's Curse* (New Directions, 1938), is sub-titled "Seven Studies in the History of American Obscurantism." The seven studies are on Hawthorne, Cooper, Melville, Poe, Emerson and Jones Very, Emily Dickinson, and Henry James. The most valuable of these are the essays on Cooper, Melville, Henry James, and Poe, though every chapter contains much sharp analysis.

The one on Poe, it may be noted in passing, is a refreshing bucket of cold water thrown in the face of the seriousness with which American scholars study Poe as a fine literary artist; Winters argues in a convincing manner that Poe's poetry is of little value other than for historical and critical interest and that his critical theories were not only false but also wrong-headed.

Obscurantism is for Winters "the ultimate development of Romantic aesthetic principles qualified to a greater or smaller extent by certain aspects of American history." It results from a dilemma of the artist, a dilemma "tragically characteristic of the history of this country and of its literature," which presents itself as a chooice between "abstractions inadequate or irrelevant to experience on the one hand, and experience on the other as far as practicable unilluminated by understanding."

There is not space left to discuss Winters' analysis of obscurantism as it appears in the eight American writers listed above. But it is to be observed that Winters has developed a valuable critical approach useful in analyzing the work of any writer; for example, the fact that Spenser moved away from experience to "abstractions inadequate or irrelevant to experience" ruined the most ambitious body of his work. And Winters' criticism should be fair warning to those present-day writers who are so excited about the work of Franz Kafka and who, under Kafka's influence, are turning to an abstract and allegorical method, both in poetry and in fiction.

Finally, two more observations on Winters' critical work are of particular importance. The first is that Winters has largely resisted the tendency of modern criticism towards specialization. Ours is undoubtedly an age of critical importance, but we have produced few critics of broad insight; rather, each critic has marked off his own little patch in the field and has set to work with vigor. The Marxists have stayed pretty close to the social significance of literature and to the social influences upon the writer; R. P. Blackmur has made some penetrating studies into the use of language in poetry; Kenneth Burke has strayed away from the particular art object to talk about general theories; John Crowe Ransom has followed a somewhat similar process, though talking about different ideas; T. S. Eliot has probed around a lot in the past with a number of stimulating critical essays, but without attempting to state an integrated critical outlook; William Empson has played a sort of parlor game with his quick fancy, excitably pursuing every minute ramification of a poetic image. All of these have produced useful studies, but no one has appeared to integrate them. Of the better critics, only Allen Tate and Yvor Winters have combined a close analysis of the individual work, a varied approach for the varied objects, and an apprehension and development of fruitful general theories; and of these two, Winters has so far done the more extended work.

The final suggestion, hardly suggested by the considerations above, is that some of Winters' most valuable work consists in detailed analysis of particular poems, and at last in *Maule's Curse,* of works of fiction. He possesses one of the most penetrating critical perceptions of our time. He will do us a good service if he, unlike so many critics, never lets his theories get a more extensive control over that perception.

AN EXAMINATION OF MODERN CRITICS:
6: YVOR WINTERS
Western Business, 1947

1.

Recently the great critical renaissance of our time has seemed to turn in upon itself. Much effort on the part of the critics has gone into examination of one another. In fact, the examination of a critic's position has become a sort of favorite parlor game for the literary reviews. One may reasonably expect this of the small critics, but it has been indulged in also by the best of our critics.

It is difficult to be certain of the reason for this. There are at least two possible reasons. One of these may be that the criticism has turned upon itself as a defensive move against recent attacks from the Brookses and MacLeishes. By the smug and easy phrasers, making capital of the emergency national awareness, this criticism has been called "coterie." Thus grouped together, the critics have become more self-conscious, perhaps, and certainly have discovered that though in the eyes of some they are a group, the group is fractured by many divergencies of opinion and method. Self-consciousness, defense of a rigorous yet truly high regard for literature, mutual effort to clarify and to consolidate the gains of a great critical period: one has reason to believe that these are the causes of the shift from critical examination of literature to the critical examination of critics.

The other possible reason is less flattering and less hopeful. Perhaps our critical period has petered out and we see its dying throes as the critics wrestle with each other rather than with the literature which is their proper concern.

Whether the critical period is near its end or not, enough work has been done in the last thirty years to make it the greatest period of literary criticism, consciously expressed, in the history of English and American literature. If it is true, this is an important judgment, and it must be made cautiously. There have been many poor studies, many wrong-headed opinions in this critical renaissance. But despite them the renaissance has flourished so that we now take for granted a critical vocabulary and a critical method which is more detailed and more capable of discussing literature without complete dependence upon the vocabularies of philosophy and history than at any previous period of our literature. This is the great contribution of the critical renaissance, and it is worth remarking, even though in truth there is more than one method, or strategy of vocabulary, as Kenneth Burke would probably call it.

Perhaps the next most remarkable thing about this critical period is that it has been various and, in a sense, greatly departmentalized and specialized. There have been both good and ill effects from this specialization: on the one hand it has led to detailed pursuit of interesting ideas within the abilities of each person, and on the other it has made the total picture of critical activity a patchwork of interesting studies but very few critical compositions in the large sense.

If one thinks of the more important names in recent criticism, one can see this specialization clearly: the Humanists, self-described; the criticism from an undynamic psychology of Richards; Ransom and his approach from his study of Greek philosophy and of German idealism; Edmund Wilson, if he may be dignified by the true name of critic (witness his recent change to the name of reviewer), with his approach to literature from a varying set of liberal ideas; the intellectual game of Empson; Blackmur and the study of language in poetry. With the spread of the ideas of these men, and of the ideas of three persons I shall mention last, a number of interesting and very valuable studies, particularly of specific literary works, have been contributed by Robert Penn Warren, Cleanth Brooks, Horace Gregory, Lionel Trilling, Leavis and Bateson in England, and ten or twelve others.

But only three critics have seemed to achieve any important all-around critical work, combining both critical theory and detailed examination of particular pieces of literature. These three are T. S. Eliot, Allen

Tate, and Yvor Winters. Of the three, Eliot's contribution has been perhaps most widely influential but surely least consequential in quality. His critical repute was partly a matter of fad and partly because his work provided a rationalization of modern experimentalism in poetry and fiction. Actually Eliot's critical position is too inconsistent and too shallow to be that of the great critic. The importance of Allen Tate's critical work has been vitiated in part by the fact that it is essentially fragmentary. His critical books are collections of isolated essays, not developed studies of book length. Further, his study of metrics in poetry has never been full or adequate. But within his essays is a wealth of insights, both into particular works of literature and into the nature of literature, excelled, probably, only by the work of Yvor Winters. Winters has combined all these aspects of criticism with an ambitious program in a sense expected of the full and great critic. If one has followed the argument thus far, he must conclude that, despite most any difference with particular judgments or ideas in the work, Winters is the greatest critic of the recent critical renaissance.

2.

I suspect that an important reason why Winters has not received his due and why he has been widely misunderstood and sometimes reviled is that the broad plan of his work has not been appreciated. (Another reason, of course, is a personal factor exhibited in his work, a sort of uncompromising determination and perhaps even arrogance which have offended some soft-minded people but which are virtues of the creative intellect.) If one turns to the page facing the title page of *Maule's Curse*, with an awareness of what work has been done since that book was published, he will be able to grasp something of the large plan initiated by Winters. It appears that Winters approached the problems of criticism first through an examination of the methods and the ideas underlying modern poetry and criticism. Apparently he is trying to explain the failures of much recent work, to study the history of the methods and ideas underlying those failures, to indicate what he considers a better tradition of method and idea, and to study the history of that tradition. This may be a statement of his overall plan to which he would not agree in particular; yet I believe it will indicate the general outline sufficiently to show his ambitious pattern. It will show, also, that his critical work is tied together in a plan; no one piece is an isolated study. Thus no one book is entirely complete in itself; the steps so far taken are these, considering here only the four largest and most important so far published: In *Primitivism and Decadence* Winters has analyzed in detail some of the methodological failures of some recent poetry, plus laying down one of his richest critical contributions, the foundations of his study of metrics. In the third book, *The Anatomy of Nonsense*, Winters has studied four of the most widespread ideas underlying recent failures in literary work. In both of these books, and particularly in *The Anatomy*, he has also indicated very briefly the position, both in method and in idea, which he feels provides a better tradition for literary composition than do those he attacks. In the second book, *Maule's Curse*, are studies in the backgrounds of the methods and ideas of modern work which he has attacked. And in his long essay on sixteenth century poetry published in *Poetry: A Magazine of Verse* is initiated a study of the history of what he considers the wiser tradition of method and idea.

3.

So far I have attempted to indicate Yvor Winters' position with relation to the critical renaissance of the last thirty years, and to indicate what appears to me the general plan of his very ambitious critical study. Now it is time to turn with as much brevity as is possible to particular contributions Winters has made within the work published to date. Winters is a man in early middle age; I have no doubt that he will be able to complete in large measure the study he has started. Thus any list of accomplishments to date is provisional in the light of later work, and I shall content myself here with a few rather random notes rather than with a developed argument.

One of the first striking aspects of Winters' critical position is that it involves a rigorous standard for the poet and the critic. He has no sympathy with halfway measures or with great or little rationalizations to escape a part of the artist's responsibility. In a sense his general objection to much recent work is that it does not have this rigor; critically it attempts to justify the aberrant or semi-successful, and creatively it uses only a portion of the possibilities which the nature of writing can offer. Here is a statement from the first paragraph of *Primitivism and Decadence*: "The very exigencies of the medium as (the poet) employs it in the act of perception should force him to the discovery of values which he never would have found without the convening of all the conditions of that particular act ... The poet who suffers from such difficulties instead of profiting by them is only in a rather rough sense a poet at all."

This rigorous standard is the foundation, also, of his objection to that work which tends to abandon coherence of meaning in favor of "pure feeling" or whatever the protagonist of the mode might name it. The argument, badly put, is that words have both denotative and connotative meanings, and that to abandon one aspect is to abandon one of the faculties at the poet's command as one might blindfold his eyes and smell his way to New York; the best poet will use all possibilities of his art. "Further," Winters says in his first book, "when the denotative power of language is impaired, the connotative becomes proportionately parasitic upon denotations in previous contexts, for words cannot have associations without meanings; and if the denotative power of language could be wholly eliminated, the connotative would be eliminated at the same stroke, for it is the nature of associations that they are associated with something. This means that non-rational writing, far from requiring greater literary independence than the traditional modes, encourages a quality of writing that is relatively derivative and insecure."

A similar argument lies behind Winters' objection to the formlessness and the "qualitative progression" of much modern poetry and prose. He calls the attitude responsible for such work "the fallacy of imitative form," and he discusses it thus in a footnote in *Primitivism and Decadence*: "It might be thus formulated: Form is expressive invariably of the state of mind of the author; a state of formlessness is legitimate subject matter for literature, and in fact all subject matter, as such, is relatively formless; but the author must endeavor to give form, or meaning, to the formless—in so far as he endeavors that his own state of mind may imitate or approximate the condition of the matter, he is surrendering to the matter instead of mastering it. Form, in so far as it endeavors to imitate the formless, destroys itself."

There is a converse to this attitude, and Winters argues it closely. If abandonment of some of the resources of poetry displays weakness of attitude and in fact produces a limitation upon the poet, the effort to use the rich resources leads to stronger poetry. One of these resources, of course, is found in the tradition of form in English poetry. As one approaches the tradition, he has the great abilities of that poetry for his use. Further, the tradition provides a means, through controlled variations from its norms, to communicate exact shades of meaning and feeling. Again I quote from *Primitivism and Decadence,* "As one approaches the norm, one's variations from that norm take on more significance." If there is no norm, there is no variation; or perhaps one should say, if there is no norm, here is nothing but variation.

Attitudes such as these explain Winters' quarrel with free verse (a quarrel which apparently has been overemphasized by some of his readers, since it is obvious that Winters admires many free verse poems and many products of "primitivism") and his argument for a strict metrical norm. From *Primitivism and Decadence*: ". . . two of the principles of variation—substitution and immeasurably variable degrees of accent—which are open to the poet employing the old meters, are not open to the poet employing free verse, for, as regards substitution, there is no normal foot from which to depart, and, as regards accent, there is no foot to indicate which syllables are to be considered accented, but the accented syllable must identify itself in relation to the entire line, the result being that accents are of fairly fixed degrees, and certain ranges of possible accent are necessarily represented by gaps . . . It is a question whether such effects can be employed with a subtlety equal to that fine substitution. Personally I am convinced that they cannot be; for in traditional verse, each variation, no matter how slight, is exactly perceptible and as a result can be given exact meaning as an act of moral perception."

The reader will have noticed that I have so far confined my quotations to some taken from Winters' first book, *Primitivism and Decadence*. In that book he set down most of his fundamental critical attitudes. The later books are enrichments and extensions of those attitudes. At first glance, in fact, *Primitivism and Decadence* may appear very enlightening but also a little bald and spare. It is a packed book, with some ideas not completely defined, at least with illustration and full argument. But all of the books are closely linked, and as one reads the later work, he will find himself again with the ideas met before, and find them becoming more definite and realized in his mind. For example, I believe it takes a reading of the three books so far published to get a thorough understanding of three of Winters' most important concepts, those of "primitivism," "decadence," and "obscurantism." It may be noted in passing that the long essay on sixteenth century poetry has a quality similar to that of the first book; it rather sparely introduces us to new conceptions of that poetry, and we are forced to reserve some judgment until we can see where the ideas lead in our reading of English verse.

The second book, *Maule's Curse*, extends the ideas we have met before into a study of eight nineteenth-century American writers. These are studies in what Winters calls "obscurantism," or "the choice between abstractions inadequate or irrelevant to experience on the one hand, and experience on the other as far as practicable unilluminated by understanding." Much of the work is richly documented not only with detailed argument but also with Winters' readings of poems or prose. The essays vary considerably in general kind, on the one extreme being the closely reasoned attack upon Poe's whole esthetic, and on the other the essay on Emily Dickinson containing almost entirely very enlightening discussions of individual poems. And both kinds have very great values.

In *The Anatomy of Nonsense* we turn, in a sense, to the "obscurantism"—or at least to the difficulties and inconsistencies in position—of four important recent writers, Henry Adams, Wallace Stevens, T. S. Eliot, and John Crowe Ransom. The studies are a fine mixture of abstract argument and analysis of particular works of the men considered.

What is carried out in these last two books is something only suggested in the first book—an examination of the relation between ideas of art and technical methods used in the work. Winters has demonstrated with care and with a number of persons, from the nineteenth century to the present, that there is an exact relation between one's conception of art and the way he will write. Except in such general principles as I have already indicated, or in the set provided at the first of *The Anatomy of Nonsense,* this relation perhaps cannot be defined more clearly; the proof is not so much in argument as in example. And Winters has provided analyses of the relation between "the fallacy of imitative form" and its poetry, between the hedonism and the poetry of Stevens, the Romantic theory and writing of Poe, the transcendentalism and poetry of Emerson and Jones Very, and many others.

Thus Winters' rigorous standard for the writer and the critic comes to a full, round, complete position. Perhaps it is defective; I shall not try to discuss that here, but I think that in any way in which it is defective it is so in minor judgments, that it is not only the single complete position offered by modern criticism but also a most intelligent and fruitful one.

The position is complete because it provides us with an intelligent way of thinking about poetry, for instance, and also with good means of examining poems; it is fruitful because it contains important directives for both the poet and the critic. The crux of the matter lies in Winters' position that writing is a "moral" judgment. The term *moral* has been misunderstood, Winters' critics commonly believing that he is trying to lead them away from art-as-an-entityin-itself position to art-as-an-adjunct-to-morals, to the commonly professed position of older critics. Winters' position is closer to that of traditional criticism than is common among modern critics. However, the term has been misunderstood, these critics having failed to notice, for example, that in one place in *Maule's Curse* Winters uses the term *human* as a parenthetical expression for the term *moral*.

In a criticism so important as is Winters', such a source of misunderstanding must be examined closely. I shall do so in my own words, aware that Winters may need to repudiate my interpretation. Winters' position is that of the Christian. He believes that within quite large limits man has choice. As I have shown, he has no sympathy with the position that poetry in a directionless period must be formless. The poet has faculties and brains with which to make decisions. The kind of choices and the kind of decisions he makes will be governed, of course, by the immediate range of choices, but, what is more important, within that range by the set of beliefs, emotional controls, intelligence, and perceptions which he has. All of these are intimately interrelated, and to them are available various technical resources of poetry. The resources used by the poet are a judgment he makes and, in the end, a judgment upon him; it is a judgment which he makes and which he calls down upon himself as intelligent, moral, human being. Winters indeed has stringency, but it is a stringency which I think no real poet will try to avoid.

WINTERS' "A SUMMER COMMENTARY"
The Explicator, March, 1951

A SUMMER COMMENTARY

When I was young, with sharper sense,
The farthest insect cry I heard
Could stay me: through the trees, intense,
I watched the hunter and the bird.

Where is the meaning that I found?
Or was it but a state of mind,
Some old penumbra of the ground,
In which to be but not to find?

Now summer grasses, brown with heat,
Have crowded sweetness through the air;
The very roadside dust is sweet;
Even the unshadowed earth is fair.

The soft voice of the nesting dove,
And the dove in soft erratic flight
Like a rapid hand within a glove,
Caress the silence and the light.

Amid the rubble, the fallen fruit,
Fermenting in its rich decay,
Smears brandy on the trampling boot
And sends it sweeter on its way.

Of all modern poems, I believe that several by Yvor Winters contain the richest sensuousness, the greatest evocation of sensory detail. Perhaps the closest competitors would be some of the early poems of Wallace Stevens; indeed, I sometimes thing that Winters has, among his various reasons for liking that remarkable work of Stevens, a great appreciation of its tremendous richness in sensory data. I cannot, in this brief comment, evoke the whole intellectual history which once permitted such immersion in sensory awareness (not to be confused with William Carlos Williams' "primitivism" of naming a "thing"); nor evoke what has happened in subsequent intellectual history. But the accomplished fact is found in such a poem as "A Summer Commentary."

Stanzas 1 and 4 have this immersion, as I call it, most deeply felt in the language. I suppose that such sensory feeling is not found in much verse since the sixteenth and seventeenth centuries, except for French poetry of the nineteenth century, to which Winters owes more than to the Renaissance.

The management of word-placement in stanza one is particularly to be noticed. After the one run-on line we come suddenly upon the three syllables which open the third line; we are projected into an unexpected closing of a thought, with each of the three syllables receiving at least secondary accent. This is fine verse management to demand the meaning of "Could stay me," a most important perception at this place in the poem. With the slow, demanded reading of these words, the fact of "stay" (not "stop," for example) is realized in the verse: its quality of pause, concern, wonder, but at an inexplicable, nonintellectual level. Likewise, the commas about the word "intense," which is further isolated by its position at the end of the line, evoke the true quality of the whole image: it is as if intensity of feeling, and not thought, were the central quality of the whole image; it is as if the trees, the boy watcher, the hunter, and the bird were all caught for a moment in true intensity.

The sensory immersion of the first stanza is one of intensity of feeling, non-intellectually explained; the quality of feeling of the fourth stanza is softness, giving up, hedonistic immersion. In the stanza are auditory, visual, and tactile senses at a moment of awareness; "soft" and "dove" appear twice and might be joined; in the one case the "nesting dove" is evoked with its feeling of hominess and sensory love, in the other case the "soft erratic flight" of the dove delighting in the fact of flight but a flight without immediate direction. There is "caress," to add to this sensory feeling. And in between, that most remarkable simile, "Like a rapid hand within a glove," which, like "intense" in the first stanza, refers both ways and evokes the pleasure which is itself delightful at the sensory level, rapid without direction of its own, and perhaps determined by the shape of objects outside the feeling or the sensory data. The simile is quite inexhaustible; it is marvelous, indeed, when we recall that, after the habit of our concern with "ambiguity," we normally think only of the metaphor or the extended metaphor as having the quality of being inexhaustible in its reference and evocation. One thing to be noticed is that it is a fulfillment of Winters' own demand that in writing about "soft" or undirected experience the verse should itself have definite outlines, definitive form and feeling. The line is a direct contrast to any line built upon the notion of "imitative form."

I must stop for a glance at the metrical accomplishment of stanza 4, as well. The trochaic substitution in the second foot of line one strongly evokes the feeling for the "soft voice," a feeling held throughout the stanza. The second and third lines of the stanza start with extra syllables—with a slight suggestion of change to a trochaic metre; the sense of delay over the connectives "and" and "like" subtly asserts the sensory immersion, as I have called it. A further important detail is the persistent alliteration of the consonant "s" throughout the stanza; it is picked up again in the last two lines of the poem. Further, the consonants "r" and "f" in the fourth stanza are picked up for important alliterative attention in the last stanza. The auditory "immersion" seems complete in its place within the movement of the poem.

Stanzas 1 and 4 indicate directly the sensory immersion which provides the basis for the poem. The real subject of the poem is to explore, to think about, the "meaning" of this quality of feeling. It is a common and important topic to Winters, as anyone will recognize who has read his other poems, his criticism, and his one published story, "The Brink of Darkness." The problem is posed directly, "Where is the meaning that I found? . . . . was it but a state of mind, . . . In which to be but not to find?"

The question is not answered so directly as it is asked; the implication is that there is no adequate answer which is direct and general. The implication is, further, that the answer is contained (1) in the richness of the experience, in a hedonism which has a quality of judgment of the kind of pleasure it will notice, and (2) in a larger perspective of the age-old knowledge of the death of pleasure and decay in nature, indeed, in what some of our modern minds may be referring to when they talk about "process."

The final stanza supremely, I think, combines a continuing sensory richness with both implications mentioned in the paragraph above. "Fermenting" is a fine process as evoked here; the decay is "rich," the boot is "sent" (not "goes," for example) "sweeter on its way," as if the process were somehow even intentional, at least as if the fact of decay were explicable chiefly because of its increased sensuousness. But through the decay strides the man, perhaps the one object in the whole scene who has the possibility of direction and will; his boot is trampling in the richness, but fermented brandy clings to it as if man had a sensory paradise in which to work his will.

SOME TECHNICAL ASPECTS OF RECENT POETRY
Western Humanities Review, Autumn, 1952

It is my intention in this essay to examine a few technical aspects of the poetry of the last fifty years in America. It is further my intention to select such aspects as, when examined in the newer poets of the 1940's, may give us some clue to the drift of poetic composition in recent years.

First, to consider rhythm and metre. All readers, I suppose, will readily think that the poetry of the twentieth century in America is characterized by both extensive and intensive experimentation in the rhythms of poetry. Yet it is remarkable that that experiment has been so confined. It has almost exclusively appeared in this country in two aspects: (1) the effort to compose free verse, and (2) the effort to push traditional English metre into most conversational rhythms.

The work of the English poets really deflates our impression, for they have had a wider experimentalism than the poets in America. If we extend our period a bit into the nineteenth century, we may recall the efforts of Gerard Manley Hopkins—nearly inexplicable as they are—to experiment with the nature of accent and the designation of accent; we may recall that

Robert Bridges worked strongly in attempts to write both quantitative and syllabic metres in English, and that his daughter, Elizabeth Daryush, also composed some very impressive poems in syllabic metre; and we are aware of W. H. Auden's attempts at Skeltonics. All this in addition to experiments with free verse.

I think one may readily be impressed with the scope of that type of experiment; that is, if one were impressed by experiment in the first place. In America we have rather few counterparts. Aside from efforts with free verse, nearly the only example is the practice of Marianne Moore in composing syllabic metre. Since Miss Moore's practice is more familiar to us, and since she has confined herself almost entirely to the long syllabic line, I prefer to quote Mrs. Daryush, with the example of her short syllabic line in the poem entitled "November":

> Faithless familiars,
>   summer-friends untrue,
> once-dear beguilers,
>   now wave ye adieu:
>
> swift warmth and beauty
>   who awhile had won
> my glad company,
>   I see you pass on.
>
> Now the still hearth-fire
>   intently gloweth,
> now weary desire
>   her dwelling knoweth,

> now a newly lit
>   lamp afar shall burn,
> the roving spirit
>   stay her and return.

Miss Moore's practice with syllabic metre has not had "lasting power," for I do not find it carried on in any of the younger poets, with reputation, whom I have read.

Of the two types of experimentation in America, the most colorful for long, of course, was that effort to move verse away from metre in any of the standard or traditional forms—in a word, to write free verse rhythms. Here, too, I trace a diminution of scope of experimentation. It is not so much an observation that free verse is over—I would suppose that nearly as much is being written today as twenty years ago, and just as ably, but perhaps largely by the old hands at it, as witnessed by a Wallace Stevens poem published in a recent issue of *Hudson Review;* it is rather an observation of a lack of interest in problems of composition, in theory of verse, which did concern some of the early practitioners.

Perhaps I can indicate this by the following: The chief problem in writing free verse, of course, is to achieve a suitable principle whereby one composes a line; in other words, where end one line and begin a new line?

As the early writers of free verse worked, it appeared that two principles were relied upon. One was a loose metrical system whereby the line normally had two or three—usually two—accents per line. This practice often includes the use of an occasional long line, thrown in presumably for some unannounced or unapparent need for variation. The second principle is to compose the line in syntactical or even breath groups.

Now free verse continues to be written, a great deal of it; but I detect little interest or awareness of the chief problem in most of the younger free verse practitioners. Recently I discussed some of his poems with a particularly able student of mine. I asked him if he could tell me why he chose to break his lines as he did. After some reflection, he said, "I say the words over and when I think they feel right, I have the line." This may be a variation of the word-grouping method; yet it was clear that he had no real principle for making his choices. And it seems to me just as clear that this is true of much of the work of many recent poets who have a reputation based on poems written in free verse. Indeed, there appears little curiosity in the matter, to my knowledge, and free verse depends very largely now upon the more impressionistic practices of such an older poet as T. S. Eliot.

In some of his poems, Mr. Eliot wrote a very conversational rhythm, although usually in free verse. A more interesting technical effort, I think, was that of forcing the traditional metre toward most conversational rhythms, under the tutelage of John Donne and other Renaissance poets. Mr. Cleanth Brooks and Mr. Robert Pen Warren have, for purposes of analysis, distinguished between the "rhetorical" line, that is, the sound of the line as actually vocalized, giving the words their quite usual accent, and the theory of the metre. With this terminology at hand, one would say that in much of the practice the rhetorical line became very dominant and often buried the theory of the metre. One can hear it in the Library of Congress recordings, for example, by John Crowe Ransom, and by Robert Penn Warren in his poem "Terror." These readings, in which metre is hardly perceived, may be contrasted with such a poem as Mr. Warren's "Bearded Oaks," in which, I should judge under the influence of a close study of Andrew Marvell, Mr. Warren shows himself greatly adept with metre.

The point is that the newer poets—among those who have large reputations from the 1940's—have chiefly followed this rhetorical method; with no exception I can think of at this time, they have neither extended nor experimented with that practice of older poets, not even tried as many modes as Mr. Warren, for example. If one might suppose that these younger poets have judged the experimentation to be of little value—a judgment with which I, for one, would agree—then one would feel that they had been working closely on the theory of poetic composition; but I cannot detect that this has been the feeling—instead, imitation of a particular practice without either understanding it fully or attempting to improve upon it.

A similar conclusion, I believe, is to be reached about my second group of technical aspects. They are two aspects of language use in poetry, and both are what I would call violence to what we know as standard English use. On the one hand, many poets of the last half-century have been concerned with enforcing original insight through unusual usage of words: the employment of nouns as verbs and verbs as nouns; the coining of words; the forging of two words together as one; and similar practices. Again, if the poets had judged that this practice was of no virtue, one would know that they had moved into another direction. However, it seems apparent that many of them have judged the practice good, but they have not attempted much except imitation of an easily imitated method.

The second word usage has a different conclusion, however. It is the use of the violent metaphor—the strained image—*where the intended meaning is evidently quite simple.* A few days ago I read a poem in which the two first lines spoke of night "crouching" in a tree. One recognizes immediately that we have here the most rife imitation of our time, one which the younger poets cannot seem to shrug off. The practice comes chiefly from the neo-metaphysical poets —such men as the later Yeats, Tate, Warren,

Empson—and these have been even more influential as tutors of the younger generation than Pound and Eliot. Although the men named do at times escape the dangers of the method, their influence has been a glove upon the younger poets. The practice is almost the union card of very nearly all the poets of reputation of the 1940's.

The last group of technical aspects I shall notice is concerned with the structure of the poem. Here, again, I shall comment on two practices.

In the twentieth century, very little of the poetry—by the most famous poets—has been built on a structure which, for want of a better term, I shall call a prose structure; that is, a structure of a series of propositions which are presumably meaningfully stated, including a concluding proposition. We might also call this the argumentative or expository structure. Although this is one of the oldest and most honorable structures for the poem, it has been relatively little used by the Romantics, the French Symbolists, and most of the moderns. Of the alternative structures, we have seen a considerable use of the dramatic. (We would find this group very large if we included as dramatic the interior monologue—the bringing together of many matters through the associational flow of one mind—characteristic of many poems by Pound and Eliot.) But poets of the last century have especially developed two structures which seem characteristic of much modern practice.

The first of these I shall call additive. I must differentiate this structure, however, from an additive structure used many times by Surrey, Spenser, and other poets in the history of English literature—a structure which consisted of taking a theme and restating it, or facets of it, over and over in differing words, images, and references. In the modern practice to which I refer, the addition is not so likely to net a sum which is a theme. Indeed, we are more than inclined to prize ourselves when we can demonstrate that one of our poems does *not* mean what a paraphrase of it means. (I am aware, of course, that a paraphrase is not a *substitute* for a poem and that a poem communicates much which a paraphrase does not say, just as two statements, although of the same meaning, will vary considerably in emotive and other overtones communicated.)

The addition is more likely, in much modern practice, to surround a moment of perception, a mood, or a feeling; we progress through a number of differing statements of presumably what is essentially the impression achieved. Certainly this structure has been much used in poetry of several poetic generations, and I should judge that it has not decreased but probably even increased in recent poetry.

The additive structure seems to have been codified into a method by a group of poets called the Activists under the guidance of Lawrence Hart of Berkeley, California. If I understand the theory of the Activists, they practice a type of additive structure for their poems, and also an interesting variation on an old bugaboo, poetic diction. It seems that a fundamental principle in the work of this group is that only the line is essentially beautiful; that the poet must work upon the composition of a beautiful line. When he has such a line, he may go on to the next line with the same intention in mind. I believe there need be no progression between lines (except spacing upon a page); there will, of course, be progression from image to image, but the connection among the images is normally, I believe, one of association around a central impression, mood, or attitude.

The second structure I shall call that of maturation. It presumes that the poem begins, if not in chaos, then at least in somewhat undifferentiated, certainly not understood, experience; it proceeds from that point gradually to the moment of insight or understanding. A poem of this structure can be graphed, for the last passage is likely to be a punch line or other statement of insight attained in the experience of the poem. In considering this structure, we are projected into the classical problem which Wordsworth regarded: What is the time relationship between the experience or occasion of a poem, and the written poem? Or, an even more classical problem, the relationship of the poem to life or to the experience which is not-poem?

It is clear that this maturation structure, as I have

called it, is based upon the point of view that the poem must recount—perhaps we may say, must imitate—the structure of the "real experience," in which we presumably proceeded from lack of understanding to understanding. I believe many modern critics would consider this as being "honest" to experience, and such a notion, I believe, is a fundamental basis for ideas of imitative form.

It is clear that this structure is greatly used—it is probably the most used structure—in the work of the recent poets. Like the violent image, and, indeed, working upon a parallel theory, this structure is also the union badge for many of the newer poets who have achieved a considerable reputation.

V

ON PUBLISHING AND OTHER TOPICS

THE LITTLE MAGAZINES
Prairie Schooner, Winter, 1942

It is difficult to find an image with which to describe the "little," non-commercial magazines. In some ways they are like the moon; changeable, often short-lived, apparently shining in the indirect light of literature, and holding in their devotees a desire which is insatiable.

But among these magazines one may expect any contradiction. Some are not changeable: *Poetry*, at least during its more than twenty years under the editorship of Harriet Monroe, maintained its sure purpose. *Poet Lore* is now in its sixty-eighth volume; *Poetry* is in its thirtieth year; *Lyric* has been published for twenty-one years, *Voices* for twenty, *Prairie Schooner* for sixteen. Sometimes the light is not reflected but is the true though wavering light of literature in our own day. And many, it must be said, are practically worthless, with poor, miserable standards; and sometimes magazines have been used as rackets by their publishers.

Thus it is clear that only two or three general characteristics will hold for most of these magazines. Admittedly they are not economically sound. Those magazines of the group which pay for contributions receive their money precariously through someone's kindness or the good will of college officials. They carry little advertising other than exchange advertising. At best their subscribers number a thousand.

Being economically unsound, the "little" magazines seldom provide any gain for those associated with them, writer, editor, or publisher. This is the second characteristic, then, which holds for most of the "little" magazines: They are published generally at a sacrifice for those associated with them. More times than not, returns will not pay for the cost of printing the magazine, with the result that the publishers must dig into their pockets for mailing, correspondence, even printing; they must take time from their busy lives to do the editorial work; and the authors must contribute their writings without remuneration.

A final general characteristic of most of the magazines is that New York is not the center of their activity. Of the 101 magazines on my current list, only seven are in New York City, a proportion no larger than that of the population of New York City to the population of the entire country. In no other aspect of literary or artistic life, I suspect, is this true. The "little" magazines realize more importantly than perhaps any other aspect of our artistic life the character of the regions of the United States.

In discussing the function of "little" magazines, one immediately begins to break up the group into factions, for some editors (and the tastes of the editors are determinants, since the "little" magazines are so often one-man or two-man organs) seem to adhere more closely to one or another function than do others. Four rather distinct functions may be distinguished, although one must keep in mind that each magazine is likely to perform in varying degrees more than one of them.

Perhaps the function most emphasized by "little" magazine editors is that of introducing new talents. There is a real task here, for many of our most respected writers saw their first publications in the non-commercial magazines. Almost the whole of a recent "generation" of writers, from Sherwood Anderson to the post-war expatriates, got its start in such magazines as *transition, This Quarter, Hound and Horn, Broom,* and very many others. Today some of the lesser magazines, such as the *Latch, American Courier, College Verse,* and a good many undergraduate literary magazines, consider themselves mainly as first proving grounds for new and young talents; and almost all "little" journals are proud of their introduction of promising writers. But it is to be remembered that few of these writers graduate to success through the commercial magazines. Most of them make their mark through book publication—novels and volumes of poetry and short stories. Many of these books arise immediately out of "little" magazines: William Carlos Williams' novel *The White Mule* was serialized in these periodicals, and most important collections of short stories and poems acknowledge first publication, not so much in the commercial magazines as in the "little" magazines. Moreover, of the writers who have built a solid reputation in the small magazines, only those who later confine themselves almost exclusively to novels are likely to graduate completely away from such journals. Most of them continue publishing in the "little" magazines as the most hospitable places for their work. Thus, though these magazines do have an important function in introducing new talent, the emphasis need not be upon *introduction*, since, as will be seen in a moment, the small magazines have even more important tasks.

A second function of the "little" magazines is that of giving voice to experimentation in literature. Apart, perhaps, from book publications, such magazines are the only places in which new trends in literature may be heard. Joyce found his magazine support among such journals, and the record can be added to for any experimental development, from the imagist and free verse revolts to surrealism. Among contemporary non-commercial journals, however, there seems to be a rather sharp division between a large group and a few magazines which are almost entirely experimental. Among the latter are the recent *Diogenes*, the publications of the *Little Man Press*, and *View*, the main surrealist magazine in this country now. Others, such as *Partisan Review* and *Iconograph*, devote considerable space to experimental work in the story and the poem, but without maintaining a complete partiality for the experimental. A few others, such as *Crescendo* and the *Span,* encourage experimentalism not so much in technical movements but in boldness of commentary and thought. Experimentalism is thus a very real and a very important function of American "little" magazines. By following such magazines, one is aware of new movements in their infancy; for if a newly formed group does not find a magazine which will give it voice, it will soon establish a "little" journal of its own.

A somewhat more general function of the non-commercial magazines may be called "cultural." It has been noted already that these magazines are not concentrated in New York, as are our commercial magazines, book publishers, radio, and other institutions of our intellectual life. In fact, the "little" magazines form a small but more or less integrated protest against the centralization, commercialism, and urbanism found in these other institutions. Non-commercial magazines sponsored the Midwest group of Sandburg, Masters, Lindsay, and others. The Southern Agrarians found their voice in "little" magazines and continue to publish in them. Marxists of all groups have had their "little" journals. Almost every region has its non-commercial magazine devoted primarily to the comment and literature of its area—the *Southwest Review, Rocky Mountain Review,* the former *Frontier and Midland,* and many others. In truth, the "little" magazines are not solely devoted to stories and poems, but nearly all contain commentary on our modern civilization. In them will be found the non-commercial in idea and attitude as well as in poem and story. This function is taken more seriously by some than by others, but there are few that do not perform the function at least in some small way.

The final, and perhaps the most important, function of the "little" magazines is the publication of good, at times even great, literature. Here one is likely to feel uneasy, speaking about something which apparently is quite relative. But since I am speaking to readers of a "little" magazine—to people who are not likely to hold as their bibles of literary worth the four great book-selling media of our country, the *Saturday Review of Literature,* the New York *Times Book Review,* the New York *Herald Tribune Books,* and the Book-of-the-Month Club *News*—I may be quite dogmatic. For one thing, where but in the "little" magazines are we likely to find the great stories and poems of our day? The only other possibility, of course, is books; but most poems and stories in books are first published in these magazines. The great novels, because of their length, will escape all magazine publication. But even the "literary" among the commercial magazines, *Harper's* and the *Atlantic,* cannot publish much great literature and in fact do not maintain so high a standard as do many of our non-commercial magazines. Furthermore, which poets, short-story writers, and novelists of ten, twenty, and thirty years ago do we now read? They are writers who published in "little" magazines of the day and who, unless they now produce commercial writing or write only books, are likely still to be publishing in such magazines. Finally, the work of Edward J. O'Brien provides further documentation. Although any one person is likely to be deficient in one way or another in literary taste, and O'Brien's taste surely was deficient, his annual book—now edited by Martha Foley— provides our most considered public selection among our contemporary stories, and its dependence upon the "little" journals for such a large proportion of its stories speaks for the standards of the best of those magazines. I do not need to maintain that our literary production which is to be called "great" is the exclusive property of the "little" magazines. But the larger proportion of it which appears in magazines at all does appear in those magazines. And to provide a publishing medium for such writing is the most important function of the non-commercial magazines.

A few of the "little" magazines are able to pay for contributions. And through this ability to pay, they are able, in proportion to the foresight and the taste of their editors, to draw off a large part of the best material available to non-commercial journals. Most of these are supported by educational institutions. They include, for example, the *Southern Review*, one of the most distinguished literary and critical magazines our country has ever produced. The failure of the *Southern Review* is a blow to American letters and one may well presume, to the educational institution which let it lapse. Others in this group are the *Kenyon Review* (which has taken over at least some of the work of the *Southern Review*), the *Yale Review*, and the *Virginia Quarterly Review;* and, among magazines not subsidized by educational institutions but still able to pay for contributions, *Partisan Review, Poetry, Direction, Accent,* and two or three newer ones, including *American Poet* and the *Poetry Chap-Book*. With the exception of the latter two, these magazines give considerable space to critical comment as well as to stories and poems. By and large they have been the publishing media for the magazine work of the great critical renaissance seen in this country during the last fifteen years.

There follows a group of distinguished magazines which are unable to pay for contributions and are thus somewhat limited in the material available to them. This group numbers more than can be mentioned conveniently here, but the most representative names are *Prairie Schooner*, the *New Mexico Quarterly Review*, *American Prefaces, Decade, Matrix, MS, Rocky Mountain Review, Opportunity, Tanager, Trend, Sewanee Review, University Review,* the *Writer's Forum,* the experimental magazines already mentioned, and such poetry journals as *Voices, Lyric,* and *Fantasy*. These magazines publish much of the distinguished poetry, short fiction, and commentary of our time.

Below these in quality (one may lump them together, however, only when pointing out that differences in standards are very great among them) is the great bulk of poetry journals and many magazines which are not exclusively devoted to poetry. Their most important function is the first I have mentioned, that of introducing new writers, besides that of offering a publishing medium for experimentation and for cultural comment. Then there is a small group of magazines which publish without critical selection and which are often used as a means of preying upon people who are willing to pay to see their writings in print.

Unlike the commercial magazines, the "little" journals nearly always find a place for poetry, even if it is used only as filler at the end of a story or article. I know of only two magazines included in the noncommercial group—*Decade*, devoted exclusively to short stories, and *Decision*, mostly devoted to commentary, but publishing an annual summer fiction number—which do not publish poetry. On the other hand, the magazines devoted exclusively to poetry are likely to have lowered their standards because there is not a great deal of really goood poetry available in this country and many pages must be filled with verse of inferior quality. Only two or three of the magazines devoted exclusively to poetry are able to avoid this lowering of standard, and, because they may be more selective, two or three magazines which have only a poetry section among stories, articles, and critical essays are able to maintain a general standard above that of any poetry magazine.

The "little" magazines are not to be mentioned without thinking of an analogous activity, in reality quite closely connected with those magazines in function and by reason of involving the same groups of people. This activity is that of the "little" publisher of pamphlets and books. Perhaps the best known of these publishers is New Directions, directed and supported by James Laughlin. New Directions has provided successful means of publication for books which would not meet commercial needs and standards. Mr. Laughlin has devoted much of his publishing work to experimental writing, demonstrated in his annual volume *New Directions,* and to the introduction of foreign writers. Judging from his advertisements and the authors on his list, Mr. Laughlin has depended upon the non-commercial magazines for the main part of his sales and for his American authors. He has maintained good workmanship in his books, equal to that of the most exacting commercial publishers. Another ambitious publishing project in a non-commercial pattern was that of The Colt Press, now unfortunately reducing its work and perhaps even stopping altogether. A third among the "little" publishers is James A. Decker, who prints more poetry, I believe, than any other publisher, and practically all of it on a royalty basis—an achievement for which Mr. Decker is greatly to be admired and supported. As a fourth, I mention my own publishing work (for six months known as Swallow and Critchlow, but now again publishing under the name Alan Swallow), much more modest in extent than any of the three mentioned above. There are several other "little" publishers who occasionally issue a book or pamphlet of real literary interest, and on occasion others appear.

One of Jack Woodford's comments on the "little" magazines is that they are published for writers, not for readers. Unfortunately, this comment is largely true, for the upper limit for the circulation of such a magazine seems to be very infrequently above one thousand. Of course, Woodford's comment does not really constitute a damaging charge against these magazines, for their very real and important functions, both literary and cultural, are carried on despite their small circulation. But it does seem a pity that such journals, performing important functions, should not receive more support.

The situation is analogous to that of the sales of poetry books. Poetry sells badly in this country, and the only conclusion possible is that even poets do not support poetry by buying it. A conservative estimate would be that there are more than a hundred thousand people in this country writing verse. If each of these verse writers would buy two books of poetry a year, most of the poetry books now published would be assured a modest commercial success. Similarly, there are surely as many people in this country who write material which is not commercial in pattern (at least almost every poet would belong to this category) and which could be "marketed" only in the "little" magazines. If each of these writers would subscribe for two of the non-commercial magazines at a cost of from two to five dollars per year, there would be an average circulation of two thousand for each of the "little" journals.

Such a circulation would make each of these magazines independent and would in many cases provide some payment for contributors to the magazines. It would mean less self-sacrifice on the part of the editors and publishers. This self-sacrifice is one of the interesting facts about the publishing of these journals; still, additional commercial enticements would not be great enough to bring many editors to change their standards to purely commercial ones or to disrupt the fine cooperation and camaraderie which now exist among these journals and among their editors and writers.

Additional support for the "little" magazines would indeed be very helpful during the present period. All of them devoted to American writing are now home from abroad; Paris is no longer a home for such writers and publishers and we need to find a place for them here. Now, because of the war, the magazines are having a difficult time. Universities find their budgets pinched, costs of production have gone up, many young writers are in the army, and the margin of financial loss which the editors and publishers need to make up is likely to increase. But we may be certain that a good many of the non-commercial journals will be continued at whatever sacrifice and that when the new post-war literature develops—or any other important literature—it will find its first hearing in the "little" magazines.

POSTWAR LITTLE MAGAZINES
Prairie Schooner, Summer, 1949

Developments occur among the "little" magazines year in and year out. But a new restiveness has seemed to strike them since the war—restiveness evident in comments in the magazines themselves, in the newest magazines, and among the youngest writers. Perhaps it is not too early to try an assessment of this restiveness.

Editors of present noncommercial magazines frequently had their first experience with such magazines during the thirties and early forties. By that time, it seemed, the exciting and often expatriate days of the littles was over; *Broom, The Little Review, S4N, transition, The Dial,* and many others were gone or were taking their last breaths. The thirties saw primarily two great efforts in the noncommercial magazines, that to seek out and to encourage a left writing of importance, and a much more successful effort to establish the critical reviews. The thirties were the days of the first *Partisan Review, Left Front, Kosmos, Pagany, Direction,* dozens of similar magazines—and also of *Hound and Horn* and *The Southern Review.*

From the left, only *Masses and Mainstream* remains, a single magazine attempting all the functions of former journals and too little occupied with creative work in story and poem. But the critical review has become triumphant, even greatly dominant, now multiplied into the established *Partisan Review, Kenyon Review, Sewanee Review,* and *Accent,* and the newcomer, *Hudson Review,* representing the chief names in the field. Behind them a bit, but proud in their shadow, work many others—the reviews which started out in the critical pattern, or, like *Rocky Mountain Review* (now *Western Review*), started in a different pattern but later changed to the status of yeoman in the service of the review.

Charges published in established magazines, manifestoes of new magazines and, particularly, comments I have heard from many young writers over the country all indicate that the pattern of the critical review has now become something against which to revolt. Thus the longest tradition in the little magazines— hate of anything staid and unbending—is fulfilled again.

What are the charges against the critical review? First, that it is dull, repetitive, inbred. One opens the quarter's issues of the critical reviews to find the same names over and over again—worthy names, indeed, but saying much the same things they said two years ago and five years ago. The language is commonly the same, but whereas it once led us to new insights, it now spaces those insights out through many pages; rather like the scholars of literature before them, the new critics now have a method fairly satisfactory to them and are most occupied with flashing its light into all the many rooms of the mansion of literature. Inbreeding is shown not only by the appearance of the same names in many different magazines but also by the appearance of an editor in his own magazine or in the pages of a magazine edited by someone else. The magazines scramble for contributors, not contributions; the advertising they do is a list of "names" as contributors.

The second charge and perhaps a more serious one (since dullness and inbreeding, like sin, seem to be characteristic of human thought), is that the critical reviews are not using their distinguished editorial and critical powers to discover and foster new talents and new writing. What growing young poets and writers of fiction have these magazines discovered and sponsored in the last five years? There are not many new faces among them, and frequently these new faces have the look that sits upon the masters. How long has it been since these reviews have discovered any relatively "important" book which was relatively ignored by the commercial press? Review space anywhere is too limited to cover more than a fraction of the new books published; but in the selectivity involved in the narrow space in the critical reviews, the many "name" books must first be given analytical praise; there is even less attention left than in the commercial reviews to give us the analysis, of which the critical reviews are so capable, of the new writer who may not be critically "successful" as yet, but who may have enough on the ball to be our next Faulkner or Tate. Nor does the new writer get the benefit of this critical examination. But so it was for the "names," too, once upon a time.

The critical reviews may point out certain defenses against these charges. *Sewanee Review* has instituted a periodical review of first novels. *Hudson Review,* after its first two issues devoted, apparently, to contributions it could secure, as a new critical review, from such well-known writers (who did not need a new magazine) as R. P. Blackmur, Kenneth Burke, Allen Tate, and Herbert Read, has, in its next issues, published several talents relatively new to the critical reviews. But these defenses are small in comparison with the restiveness which has been displayed. That restiveness indicates that the critical review is at its zenith. No one, I suppose, would wish the complete downfall of the pattern of the review, since these magazines have great abilities. But the restiveness indicates that the critical review does not by any means perform the many functions of the noncommercial magazines.

To understand what confronts the non-commercial magazine today it is necessary to consider two matters which provide an over-view. The first of these is to examine briefly the pattern of the critical review at its best, so that its success and failure may be understood; the second is to consider the various functions performed by the little magazines.

Perhaps the best magazines in the pattern of the critical review have been *Hound and Horn* and *The Southern Review*—and surely it is no stretch of the imagination to consider them the two most important literary journals ever to appear in the United States. What made them so excellent? In the first place, appearance. The best of the reviews have been designed and printed with a consciousness of their literary worth. This consciousness is largely lacking in present reviews with the exception of *Sewanee Review*. In the second place—program—not merely eclecticism, or definition of program by negatives, but a powerful sense that some new ideas were being developed into literary form and significance. This required, in addition to the program itself, a group of writers reasonably agreed upon the program. The editors of the magazines could select, to the best of their abilities, the best creative and critical pieces which came to them free lance; but they could also turn to many an able writer—perhaps a writer not well known with a literary reputation—who could be depended upon (a) to follow through a point of view within the general objectives of the magazine and (b) to deliver a manuscript which was a good handling of an assignment and an extension of the editorial objectives in a thoroughly sound manner. Among today's magazines, the program and the group of writers seem now too firmly established, even entrenched; and the point of view common to any of the magazines seems little more definite than the general term "new criticism." In the third place, *Hound and Horn* and *The Southern Review* were edited with a feeling of creativeness, of being in on the ground floor in the development of something tremendously arresting and important in our literature and our culture. This feeling grew out of the program, yes, but also out of a good nose for what had the vitality of development ahead of it. Today, the critical reviews seem to lack that sense of creativeness; with their point largely won, they are preoccupied more with the pedagogy of the point of view, as it were, rather than with new developments and new vitality.

These three characteristics are needful, apparently, to make a great magazine in the pattern of the critical review. Today they appear lost. A point has been won, and a new point has not been established for any of them; dispersion has now wreaked havoc on the concentration of talent which supported the best of the reviews, particularly the concentration in the South which supported *The Southern Review*. I should not presume that myriad New York could provide the necessary point of view or the concentration of talent reasonably agreed on objectives and methods to create another review of great character. This is rife speculation, but I wonder if the next spot for these requisites to appear isn't the West. The necessary talent is richly accumulating there, but so far the talent does not seem sufficiently diversified in specialties nor sufficiently agreed upon the objectives and methods.

The second over-view which is helpful is the consideration of the functions performed by the little magazines, not by any one magazine of the group but by the entire groups. These functions include at least the following: (1) A publishing outlet for most of the fine writing in short form produced in this country. In poetry and criticism, particularly, there is little market of quality among the commercial magazines; only in the short story is the market for quality work largely divided between the commercial and noncommercial magazines. (2) Providing early publication and training ground for new writers. Many observers of these magazines would place this function first. I would not quibble except that too much emphasis upon such a function tends to obscure the other important ones and also to give the implication that the writers here learn how to write for commercial magazines. The talent published in the little magazines is not likely to leave the magazines entirely so long as it produces magazine materials but to "graduate" from the little magazines, if at all, only into the writing of books. (3) Sponsoring experimentation in writing, either as that writing finds a place in ecletic magazines or as it creates journals of its own. (4) A publishing outlet for much nonfiction which, for various reasons, cannot find a haven in the commercial magazines; "noncommercial thinking" as well as noncommercial creative writing is sponsored in the little magazines.

Critical reviews of today have tended to narrow their functions to the first of those mentioned above and to neglect the other important ones. Thereby, I believe, arises the restiveness against them; and the restiveness would charge, if I understand it correctly, that in narrowing its function the critical review does not perform even that function adequately enough. As the restiveness shapes itself in other magazines, presumably it would concentrate upon the other functions.

My observation indicates that this is true of the magazines established since the war and outside the pattern of the critical review. But, interestingly enough, few have specialized in any one of the functions indicated. With the death of *View,* hardly any magazine today is devoted rather singly to experimental writing of any new school or development. *Experiment,* published cooperatively, is devoted to experimental poetry but accepts verse of many types. *Illiterati* and *Circle,* both older magazines and both now published only occasionally, similarly ride no particular experimentalism. Perhaps these are straws to indicate that the literary winds have not blown up any new developments upon the experimentalism of the twenties and thirties.

A few magazines among the new ones are devoted

as much to nonfiction as to creative work and are notable for their interest in the fourth function noted above. *Berkeley: A Journal of Modern Culture* has been devoting large space in an issue to new thinking in one field or another: architecture, music, city planning, publishing, modern art. *Neurotica* has embarked upon examining the neurotic conscience in our culture, particularly as it relates to creative activities. A number of magazines are now published in the interest of the anarchist movement, most of them devoted more to nonfiction than to creative writing. The notable exception is *Retort*.

Most of the new magazines have taken the direction of eclecticism. They apparently are not so much devoted to a sense of new development as to providing a hearing to all genuine talent, new or old. It is quite possible that the editors have so far been unable to sense a new development of vitality in postwar writing; awaiting the time when such a direction may be evident and may be sponsored by one of them or by a magazine yet to be created, these magazines want to give a hearing to all and to be followers instead of leaders of directions in writing. The new magazines have been most notable, other than for this eclectic policy, for interesting typography and for concentrating upon creative writing rather than upon critical or other nonfiction.

The Tiger's Eye has been challenging for its experimental and costly printing, nearly unique among the little magazines; and for its financial support for the contributors selected mainly upon an eclectic policy. *Here and now* has provided an interesting Canadian counterpart. *Berkeley* is worth mentioning again for its adaptation of a newspaper format. *The Golden Goose, Imagi, Gale,* and *Poetry Book Magazine* are new journals devoted to poetry and working mainly with a diverse taste. *American Letters, Contour, Epoch,* and *Line* combine prose and poetry in an editorial pattern chiefly characterized by eclecticism.

Such eclecticism—since it provides the editor and reader with one of the chief delights of the little magazines, the discovery of new talent and of unexpectedly valid writing—is old to the little magazines and may be considered nearly as dominant as is the pattern of the critical review. Among the older magazines, *Decade, Interim, Matrix,* and *Prairie Schooner* have worked these functions for years and now count as legion the services performed to promising and successful writers. The pattern has even encroached upon the former regional quarterly so much that most such magazines now published, including *The New Mexico Quarterly Review, Arizona Quarterly,* and *University of Kansas City Review,* are edited chiefly with eclecticism for a policy and devoting only partial attention to their regional or scholarly specialties.

Nor is eclecticism sufficient to all the needs of the group of little magazines. It provides the dominant pattern for the magazines which will serve writers greatly during the next few years, perhaps more than ever before. For in them will appear the early seeds of whatever vital developments may be coming. Such developments are then likely to spread their influences throughout all the established magazines as well as to push the establishment of magazines devoted more single-mindedly to those developments. One of those new magazines might well use the pattern of the critical review, vitalized by new groups and new feelings of creativeness. Meantime both the critical review and the eclectic magazine devoted to creative effort serve us well. And both, we may be certain, are patterns which can be shaped to the needs we will have in the years ahead.

WHY THE LITTLE MAGAZINES?
Author & Journalist, October, 1952

For many years, the best image I could think of for the little magazines was the moon. Like the moon, they seemed changeable, sometimes short-lived, capricious. In the first three decades of the little magazine movement—approximately 1910-1940—this image did appear to be an apt one.

During the last couple of decades, approximately, a change of tone has set in so that the likeness seems more substantial than that of the moon. Perhaps not a sun, steady and brilliant and life-giving; but very close to that image.

Indeed, there are many outcries today that the little magazines have lost much of the "life" that they had 20 and 30 years ago—much of that capriciousness but also that energy which seemed to bring to us, then, so many new ideas, so many new vigors of literary experiment and challenges to our thinking.

These outcries are not entirely just. To the reader who watches these magazines with some care, the number of new ones each year is still satisfying to the demand that freshness appear.

Yet the little magazines show much steadiness. The "movement" which demands that they be published remains undiminished year by year. And a great many of the magazines can now point to steady appearances over many years. Such magazines as the *Sewanee Review, Poetry, Voices,* and *Prairie Schooner* have published steadily more than a quarter of a century! And many others have careers extending far more than a decade of service to American letters.

Why do we have little magazines? And why are they called *little magazines?* The reason we have them is that in the realm of publications devoted to mass circulation—the commercial magazines—there is not the market available for much that our writers wish to write and feel to be truly significant. They are called "little" because they are not devoted to the mass market, even though many of them are substantial, large journals. They are commonly supported, not by advertising and sales, but by the devotion and sweat of the editor or publisher, by colleges and universities, by contributions from individuals and foundations. I have frequently suggested that they may be more properly described as "non-commercial" magazines. This is not to subvert the term *little*, however; it has become the recognized name and, as understood, is perfectly apt.

The functions of the little magazines naturally grow out of their reason for being. Indeed, there is only one reason for them; to publish writing which is not suitable for the mass-circulation, commercial magazines according to the concepts of the editors. In my own thought there are four functions for the little magazines.

First—and surely foremost by a wide margin—is to provide a market for the "great" writing of our time; that is, such of that writing as is to be published in magazines rather than exclusively in books. Without casting unfair aspersions at commercial magazines, which do, often, publish writing of some real significance, the reader and the writer of our time must recognize that this is not the primary function of the commercial magazines. It has become the function of the little magazines.

Sometimes it appears that the little magazines do a pretty poor job of this function. Many publish writing which is downright bad—and writing which varies from that grade to the very best that we produce. And it sometimes appears there are too many of these magazines—too many for the amount of really good writing available. When one considers how little of the writing coming from the presses today will probably be recalled as significant two and three generations—and more—from now, one knows that these magazines are publishing much that is several grades below the best.

Yet there is practically no other place for our best writing, except as it appears in books, sometimes after such magazine publication. The editors of little magazines have the virtues and the vices of their tastes—but they exercise *their* tastes rather than carry out some editorial policy set up in terms of a mass market as the publishers, say, of the *Saturday Evening Post* conceive that market.

Thus the magazines vary greatly in value, according to the abilities of the editors to choose the good; their dedication—at least for most of them—insures, however, that none is likely to be completely insignificant and only a perusal of all of them would truly offer a chance to pick the greatest writing of our time.

A good example—and one which has at times influenced the commercial magazines—is the short story. By the end of the 1930's, editors of our large-circulation magazines woke up to the fact that a great many writers of the highest reputations had made those reputations without being published at all in their own pages! Such fine fiction writers as Katherine Anne Porter, Ernest Hemingway, Theodore Dreiser, Sherwood Anderson, William Faulkner, and many others had *never* appeared in the commercial magazines or had appeared there with inferior stories or with some other kind of writing! Yet these people had gained vast reputations and were, indeed, read more widely, probably, than many a writer for the magazines which counted circulations in the millions.

The editors of such large magazines gradually realized that they had, in some ways, missed the boat. Katherine Anne Porter was invited to contribute to some of the large commercial magazines; other prominent writers received similar invitations from time to time. The magazines of this large group have, from time to time, seriously made an effort to select a story here and there which would, from their point of view, offer more "quality" than was their custom.

The situation of the poet was often more stringent. The opportunity for the serious literary critic was worst of all. One has only to check the magazine appearances of our most admired poets of this century—Robinson, Frost, Hardy, Yeats, Stevens, Eliot, and many others—to discover that they practically *never* appeared in any other magazines than the little magazines. For the serious critic, I think there is no exception whatsoever, except as such a man might publish reviews in a commercial magazine.

Such, then, is the great province of the little magazine, the work to which the editors and publishers of these magazines—frequently with much self-sacrifice—have devoted themselves. Such devotion, even when the magazine came out pitifully inadequate, must at least be admired! In the little magazines, at any rate, our best literary reputations are generally made, insofar as *any* magazines contribute to those reputations.

The second important function of the little magazines is to keep the literary atmosphere stirred up. This the magazines do by introducing experimentation, by sponsoring controversy and new movements. Whenever a new literary group appears on the horizon, one will first see it in these magazines. Sometimes it appears in those among the little magazines which always try to look for the new; more often, the group will find no magazine particularly open to their new work and they will start a new magazine primarily to sponsor it and give it a hearing. The flexibilities of the little magazines, their changing aspects, are keys to such experiment in writing.

The third function of the little magazines is to give a hearing to the unpopular ideas. Such a function is particularly important in such times as we find today for our intellectual climate. In this atmosphere—one in which the intellectual and artist has derisively been called the "egghead"— we find a tightening of lines so that our "free press" is extremely cautious about permitting real freedom of expression. Any writer today recognizes that he cannot publish in the mass-circulation market of the commercial magazines any ideas which are truly sharp criticism of the status quo. The ideas found in such magazines must, by the nature of the magazines, fall within a circle of the expected and "safe."

For those of us who now and then feel that the status quo has a few holes in its armor, the possible magazines for publishing such ideas are primarily the little magazines, in addition to those "liberal" magazines which fall rather betwixt and between the "little" and the "commercial" class—such magazines as the *Nation,* the *New Republic,* and the *Reporter.*

These "liberal" magazines themselves are not entirely open to all thought. Thus, the little magazines are a basic, primary source for the introduction of new thought in various realms—philosophy, politics, artistic endeavors.

Such a function cannot be too importantly stressed. In a democracy which depends for its longevity and its greatness upon the ability to adapt, by peaceful means, to changing needs and conditions, the possibility that any new idea can be expressed somewhere is to be prized as the true cornerstone of the nation. In our time, the little magazines provide sometimes the only place for the new to be heard and to be assessed for its value.

A fourth function I hesitate to mention. To me, it does not seem a signficant one; but I mention it because it has been said so often of the little magazines. That is, that these magazines provide a training ground for the writer.

It is true that writers very often publish their first writings in such magazines. But it is not so true that these magazines provide a training ground, as such, for the large-circulation magazines; not many graduate from the little magazines to the slicks, for example, in a direct line. Many an important writer has never appeared in the large-circulation magazines, but has continued to publish during all his literary career, in the little magazines—plus, of course, books.

The market place for literary materials is always

a changing place. There was a time when such writers as Dickens and Thackeray, Hawthorne and Emerson, published much of their significant work in popular journals. We have been passing through a long period in which this, largely, has not been true of the comparable writers of our time. One day we may see a return—at times, I am confident in expecting it—to a situation in which the imperative need for the little magazine will be gone, or at least reduced. Once again we may see a greater adaptability, a greater "literary significance," in widely circulated magazines.

Until such time, the little magazines are necessary to our sanity, to our literary and intellectual life. Poor as they often are, little as sometimes the editors do conceive their functions, they are what we have to work with and to support to fill those needs.

Some of us feel so strongly about their importance for our own times that we are pledged not to submit our own writings to the large, commercial magazines. Such dedications sometimes are false, sometimes foolish; but it would seem to some of us that the real dedication—to quality, to truth, to beauty in writing—must be channeled partially into a dedicated interest in the little magazines as the part of our market today which comes closest to a free and significant press.

POET, PUBLISHER, AND
THE TRIBAL CHANT
Poetry, October, 1949

The problem of publishing poetry is simple and is known to us all: poetry does not sell to any considerable audience in our culture. Only the occasional book of poetry will sell sufficiently to pay its costs; the vast majority has an average sale in the few hundreds and a loss of a few dollars to several hundreds of dollars.

If we are to do anything about bettering this situation, we have only three courses before us: to increase the audience for poetry, to work within the publishing context as it is, or to work outside that publishing context. I shall examine each of these briefly but frankly from my own experience in publishing poetry.

To increase the audience for poetry. We might attack this problem directly and immediately through usual methods of *reaching* a wide audience, in other words, through the usual book promotion methods. My own experience indicates that this is costly and quite completely a loss.

Advertising poetry is such a loss. I have seen ads in magazines—magazines in which the poet had frequently appeared and which had presumably made the poet well known to their subscribers—pull no orders at all. And mail advertising, other than to a small list of friends and well-wishers of the particular poet, will not pull a percentage of orders which the business people in mail advertising would consider worth the effort and cost. Indeed, I have finally and reluctantly come to the conclusion that there is no specific audience for poetry which can be reached in any business-like way. If one published a book on horses, for example, he would have a specific and concentrated way of reaching the audience for the book by advertising in magazines devoted to the horse and by mail advertising to members of horse-breeding associations. In the case of poetry, the situation seems to be this: each poet starts with a small audience which, as he continues, may gradually widen from a particular group of friends or a particular place to a larger group and place. The great help would thus be to find means of speeding up that process whereby a poet may increase his individual audience. Advertising will help a bit; meantime, advertising is necessary, or we would be afraid we would sell no books at all. But chiefly we must look elsewhere, and our problem would be simplified if the readers of poetry—even of a poetry magazine—would constitute themselves a specific audience for books of poetry, just as breeders of horses constitute a specific audience for books on breeding horses.

I believe that anyone examining the situation will

conclude that reviewing of poetry (and of most other "serious" books) is in a bad state today. This is easy to demonstrate with regard to the three large weekly reviews, which ought to realize more clearly their news and topical function rather than their pretensions to literary judgment, of which they are incapable within the confines of their work. But the situation is little better elsewhere. As one who thinks that the "new criticism" is the best criticism the world has ever had, perhaps I may be permitted one remark in good spirit: its chief fault is that it has become repetitive; it is not being used now, *as it once was*, to define helpfully the deficiencies and the virtues of new work; in the hands of its second generation, it encourages a review which demonstrates the reviewer's own sweeping brilliance and ability with the terminology without encouraging the reading of new work with taste and understanding. It is a legend in publishing that reviews do not sell books; and, except for certain great extremes of nearly unanimous praise or condemnation, I am certain the legend is correct. I suspect that the reason is that the reviewers are not performing their function with any real help to the reader or the writer, and I think we need not be concerned about what they are doing for themselves.

Since poetry does not sell, booksellers cannot stock it widely. The publisher is supposed to create the market, and this he can hardly do, since he can't advertise poetry widely with any effect and since reviews so little influence buying; meantime, the bookseller hasn't the means of creating the market. A few booksellers, as with a few publishers, carry most of the burden of conviction about poetry. These are likely to be the booksellers doing a "personal" trade, and they are by no means to be identified with the six or eight best-known "advance guard" booksellers in the country. My own experience with the latter has been quite sad. One of the best known has owed me, for sixteen months, enough to buy composition for a new book of poems. Another, well-known in another section of the country, owed me a bill for so long that finally a friend, who also was an author on my list and a customer of the bookseller, walked into the store and emerged with a check which he sent me; I still do not know how he got it. Of course these booksellers have a difficult time of it, but it is too bad that they must live so directly upon the publisher. In the end, booksellers will help with poetry, I believe, if they finally do develop toward specialist and personal bookselling as their primary function; then perhaps they will be able to devote more of their time profitably to contacting an audience for poetry. But they will be disappointed in this unless that audience can be encouraged and can be specifically tapped.

Advertising, reviewing, and bookselling are of little help to us in publishing poetry, at least until other conditions or their own conditions may change. We have two other possibilities, then, with regard to the audience for poetry.

We recognize that a very wide audience exists for a certain kind of verse—it gets into newspapers, popular magazines, popular books, on radio shows. We might, then, change the nature of our work to make our poetry available to that wide audience. We tend to dismiss this suggestion lightly, for we know that it really asks us to write and to publish something other than poetry or at best some surface manifestation of it. But the demand for such a change is persistent among many people and lies at the basis of much criticism of modern poetry. Even in a more serious way it may be regarded carefully. Perhaps poetry does not offer a mode of communication, in this and future cultures, which can survive. Perhaps we are to become addicted, in the future, to the incipient and uncontrolled rhetoric of careless language rather than to maintain the formalized and controlled language of poetry. This way, as Mr. Yvor Winters and others have observed, lies madness; but madness, of course, is not an impossibility.

Being of a generation which has tried to think deeply of social and economic change, I have a sympathy with those who would work directly to change the audience for poetry. They seem to me, however, to work upon a further belief—in the value of mass activity of some sort. To this, too, I can give support, but upon a more guarded basis. The dangers in such activity have long been indicated in thinking in ethics, politics, and literature; the problem provides one of the great themes of literature, including the fiction and poetry of our time. The problem is serious, and much is involved. One danger we risk is that poetry and art should survive at all in our well-meaning efforts at change. Next to survival of mankind, survival of poetry and art seems to me most important; indeed, survival of mankind without poetry is the survival of a humanity of which I should not wish to be a part. Because I think that assenting, per se, to "changing mankind" is a colossal pride and egoism, because it moves one away from the core of interest in poetry and art, and because it demands the balancing of the dangers of the undertaking in momentary and shifting and tenuous decision; I think, further, that no one ought to commit himself completely and unreservedly to the effort. In addition, the effort takes one away from what Mr. John Crowe Ransom, in discussing poetry, has called "texture," in this case the texture of living.

With this thinking, to be quite personal, I have tried to make an integrated work out of teaching, out of editing and publishing, and, with what energy might be salvaged, out of writing. All, I think, contain a similar approach and a similar feeling which perhaps is indicated in these two lines:

> And I, who read and printed words,
> Worked warm within that marvelous air.

Once one makes another commitment, he breathes another air.

To work within the publishing context as it is. We are aware that at present the process of getting the book from the writer to the reader is divided into three rather clearly distinct operations, printing, publishing, bookselling. A brief reflection that the process did not always have these distinct operations will indicate that it need not always have them. When printing was first invented, the printer himself combined all the operations. He selected the manuscript, manufactured the book, and sold it. Within approximately a century, by Shakespeare's time, the process had been split between printer and bookseller, the bookseller hiring the printer and becoming the entrepeneur. In the nineteenth century arose the great publishing houses which have established the pattern for today. This pattern involved a third division in the process, the publisher, who took upon himself the responsibility of selecting the manuscript, hiring the printer, and creating such interest in the book that, when it was turned over to the bookseller, the seller might have a reasonably ready-made market. The publisher became the chief entrepeneur, the chief source of risk undertaking.

That publishing is now in difficulty has become public knowledge. The crisis proportions have been reached in post-war years; the publisher's costs, all along the line, have approximately doubled, whereas returns from book sales have been dwindling. But the crisis is not merely temporary; it is direct indication that publishing is in the process of deep change which is already partially completed and which has yet to run its full development.

Because general education has provided a potentially mass audience for books, the publisher has been forced to adopt the methods of other mass media of communciation—newspapers, magazines, radio, movies—which already have reached that audience; if he will not adopt them, the publisher is forced to submit to them. The problem for these methods is primarily one for the inventive economic mind—how to reach and "sell" the audience. The answers are not all achieved as yet, but for many years now publishing has been developing a tradition—counter to its tradition of the "gentleman publisher"—of using that inventive economic mind. Some answers successfully tried so far are these: reprint publishing, which, once mechanical problems were solved, placed inexpensive books before the whole public, not just bookish people, in department store, drug store, and newsstand; sale by mail through the book club to reach a tremendous audience efficiently; borrowing from other industries vast techniques of publicity and of advertising.

One consequence of this trend is that the bookseller

is no longer essential to book distribution. He is now provided with direct competition which uses more efficient methods than he can use. It is true that the bookseller is still needed in book distribution, that he is much like the cake which is both had and eaten at the same time. For the successful methods of mass distribution so far apply to only a small proportion of the titles published each year, and only the bookseller so far provides the means of distributing the majority of those titles.

The other consequence is that the publisher has become more and more dependent upon what he once considered "subsidiary rights"—reprint rights, book club rights, serialization and condensation rights, movie rights. It is to be noted that these rights are those exploited by the means for mass distribution and, further, that the average publisher is today showing profit, if any profit, only from income from those rights. The economic role of the original publisher is gradually changing, so that more and more he becomes front man (and a precarious one who may not be needed much longer) for other interests in the book.

With interdependence of "subsidiary" and original publishing interests, the logical step is capital interdependence so that the formerly separate decision of each may become one decision. Prototype of the direction indicated is, today, the vast Doubleday enterprise, which has in one organization a very large "trade list" of new books, several book clubs, including the two largest, and one of the three largest reprint organizations; it has a chain of bookstores and large book manufacturing facilities. ▸The economic tie-up among Simon and Schuster, Book-of-the-Month Club, and Pocket Books is another example; a third is the ownership of Grosset and Dunlap and the development of Bantam Books by five other trade publishers. The movie industry, through prizes and through support of certain editorial practices, has begun to influence publishing decisions directly and at their source instead of indirectly; in time, television may well provide a similar direct influence.

Although I am not here attempting an essay of conjecture, my personal concern in this matter prompts one paragraph of the sort. The mass distribution of books is gradually extending to many different titles; the reprint publishers have also successfully launched "originals." The choice of publishable manuscripts in these areas will surely become more and more determined by the needs of those interests which are now hardly "subsidiary," since they already make or break the original publisher. Perhaps many books of various types will be handled exclusively for mass distribution. The final hope that this step will not be taken is that the original publisher is needed to test books for a mass audience; it seems evident to me that recent experience has exploded this hope, and that certain kinds of books need be no more concerned about such testing than have the magazines. Booksellers cannot successfully compete with the mass methods of distribution. Those who survive the competition will do so, I believe, only in the effort to develop a larger market for books not successfully distributed in the mass, in other words, by development of specialized and personal bookselling, much of it built upon a core of selling antiquarian, used, and out-of-print books. Since the textbook industry is so far reasonably stabilized, the trend of the college bookstore to stock more and more trade books should continue and those bookstores, like the colleges and universities themselves, provide a bulwark against loss of serious taste. The public library may well have to start selling books, just as it already rents new books in competition with the lending library. Large publishing will coalesce more and more about the mass methods of distribution, and the other kind of publishing will become increasingly divorced from those commercial methods. To be supported, the latter kind of publishing will have to develop some new methods.

It is clear that poetry does not have a large audience and that it cannot be adapted to the methods of mass distribution of books. Consequently, it has no logical economic existence in commercial publishing today. The exceptions are two: (1) Sales are occasionally sufficient to warrant the commercial publication of a book of poems. The book of poems will be one of three kinds: the popular anthology, in many cases having a double sale as trade and textbook; the book of the momentarily popular poet, such as the Edna St. Vincent Millay of the 'twenties or the Walter Benton of the 'forties; the book of the poet, like Robert Frost, who has achieved a gradually developing market sufficient to make his poetry a profitable commercial publishing venture. But even few of these can make the grade in the mass market and will do so only as they are fed by other publishing activities. (2) So long as the tradition of the "gentleman publisher" continues and matters of literary prestige and taste are important in commercial publishing, poetry will continue to be published as an item of costly prestige. This tradition is being detroyed. A majority of publishers today find that they need not be concerned with such prestige.

If the spring 1949 lists of the publishers are evidence, this year marks a continued decline in the commercial sponsorship of books of poetry. This involves both continued cutting of poetry from the lists and continued use of English poets for a large proportion of the books issued. (To the uninitiated, a book of poems by an English poet can frequently decrease the loss involved in publishing poetry because the American publisher can import sheets for his edition or can manufacture his edition by off-setting the pages of the English book.) One thing is quite certain; just as we have come to look for our best literary magazines among those which are privately, institutionally, or charitably supported, so we must come gradually to look for our most helpful publishing of poetry in the analogous small publisher. Clearly most of our poetry publishing must be outside the commercial publishing pattern, since that pattern and poetry cannot support each other.

To work outside the commercial publishing pattern. Poetry does not have a considerable audience in our culture. To publish poetry means to make up certain losses. How does one make up the losses?

I do not mean to be facetious, but there are two ways: with wealth, and with work. If one were wealthy, he might support the losses according to his willingness to give of his wealth. If he were not wealthy, he might support the losses by securing wealth from "angels" or from other sources of wealth which have taken an interest in such problems. The difficulty in this latter case is that one runs the danger of certain commitments in return for the support.

But persons of means, as publishers in their own right or as supporters of publishers, can greatly help by meeting some of the financial losses in publishing poetry. The large foundations should surely revise their plans so that they can support serious publishing as well as individual writers; this they have recognized more in the case of scholarly publishing than in the case of poetry publishing, although the problems are similar. And the institutional press (chiefly the university press) needs to support serious publishing of poetry just as it supports some of our best literary magazines.

Without wealth to make up the losses of publishing poetry, the other possibility is to make them up with work. For example, my own original premise in publishing was that if I could put my labor freely into the work, so that against the book there would be no charge for labor of printing and distribution, sales could be sufficient to pay for binding, paper, ink, wear on type, and postage; and I discovered that it will work approximately. This is frequently the pattern of the private press, to which we have long looked for much of our best publishing of poetry, unless that press have other support. When the effort gets larger, as I have tried to make it in recent years, one must still use all devices possible to substitute work for money: set type, print, bind, reduce the cost of advertising by labor as much as possible, bill and ship the books. And when one can find, as I have discovered possible, that other individuals are willing to contribute their labor, the possibilities for cooperative effort become extremely significant.

By individual dedication, as it were, the problem of publishing poetry can at least be met. To be met more adequately, dedication is probably not so much needed to provide more publishers of poetry as it is needed to provide better ones. Through work and conviction in the right and duty to do so, individuals can see that poetry is published; their further duty is to learn to do the job of publishing as well as possible, that is, with good judgment of the value of the poetry attempted, and with a willingness to learn the best ways possible to help the poet involved reach his best audience and his best reputation.

This dedication and this conviction are not unusual. The writing of poetry in our time requires a kind of conviction. A similar conviction is found among many of our best literary magazines today. I have indicated that it is also necessary to any effort to solve the problem of publishing poetry. More than this, I believe that the reading of poetry requires a conviction of its importance—it is too easy to turn elsewhere nowadays. But among us who have the conviction are many relative failures. We are almost as addicted as the follower of popular songs to fad and to talking-up and bobby-soxing the latest critically-approved poet. How swiftly they fall from the scene!

The level of conviction among readers must be a little higher than this if the problem of publishing poetry is worth any effort at all. The level of conviction must involve searching through the news media about poetry; reviews must be read primarily as news information about what is published and available, except in the rare circumstance when reviewing performs a decent critical job; magazines, critical books, and libraries must be searched intelligently; the bookseller must be encouraged to stock some titles in poetry, and those titles must be sampled —all this in search of several books per year which the individual can read to his growth. And the conviction must involve buying those books, too—at whatever cost.

The reader, just as the poet and the publisher, can learn to work and to enquire and to read actively, not passively, for fear he should be the dupe of other tastes and convictions. In each of us, with poetry as with other concerns, is the possibility of making our lives important to ourselves and to others.

THE PROBLEMS OF PUBLISHING POETRY
Poetry Broadside, April, 1957

The problems of publishing poetry in this country are obvious and well known: there is no general market of size for poetry, except for those volumes and persons who prey upon the original works, namely, the anthologies and anthologists. It is a strange aspect of our culture that anthologies often sell very well and make a good poet known by a couple poems but do not entice many purchases of the poet's more complete works.

With this lack of a general market for poetry, one economic consequence is clear: one cannot publish poetry and pay the regular prices for printing and binding and sell enough copies to bring back the cost —let alone any returns for labor, cost of handling, etc. There is an occasional exception, but I believe that this exception would be less frequent than one in a hundred volumes of verse.

To publish books of poetry, then, over a period of time, on a continuing basis, involves finding a method of "making up" the financial losses involved in this situation. There are three ways of doing so:

1. To ask the author to cooperate. This is by far the most popular method used today, and it has

clearly entered our respectable, large, commercial publishing houses, where it is quite possible today to secure a contract for a book of verse which includes some support from the author, in foregoing normal royalties, in a cash contribution, or in some other aid provided by the poet. Thus, the vicious methods of the "vanity" and "cooperative" publishers even have their more mellow counterparts in the big houses.

2. To find an "angel" to make up the monetary difference.. This is frequently done, particularly for new firms entering the field ambitiously. The difficulties with "angels" are, from what I have observed (never having had one myself), something like this: (a) Inevitably, no matter how honorable may be the motives of the angel, he or she will begin to exercise some influence and actual control over the editorial judgment involved in selecting the manuscripts to be published. Thus, the original purpose of the effort will be perverted. (b) When results are not forthcoming according to hopes, and continuation of the project means continued demands upon the pocket, the angel will grow weary of the expense and probably find a more spectacular means of seeing "results" for his contributions.

3. To substitute work for money. This has been the method by which I have continued to publish poetry, with an interval of two years for Army service, for seventeen years. My original premise was that if I could reduce the out-of-pocket expenses to payment

for materials and work which I could not perform, I could sell enough copies to pay that out-of-pocket expense and a royalty to the author. This has worked fairly consistently. I taught myself to print, I printed at first from hand set type on a hand press, thus reducing costs to paper, postage, and, usually, binding. As I have continued in the work and my "list" has become more and more established as a serious and significant list of verse, the sales have increased enough so that now I purchase composition; the sales will, on the average, pay these out-of-pocket expenses and the royalties, if I do not figure the time that I put into presswork, preparing for binding, printing the jacket, and the distribution labor.

The above, I believe, is an accurate description of the situation for publishing poetry. The description is not enticing, and it defeats most well-meaning projects to "do something" about the situation. The "vanity" volume is clearly no answer; somehow, it places a premium upon something other than poetic values and worth. The "angel" method is warped and obnoxious, as is so frequently true of the "well-meaning" but essentially patronizing effort to come to the rescue of the arts. The method of substituting work for money is one which involves many long hours, not simply over a period of a few weeks or months, but also over many years, if it is to amount to any contribution. And before many years are gone, the time required, with so little response in return for the effort, becomes discouraging, and the effort is dropped. I recall that of the small presses which were publishing poetry honorably in 1940, when I issued my first volume, not a one has continued regularly until today. I exclude from this consideration the firm of New Directions, which, with money behind it, seems to me not to belong in the same category; further, in recent years, it has not been an outlet for the publication of new American poets, devoting so much of its work to foreign authors and the occasional publication of volumes of Tennessee Williams and Kenneth Rexroth. The Cunnington Press—that extremely beautiful printing!—ceased for a time, revived two or three years ago briefly, but, I understand, through the tragic death of one of the participants, is again dormant. Carroll Coleman, that very fine printer at The Prairie Press, got involved in university work which demanded all of his time; occasionally he has been able to issue a volume (as he did last year of my own poems), but unfortunately his university work makes continuation practically impossible for him.

In the intervening years a number of promising efforts have been started. Quite often, these little presses will be started to provide an outlet for the work of a particular person or a particular group. Somehow something gets hold of them—weariness, or the accomplishment of a certain limited objective when two or a half dozen volumes are issued; but they are normally short-lived. This is not to belittle their important contributions, however—to introduce one or another poet. Most often, I suppose, these efforts are not editorially equipped or inclined to carry on a continuing, eclectic effort; the real contribution they can make resides in the volume or few volumes they get out. I think these efforts are vastly to be encouraged.

There are a couple of factors in the over-all picture which should be mentioned:

1. I think that an enduring effort at publishing poetry must be informed with an effort at good judgment. First of all, it makes sense that if one puts so much work into publishing verse, one is rewarded only if it is *good* verse. For a personal example, I have often said that by the time I'm through with a book, having read it in manuscript several times, having gone over the proofs myself, having read it as I actually printed it, I am completely familiar with it. If it stands up under such readings, and I measure it against my own weariness and desperation at times to try to fulfill my commitments and plans to get it out; if it still has the spark of life after such concern, then I can proudly offer it and feel that I know it better than any reviewer who will read it once or a few times before writing his review! I must confess that at times, at the end, I've decided my judgment was faulty, that my enthusiasm for a manuscript was not born out by the other tests of the work! At any

rate, I recommend such kind of concern to anyone who really wants to get "inside" some poems! A few editorial "errors" by such tests will make one cautious about committing the time to another manuscript unless one gets pretty convinced of its value; otherwise, one will feel that his commitment of time has been abortive.

With the sharpening of judgment, the willingness to put the time only into volumes which one feels bear up under these tests, the "list" has a chance of becoming gradually recognized as one in which some careful judgment has been placed. There will be a few benefits coming just as gradually—the grudging winning of more review space of the books one offers, a few sales picked up here and there from the small general audience for poetry, since that audience will begin to realize that to maintain any eclectic following of rising poets, this "list" needs to be examined now and then.

2. If one persists, and if one exercises reasonably sound judgment of poetic value, one will gradually accumulate some "properties" which may have some long-range economic values. At the race track, a bettor puts his two bucks on the nose of a colt which seems to show promise in his first time out; so he puts some more money the next time the colt is out. Maybe the colt has already shown what flash he had, and there's no real class there. But maybe the next time he's right up there when the racing really begins

and he shows some real class. So it is with publishing first volumes of poets. They show a good quality here or there, or else the effort wouldn't be made at all to get out the volumes. That may be the end, or it may be the beginning. For those who have the real quality (occasionally it is in the first volume, too, but often develops greatness later), continued publication may mean long-range sales, anthology rights, etc. I am very proud of a number of volumes on my list—volumes which have already demonstrated ultimate worth and promise of sales, although of course small, for many, many years to come, well beyond my own lifetime. These are great helps, but I should judge that the publishing effort must be continuous over a couple of decades to begin to show much in the way of these values, and they will seem pitifully small to the author and to the publisher, even then.

Persistence in publishing does have, however, its vicious circle. And that is the weighing of time taken for it, particularly when a living must be made elsewhere. At the present time, and for some years, I have received some 250 book manuscripts of verse *per year* in the mail. This is more than one each two days. Now then, in publishing as I do, I must find time for production and distribution of the volume; the editorial time is just the beginning. So these must vie against each other: if one devotes the time to editorial work, the books accepted won't get printed very often; if one concentrates on the production and distribution, then the editorial work falls behind. One is tempted to let some aspect of this become slipshod; yet, clearly, if either part is slipshod, the publishing effort is not realizing its real worth! The manuscripts must be examined with care, not merely from wanting to be a conscientious person, giving the unknown a full chance, but also for the ultimate value of the amount of time put into the whole effort. For clearly, that value is realized by publishing, among the volumes possible, only those which are the *most* worthy.

Further—something not realized by small presses first starting out—provision must be made for being able to follow up on first volumes by seconds and thirds and fourths, when the poet has developed worthily. If one introduces, conscientiously, twenty new poets, he has to be prepared to publish five or ten new volumes from these poets within a few years! Multiply this by several times, and the burden becomes considerable for the serious effort.

At the present time, it is my hope to have enough energy and time in which to do the editorial work (with the aid of some former students and friends whose judgments I know to aid me, gratis, in going through manuscripts) and to produce from six to ten volumes per year—more, I may say, than any other publisher attempts to produce in a year on a royalty contract. Sometimes the energy and time just aren't there; in 1956, I was able, physically, to get out only six new titles, as an example. Now then, in planning these new volumes, I should want always to have room for fine first-book collections; it seems to me this is the lifeblood, and a publisher who does not publish first collections but only collections of persons with some reputation already gained is no real publisher of poetry. So perhaps two or four of the possible titles will be first collections, and I have oganized my consideration of first collections in such a way that I believe that I can achieve some conscientious results in picking the best volumes available to me. From these, there are natural decreases: many of the poets don't live up to the achievement and promise of those first volumes. But many do, and with dozens of poets already introduced, there will be need for an indeterminant number of second and later books from these poets. At present, I figure a need of two to three volumes per year in this group —the subsequent volumes by poets already on my list who have earned new volumes. Finally, there is a need always to have room for the superior, fine book by the reasonably mature poet who may have had his first and even later volumes published elsewhere but is without a publisher at present. My thought is to provide room for one to two of these per year, although, to be frank, I haven't found very many after sincere efforts to secure some good manuscripts of the kind. The truth, of course, always is that there is not a great deal of fine verse written in any one year.

These will indicate some special problems, then, of the publisher who does attempt to carry on and to provide for the issuing of good volumes, from new poets, from poets along the way to their best achievements, and from the poets who have already achieved maturity. To neglect any one of the aspects seems to me to require the judgment that the publisher is wasting his time in large measure. Of course no two years will provide an exactly similar proportion among the three, but provision for a variable proportion of time devoted to all three must be made.

Finally, I turn to the matter of the publisher and the general small audience for poetry. I wish to remark three aspects of that relationship.

First, new publishers are always coming up with some new plans about how the audience may be extended. Books will be issued in certain new ways which the publishers feel will tap a larger market. Naturally, all such efforts are watched with interest. I, for one, will be happy when someone does come up with a new idea which will effectively tap a new audience. But, so far, I have not seen any that worked, despite many ideas offered. Proposals to get poetry out very cheap (I once did this, offering pamphlets at twenty-five cents and large books, bound by the best binder in the country, at one dollar!), to print it as broadsides instead of books, to bring poetry to the people by returning it to an oral basis—all these, I fear, are doomed to defeat. It seems that a larger audience for poetry is part of a larger problem—a matter of conviction of poets, publishers, and readers that poetry is, indeed, worthwhile; a matter of conviction that a cultural change can be achieved which will make a better "home" for poets and poetry; a matter of a long-range educational process. With many, I should be relieved happily if there were really a short-cut!

Second, reviewing, particularly in the present day, seems to be a necessary evil. Upon reviews we depend for 90% or so of our news of books, but reviewing is in sufficiently bad state that the function is not performed with any efficiency. Reviews are markedly late, not alone in the quarterlies, but in the weekly review media as well; reviews are affected strongly by the various fads in poetic tastes and criticisms which run their gamuts; reviews seem to be used very frequently by reviewers as demonstrations of some critical brilliance or other, instead of for information about the work available. I have marked a decided deterioration in these respects in the last five years. The results are clear: the building of poetic reputations out of proportion to worth; the busy fanfare for the poet who is second-rate and turns out never to be capable of becoming first-rate; the widespread public ignorance of many a good poet.

Definitely, something better is needed, but I have few ideas on how it is to be achieved.

Third, over a period of years I have come up with the theory that poets' reputations work out normally on the basis of concentric circles. With a first volume, the only purchasers are the friends and well-wishers of the poet, those who know him and of him, plus a small assortment of libraries and individuals who conscientiously attempt to cover a wide field in their interests. As this first circle of purchasers may become enthusiastic about the work, their contact with others may spread the work and make the circle a bit wider. With second and third and fourth books, new circles normally will be added, so that the reputation may extend among a larger group of individuals, more scattered than in the first circle. And so on, until conviction of a good many people and a few reviewers will have created a reputation of substance. Of course, any one of these "normal" circles may be disturbed by some unusual happening—a major award for a book, such as the Lamont award for first books, the various annual prizes, etc., or a widespread unanimity of critical reception that this is a truly significant book. Under such conditions, the circles will be disrupted and a reputation blossom (often without quality to warrant it!) far beyond the normal procedure. An interesting thing to watch concerns the mobility of the authors: a book may be selling not at all or a very, very few copies; then the author may move to a new place and make new friends who become interested and who (although not previously hearing of the poet at all) may become convinced of the poet's real quality, and a number of new copies will be sold! These "concentric circles" may be affected by even such matters. But if the quality is really there, one has a feeling that, however slowly, the process will continue; in the long run, the first-rate poet may achieve some greater sales and recognition than the second-rate who has got a lot of play right after publication. For an example, among the poets generally thought of as in the 40 to 50 year age group, I am confident that a poet on my list is a good head and shoulders above the Randall Jarrells, Richard Wilburs, and such poets who have the critical reputations right now for immediate sales, review space, and anthology representations. Yet as one watches, one sees that this poet's reputation, increasing at a snail's pace, is based upon complete conviction, the kind of reputation which is not put off but inevitably must grow as these readers express their minds openly. In twenty years quite a change shall come and a kind of justice be done. If one did not believe that, he would have no business being a publisher of poetry. Catering to the immediate taste will do him no good; he performs his job well only if he can achieve some kind of wise judgment of poetic value and then assert it by what he offers.

DIRECTIONS IN PUBLISHING
Berkeley, Number 5 (1948)

The plight of publishing today has become a topic of conversation and of magazine articles. Publishers themselves, like football coaches, have been crying in their towels and have been granting a public look at their innermost financial problems. While the rest of our economy is sitting uneasily on top of expansion and inflating prices, publishing, which is a part of that business economy, has already embarked on a depression we expect to ride before long through our entire economic life. Perhaps a general depression will mean a second depression to publishing. Publishers have reason to cry in their towels.

Like the readers of *Berkeley*, I am principally interested in this matter because of what it means for the future of the American writer and, indeed, for the future of American culture; but before this question can be examined, we need to know something about how this situation came about in publishing. We need to examine both the short-range conditions, which have brought to publishing an effective crisis before a general economic depression, and also certain long-range conditions which have perhaps even greater significance in the trends we must expect to come.

The immediate crisis stems from war and post-war conditions. During the war publishers were faced, on the one hand, with a book market which rapidly increased two and three fold over the pre-war market; on the other hand, publishers had less paper and relatively fewer manufacturing plants with which to produce the books demanded. They coped with this situation in a common-sense and business-like manner: they made their books smaller in size and introduced other economies in the use of paper and manufacturing facilities; but more importantly, they reduced their lists to fewer titles and put what paper and production facilities they could get into those fewer titles, selling, in the main, many more copies of a published title than was indicated even by the expansion of the market.

While other manufacturers were taking price increases for their wares in the inflationary war period, publishers maintained very much the same price level as before. The reason that the publishers could manage this and still come out with more profit than before lies in the nature of producing and promoting a book. Common is misunderstanding on this point, and from such misunderstanding arise the many "dodged" questions in publishing: why don't we produce cheaper books, why don't we produce paper bound books for our trade editions? In book production, economies in the cost of manufacturing a single book lie mainly in two places: choice of manner of production, and size of edition. Cheap books may be produced by the automatic methods involved, for example, in the manufacturing of the twenty-five cent "pocket books"; but the method of production can be used only for books of that general format and appearance and can be used *only* where a printing of large size can be assured. Whether we like it or not, very few of the titles published in this country (where, for example, books are purchased, on a per capita basis, only about one-fourth as frequently as in Denmark) have any opportunity of selling in even a moderate quantity; therefore, the methods of producing cheap, paper bound books are simply not available to most publishers. Further, they are not available to the trade (as distinguished from the text) book, in which sales possibilities largely have to be tested and in which customer expectations concerning quality of paper, typography, and binding are set in retail sales. If a book must be priced in the several-dollar class, which would be required of small printings of books, whether paper bound or cloth bound, the increase in price is small to make a cloth binding and the trade book we know today. To give one example, a book which now costs a publisher something like sixty cents to produce in 10,000 quantity will still cost the publisher forty-five to fifty cents if the binding is changed to paper, a cent or two less if the paper is cheapened, a few cents less if the type is made smaller and less readable; the possible savings in these directions to the purchasers of the book are likely to be only twenty-five to fifty cents or only a small percentage of the price he now pays for a well-made book.

The war forced certain economies upon the publisher: fewer titles, so that he could concentrate upon each title so that it would be given a better push into the world; reduced use of paper and manufacturing facilities; particularly, larger printings brought about by these factors and by the rapidly expanding book market. And these economies made it quite possible for the publisher to hold the old price for books and still find himself very prosperous.

Soon after the war ended, these conditions for publishing rather quickly reversed. The market started to narrow; book sales have fallen off progressively season by season for two years. The causes for this shrinkage in the market for books are many and are obvious to the reader; but I pause to notice the most pernicious of all, the attitude that reading is a luxury in democratic, educated America, and that in a market filled with all goods, books must give way to refrigerators, automobiles, and gadgets, and must compete with other luxuries.

Meantime, great increases in the costs of book manufacturing were seen season by season, so that, at present, the cost of manufacturing a book is close to twice the pre-war cost for the same book. Increases in costs hit the publisher elsewhere, too—in all overhead and promotional expenses, including rents, salaries, advertising space. (Through an unfair, late action of the last Congress, he and the bookseller are faced with a large increase in book postage, also.)

Finally, publishers used the expanding quantity of paper and greater manufacturing facilities in once again increasing their lists, reprinting out-of-print titles, loading the market with more titles as well as with an increasing total number of books. More titles in a narrowing market meant only one thing—reduction of sales per title published. And, as has been indicated, the smaller the printing of a title, the greater the cost per book in its manufacture.

When other manufacturers faced a similar situation, they promptly increased prices. But the publisher felt that he could not do this to a large extent. By the time he needed the price increase, there was much talk—but very little reality—about leveling off prices and even reducing prices. The publisher had come upon an inopportune time in which to increase. And whenever he tried it, he felt that he met resistance on the part of his bookseller outlets and on the part of the purchaser. Thus he was stuck with a price which represented, in its increase, only a fraction of the increased costs he must pay for production and overhead.

As a result of these factors, the key word in publishing these days is "the break-even point," that is, the number of sales needed, given a particular book with a particular plan for promotion, to bring back the outlay for the book. In pre-war days, the structure of cost to price in publishing was such that, given an ordinary first novel, modestly presented to the trade, a break-even point might rest somewhere between 2000 and 3500 sales, depending upon the practices of the individual publisher. Today, the same novel with a comparable modesty in presentation, will reach a break-even point only with 7500 to 10,000 sales, depending again upon the practices of the particular publisher. In a shrinking market, the number of books which could make those sales or larger ones grows ever smaller. (And to speak of an average is impertinent, since each title must be individually manufactured and cannot assume a portion of the sales of a book which has sold a great deal better.)

These are the conditions which have brought the immediate crisis to publishing. The common-sense step indicated for the publisher is to decrease the number of titles and to hope to spread the available sales over fewer titles, thus increasing the percentage of titles which sell over the "break-even" point. Indeed, the matter seems quite simple, in theory: no longer accept the book which will sell in the 2500 to 10,000 bracket. In theory, again, the books which expected to sell in this bracket would go unpublished.

This matter is of tremendous import to the serious writer and the serious reader, and, we may assume, to American culture. If publishers took this step completely, probably half of the books published in the past would be placed out of the reach of the commercial publisher today. Many of those books, it is true, we would not miss sorely; but a great many we have needed, and we will need many more like them in the future. Poetry, early work of many a recognized writer, and many a valuable book, even though twentieth of an author, never reaches this sale.

The trouble with this picture of arbitrarily lopping off those titles which do not sell at least 10,000 copies is that it is largely theory. Despite the common-sense step indicated, publishers are not paring their lists markedly, two years after the impact hit them; 1948 will see more titles published than 1947 or 1946, and 1949 is likely to reach very close to the same number. Almost like cultural lag, changes in the patterns of book acceptances are only now operating with any completeness, and only now is the full danger to the good but poor-selling book quite likely to be realized.

Why has the publisher responded so slowly to the need indicated? Here we need to think, for a moment, less of publishing in the over-all sense and more of the individual publisher. To decrease his list was very difficult for that publisher. During the war, because of need for paper for rapidly selling books, he had let go out of print many titles which had a smaller but perhaps more steady sale. With paper freer and with a narrowing market, these substantial titles needed to be in print, and the authors, now that the publisher *could* get them into print, demanded that he do so. During the war the publisher had been aggressive in his prosperity, encouraging new talent, granting considerable advances for unfinished work, looking forward to expansion; he had to add to his list to fulfill commitments; the momentum had been generated. Further, a publisher cannot spread his sales to make an average sale and thus bring each title over the break-even point; many factors other than those of a publisher's presentation and promotion control reception of a book; and should a publisher arrange his presentation and promotion and other controllables so that a "natural seller" would be given little stress in favor of a less fortunate book, he would gain the wrath of a valuable author and lose the possibility of a very large profit on a tremendous seller.

This matter is complex, and we have not reached nearly all the complexities. But I shall mention only two other important reasons why a publisher has difficulty in reducing his lists. One of these can best be discussed, perhaps, under the heading "investments." Besides obvious investments in a quick-moving book, a publisher normally expects to make other investments. One of these is in a full list, that is, in a list sufficient in size and diversity that the chances of having a number of good sellers will be increased, since good sellers fall into many types and are not always to be predicted. Another investment, of a long-range sort, is in an author. The publisher is as conscious as anyone that, although some early books of an author can be very popular, in many cases an author gradually accumulates the reputation, backlog, and skill which make him a valuable author to a publisher. The records of the early books by such people as Hemingway, Steinbeck, Maugham, and many others are well known and sufficiently illustrate the investments needed in the careers of promising writers. And a third type of long-range investment is in the book which does not follow the usual pattern of quick sales but is likely to sell, perhaps modestly, but over a long period of time. A personal illustration may indicate what is involved. On one of my recent lists is a tremendously valuable book of criticism, a type of writing considered a poor publishing risk at any time. By careful management of as many factors as possible and by reason of the fact that my rather unusual publishing procedures allow a lower overhead than is customary, this book has a lower "break-even" point than is common today. The first printing will just reach this break-even point. Sales of approximately three years promise to reach that point, with the three-year investment just returned. A second printing would call for new investment but would insure that when the second printing was exhausted a little more than the investment could be realized. Thus sales over a period of six to eight years and exhausting two printings might possibly return a little more than the investment which was made during this long time. And a similar but monetarily more optimistic picture may be expected of many a book.

The final consideration for the publisher who needs to reduce his list is that many people in publishing, just as the readers of *Berkeley* and just as I, are much concerned about the "serious" book which may not have large sales possibilities. These people would feel that a large satisfaction in their work would be denied them if they could not see on their lists an occasional book to which they might point with other than monetary pride. Even for the publisher most callous to these matters, a list without such books is likely to seem to lack prestige in the eyes of the trade, other publishers, and readers.

My feeling is, then, that we may expect the shrinkage in books to be published to come not so much through the reduction of lists by the individual publisher as through the failure of publishers or at least of their trade departments. It is well known now that many publishers are afloat because of the great sales of their textbooks in recent years or because of similar results auxiliary to the job of publishing in the retail field. And many another publisher has practically closed his trade department, keeping just such small staff as can handle the few books which are committed or otherwise indicated for publication. Failure of publishers and of trade departments may even sharpen as conditions continue, resulting in a marked shrinkage of the total number of titles published;

this shrinkage will probably be temporary in large measure, since those publishers who can survive on whatever terms will look for any opportunities to expand trade lists again.

As trade lists of commercial publishers shrink, it is possible that other publishers may take up some of the titles. These publishers are two, the university press and the private press. During the last twenty years, particularly, the university press has established for itself a leading place in publishing, largely through books of non-fiction closely associated with scholarly activities and selling in the 1000 to 3500 class. With the increased difficulties for those books which might be expected to sell in the 2000 to 10,000 class, and with increased costs boosting the break-even point for university press books as well, the university press has the opportunity of stepping into a new field. To take full advantage of this opportunity, editors of the university presses would need to change their policy so that they could accept fiction and other books formerly considered the province of the commercial publisher. It is to be hoped that the university press will rise to its opportunities and its responsibilities during this crisis. The private press, such as one of the imprints I am maintaining and such as are found in several places over the country, likewise have a new opportunity and a new responsibility to the writing they would sponsor. It is to be hoped that their number will increase and that their stormy, difficult paths may be smoothed by renewed interest in their work on the part of the booksellers and book buyers. These presses do not have the wide facilities of the commercial publisher for making their works known to a large public; the review, the seller, the buyer in books need to make special effort to discover what these small presses are doing, for during this period we are likely to be more dependent than ever before upon their services to our literature.

The conditions so far sketched I have called short-range, but they fit neatly into certain long-range developments in publishing and serve to deepen to crisis proportions a development which at some time must surely have brought the crisis anyway. There is not space here to sketch a history of publishing, but I would have the reader pause for a moment to think back over such history as he knows, from the days the scribes copied books laboriously and often beautifully by hand, to the printer-publisher, to the bookseller-publisher, to the more recent tradition of the publisher and an entrepreneur economic unit separate both from the printer and the bookseller. During this last phase, the tradition was of the publisher as a man of taste who would accept a manuscript from an author, hire a printer, and produce a book for sale. The books were actually sold by other entrepreneurs, the booksellers, normally, also, people who had some affection for books. The realm of books was reasonably centered in a few people, the writer, the publisher as man of taste, the bookseller as man of taste, and the few buyers also men of taste. In a day when oil monopolies were being made out of little entrepreneurs in oil, or a similar process was going on in destroying several hundred manufacturers of automobiles in favor of the ten or so left—or in a hundred areas—publishing and books were left to their gentlemen of taste.

But publishing also had its inventive geniuses and its people willing to see publishing made into a big business. Too few people visited bookstores and bought books; magazines proved that reading matter could be sold to many millions instead of to a few. So new patterns for merchandising had to be devised. To my mind, there have been three of these, all devoted to getting books to a larger number of people than can be sold through the bookstore. First of these was the device of selling books in department stores, drug stores, five and dimes; the material needed for this outlet, like the store's other merchandise, had to be price conscious; therefore, books were manufactured for this trade in reprint editions, priced at 59 cents or 89 cents or $1.49, a price possible after a book had proved itself by its sales and some of the costs and royalties could be reduced for these editions. And these books reached a "new market." In fact, these editions reached a new market not only through such department stores but also because they provided the basic stock, often placed there on assignment by the reprint publisher, for hundreds of would-be bookstores over the country.

Second of the merchandising methods was that of mail selling, resulting in book clubs, from the two giants to the many lesser ones. Selling books in large quantities of a single title, a club could realize all the economies of quantity production, undersell the retail outlet for the books, and add, again, a "new market."

Third new merchandising idea was to get books into the corner drug store and newsstand, alongside magazines. This involved use of the elaborate and efficient methods developed to merchandise magazines; it enormously extended the possible market but required books priced to compete with magazines. Manufacturing methods were developed to produce books which could compete on a price basis.

Since each of these was a merchandising method and a distribution and manufacturing problem different from that of the traditional publisher-bookseller method, new firms normally sponsored the new developments. They resulted in "subsidiary rights" for the original, or trade, publication. Closely associated with these was the development of the movies, which added a new outlet for stories and provided still another "subsidiary right" to an original publication.

Gradually the position of the publisher has shifted in response to this developing situation. Particularly under the stress of the recent crisis conditions, this changed position is clear. Many a publisher now is not making money or is frequently losing money on his activities as a trade publisher; he is breaking even or showing a small profit because of his share in the subsidiary rights to the books he publishes. His economic role, in fact, has changed; he is hardly any longer an entrepreneur in his own right but, instead, is entrepreneur *for others* interested in his books. He is the principal proving ground for books which can be successfully handled by those interested in merchandising the literary material in reprints, book clubs, or movies. He is now more successful economically as a publisher, the more material he can deliver to those who stand behind him; indeed, today he is largely dependent upon them for his continuing existence.

These conditions, I think even more than the crisis out of short-range conditions—which may or may not be long-range, also—have tremendous implications for the future of American writing. The type of book suitable for moving up the ascending ladder of "rights" from the hard-cover reprint, paper reprint, book club, to movies (in approximately increasing selectivity of number of titles used), we know by experience to be extremely limited. And the economy of the present trade publisher puts a premium for his existence upon good guesses regarding the books suitable for such uses, and a gradual pruning away of the books which don't have that chance.

With economic lines thus drawn, it is obvious that

"smart money" would see the advantage of having the various types of merchandising working closely together, each governing, insofar as it is feasible, the choices to be made by the others. A condition for monopoly existed, and monopoly has been growing. Prototype at present is the vast Doubleday empire, which in its associated firms, controls one of the largest trade publishing houses, one of the largest publishers of hard-cover reprints (the various Garden City imprints), and several book clubs, including the Literary Guild. Movie interests, too, have seen the folly of awaiting developments under the complete control of others; gradually these interests have participated more and more in development of manuscript material, in selection of books for attention through prizes and other devices, and, just recently, in editorial activities of various publishing houses. No Standard Oil is on the immediate horizon in publishing, but the economic conditions for such monopoly are present in publishing today, aggravated by the present crisis. Traditions in publishing may prove strong enough to resist this direction. At present, the decision seems some distance in the future; yet each day decisions are being made in one direction or the other and every reader may well govern his own choices, insofar as he can, to prevent monopoly in one of the few areas yet left to us in which the tradition of the man of taste and good will is not completely dead.

We may well note that in this picture the role of the bookseller has been changing, also. New methods of merchandising have sold some books better than he, and he has little chance for equal competition with these methods. He is faced with shrinking sales and increasing overhead; as a merchandiser, he has long made less on his capital and effort than almost any other merchandiser of goods. Efforts to increase the number of bookseller outlets are likely to endanger some already in existence and are hampered by the poor financial returns of the book trade. Many present outlets are endangered as department stores, finding that space and personnel and advertising devoted to books return less than the same devoted to clothing or other departments, either close their book departments or reduce them to smaller chances. Although relatively few booksellers have tried to develop the potentialities of the role, bookselling seems to be forced gradually toward a role comparable to that of the gift shop or similar establishment which caters to individual needs and tastes; perhaps the bookseller needs to develop even more his ability, which no other book merchandiser has, of providing a book on psychology needed by this customer, the self-help book needed by the worker, the book of poems called for all too infrequently. Such personalized service, as opposed to the vast impersonalized merchandising of the book clubs and the reprint outlets, is not normally profitable and provides a small market for the publisher; yet these books are needed and perhaps even a larger market can be developed for them through personalized bookselling.

Both the short-range and the long-range conditions for publishing are deeply, deeply disturbing. It is hardly possible to think that our literature will be defeated by complete commercialization into the cheap and shoddy, or that, in another long-range development, "serious" books would need to be charitably "sponsored" and the commercial publisher deteriorate to the level of the commercial magazines; yet, like atomic warfare, conditions for the grisly prospect confront us each day we go to our literary labors.

What will happen to provide a new direction? At this point I must lapse even more into the personal. I am a relative newcomer to publishing, having cut my teeth on the private press and still maintaining such a press as something, I believe, of great value in publishing today; this imprint is called Alan Swallow, Denver. And even as my efforts extend into the field of commercial publication, through the joint imprint of The Swallow Press and William Morrow and Company, my role is that of one interested in "serious" writing; or, through my association with the firm of Sage Books, Inc., or as director of The University of Denver Press, the role is that of sponsoring valuable writing of all sorts coming from the West. These roles hardly fit me for suggesting directions. But I should like to remark that it seems evident that "muddling through" will not provide an answer, certainly not an adequate answer, to the problems which confront good publishing today. All palliative efforts are valuable, efforts to streamline production, to hack a cent of cost here and there, or to expand our outlets; every cent in these realms becomes large in the problem which faces us all. But they are palliatives, and unless they can be pyramided into something fairly large-scale, sufficiently large-scale, in fact, as to make something like a hundred percent change in one of the economic conditions governing publishing today, they are not likely seriously to affect the general development. The stage is set for something revolutionary—for the person who can think of something entirely new in procedures. Perhaps the new could come in book manufacturing, perhaps in merchandising, perhaps in another place. Short of that, we must muddle through and do the best we can.

So far, of course, we are far short of that. Our immediate guesses can be narrowed and must be only guesses. One direction does seem indicated to me, unless the failure of houses and monopoly get us first—and that is greater specialization. As techniques have grown to set the conditions for fast selling of books of temporary interest, and as merchandising methods have been invented to handle these well, perhaps we may look forward to a specialized co-operation (or monopoly concern) to present such books. I think it conceivable that the bestseller type of book, which publishers can spot a little more easily than before and can "put over" better than before, may, through the cooperation of all subsidiary interests, including the movies, sell these books in cheap editions very widely, particularly through department store, mail, and newsstand facilities. "Originals" may well be handled in these editions as well as proved books and the screening of books for the process be done by representatives of the various interests in the book, without much use of the present trade publisher with his groping and rather uneconomic methods and without the use of the relatively uneconomic bookseller. Much as the "rental library" type of book is handled as a special type of publishing today, so perhaps our very big but momentary sellers may be handled as a special publishing function in the future.

What will be left? After the volatile stuff is gone, remains the more permanent ash, and I believe my readers will join me in thinking these the best books of all. So long as the price-cost situation is so terribly critical for these books, we must strive through any efforts we can make—choosy buying of books, encouragement to non-commercial publishers, even direct individual help* to see that good books get pub-

---
*A poet friend of mine has suggested an action which may well be helpful in many situations during this period. He has proposed that if a manuscript of poetry comes up which deserves publication and would seem to him worthy of support, but would sell very poorly, he would like to contribute a small fee to help assure publication; he would expect nothing in return except that he might wish to secure a few copies of the publication to use for Christmas gifts. Perhaps he has suggested a means for honorable, yet effective, means for widespread "sponsorship" of valuable books.

lished when they have little other chance. However small it is—and it must seem appallingly small in the strait we have entered—each person must help in his own measure. I wish that I might relieve him of his responsibilities and say that some man, somewhere, will right all the wrongs and lead us into the meadow of a great future literature, recognized as it deserves; but each of us is that person.

THE LIBERAL IN THE COLLEGE
The Humanist, January-February, 1955

Many of the great American liberals have been members of college and university faculties. Thorstein Veblen, Charles A. Beard, John Dewey, Robert Morss Lovett, several of the noted jurists—an imposing list could be compiled. Such men as these kept alive a tradition of American liberalism which dates back to the eighteenth-century liberalism of the Age of Enlightenment and the Revolution. This tradition, as interpreted by the college liberals, has kept higher education probably the freest of American institutions, despite tremendous outside pressures and despite, also, thousands upon thousands of teachers who have failed the tradition.

The liberal in the college of today has for his support and use the great strengths of this tradition. But in the battles for freedom now—and those to come—the tradition will, I think, fail the liberal unless the inheritance is re-examined or unless the liberal re-examines his relationship to that tradition. As it is interpreted in our universities now, the liberal tradition seems to have a great weakness. It is my purpose in this essay to suggest that weakness and to attempt a restatement which may provoke the liberal to whatever re-examination will aid his efforts to keep education the free institution he had so much part in creating.

To try to think about the plight of the liberal in education, it is essential to look at fundamentals. The inescapable central issue about education is the function of the institution within the society which supports it. This issue has been phrased in various words. Here I shall indulge the following phrasing: that the central issue involves "indoctrination" and "freedom of inquiry."

I am aware that "indoctrination" is a prejudiced word. It is used here to name those theories of education—and they are in the vast majority—which start thinking about education upon an unquestioned premise. This premise is that the result of education is known before the process of educating starts: that the purpose of education is to attain in the student some set of knowledge, skills, values, and ideas which the student must achieve before he is considered "educated." That is the nature of indoctrination: to achieve in the student some result already known, already premised for him.

The opposite to indoctrination is the position that there is no determined, no previously premised and unquestioned result known to which the student must somehow measure. He will acquire knowledges, skills, ideas, yes, but no particular sets or galaxies of these must be achieved as the end product of his education. This is "freedom of inquiry"—to arrive at conclusions, attitudes, and ideas according to the nature of pertinent evidence.

Upon the issue between these two positions is waged the battle over education.

The difficult situation of the liberal in our colleges is that on the one hand he desires freedom for the institution of education and for himself, that is, freedom from outside forces; but that on the other hand he is an indoctrinator in his own educational theories and practices.

The tradition of liberalism we inherit from the eighteenth and nineteenth centuries is a belief in the market place of ideas; put all ideas into the public arena, and ignorance will be overcome and the public gradually discern the truth. This is a forceful position, one which has probably made the United States such an adaptable and great nation.

The liberal educator seems to mean by the free market place of ideas, first, freedom of research, that is, to pursue knowledge and truth wherever they lead; and, second, a negative position, that *no idea, per se,* is to be excluded from the market place. The college liberal has been most noted for his distinguished research, for his additions to our funds of ideas, and, unhappily, rather little known for distinguished application of the market place of ideas to his teaching. It is the latter which constitutes the Achilles heel of his position as he seems to understand the liberal inheritance.

This inconsistency—or perhaps we may call it, more appropriately, this failure to extend his position consistently into all his work—has sometimes led the liberal to desert the strength of his position. Some years ago, for example, the liberal led the fashion of decrying "pure" research. To him, such research seemed a special pleading, a dedicated attachment to the insignificant. To the liberal, the physical scientist, particularly, had seemed to pursue his research to wake up one morning, an innocent babe, to realize that he had created a social force of tremendous power in achieving atomic fission. The scientist had been creating social forces only less tremendous for several generations. To the liberal, specialized research in the sciences and in technology had leaped far ahead of our lagging social adaptation. Research seemed irresponsible, not aware of social significances of what was being done. The scientist and any other person devoted to "pure" research had, to the mind of the liberal, to take up his social awareness and responsibilities; the research position had to be modified by the demands of social responsibility.

In taking such a stand and in deserting the fundamental position of freedom, the liberal educator has done great harm. To debate the end products of research is to place research in a position of control of forces not interested in freedom. It is to deny the market place of ideas. And this has been happening. The liberal is not solely responsible, of course, for the trend, but his inconsistency has contributed to it. Research has been slipping out of the college and university. It is now performed more and more within large corporations. Or, if it remains in the university, it is often performed directly at the behest of grants from corporations which set the problems before the research staffs. I am informed that there has been no fundamental research in basic matters of science for years in the United States except that performed by a handful of persons. Instead, research is into technology, primarily. Such research is important, of course. But the result is that research becomes increasingly the tool of groups for their own special interests instead of the tool of a whole society for its advances in knowledge. The liberal educator must recognize that he must battle for free research, for "pure" research, if you will. It is the only position that will keep the free market place of ideas—to inquire into the truth, no matter where the evidences may lead.

The college liberal has violated freedom for education insofar as he lent any aid to the decrying of pure research, but this is an error rather easily corrected in his thinking (although now very difficult to correct in institutional arrangements). He has committed perhaps a more grievous violation of freedom which is so much a part of his thinking that he will need to examine himself very closely if he is to correct himself. And that is in his *teaching*, in which he so often holds fundamentally to a notion of indoctrination.

I am continually surprised to hear, not just the conservative educator, but also the liberal educator—men of goodwill, all, and valiant fighters for academic freedom and for recognition of education as a great profession—take positions such as the following:

1. Disclose a primary and sometimes almost exclusive interest in the "superior" student.

2. Speak of "standards" which must be held in the classrooms, not as if such "standards" were high expectations of student creative development but were, instead, rather rigid sets of measuring sticks.

3. Maintain that the educator must concentrate upon the "values" which the growth of civilization has created and taught us, again as if those "values" were the one fixed constant in a sea of change. (My experience is that this is an especially popular "out" among liberal educators.)

4. Set up requirements which separate sheep from goats, that is, which deny the privilege of education to some persons because they do not think certain thoughts or do not meet some other tests of presumed ability. The pride that liberals have taken in "entrance requirements" and "entrance standards," and in the exclusiveness of colleges and universities, has always flabbergasted me; further, that there is such a ready acceptance among college liberals as among college conservatives of the thought that some persons

are simply not "college calibre" because they do not pass certain tests has likewise puzzled me.

5. Make such judgments as "John Doe is a B-minus student" seriously, as if this were a judgment of abilities straightforwardly and objectively determined. (This usually means, of course, that the student behaved in a certain way with regard to behavior expected from him by the educator.)

Underneath each of these positions lies a theory of indoctrination—that the professor already knows what the end product of education should be.

The tragic irony of the tradition of college liberalism—either in fact or in the manner in which recent liberals have interpreted the tradition—is that the liberal position has demanded freedom for the institution of education but holds to indoctrination within the institution itself. The college liberal will fight strongly for "academic freedom." He fights that no force outside education shall determine what the end product of education will be. In view of the fact that in his own practice he believes there *is* an end product of education, he then seems to be fighting that *he* shall determine the end product.

Naturally, in the eyes of the community which supports education, "academic freedom" in any such terms seems a special pleading, a pleading for a privilege for educators.

Since, in effect, the college liberal has agreed with his opponents about the nature of education, he fights on the same ground with all those forces—with the American Legion, with the Joe McCarthys, with legislatures, with Congressional and state investigating committees, with groups of citizens examining textbooks—about who shall control the indoctrination, the end product expected of the process of education. In that struggle, the liberal educator is surely doomed to failure; the forces are more powerful than he. Indeed, to fight these forces on their own ground, about the determination of the product, is to bring about misunderstanding upon the part of the community and, in the end, almost certain defeat, now that the issue is so strongly drawn and the forces so marshalled for attack.

The liberal educator has shared too much with his enemies the notion, on the one hand, that education is an institution for inculcating in the young the skills, knowledges, values, and ideas which some group, and probably not the educator, shall determine; and, on the other hand, that education is an institution for conducting advancement of knowledge into areas of need, with the particular needs being defined more and more by special, particularly commercial, interests.

The liberal educator must redefine his position today. Perhaps the liberal tradition itself has failed him, but more likely he has misinterpreted that tradition. He must remove inconsistencies in the position he has been taking, for it has left him on a losing battle ground to those who would capture education from him as an institution of indoctrination. He must positively ground his position in freedom, freedom in the classroom itself, as well as for the whole institution of education; freedom for the result of student activity as well as for the product of research; freedom of inquiry in every aspect of education, inside and out.

Toward such a redefinition, I offer the following set of principles:

1. A democracy, to survive by adapting itself to continually changing conditions, must have an institution charged with the responsibility of freedom of inquiry—to criticize, discover, create, investigate, wherever the evidences may lead. The institution in our democracy still best equipped to perform that necessary function is education.

2. The liberal position must be emphasized as freedom of inquiry, and the liberal educator must take the stand for public support of education as the institution of free inquiry, before the institution is completely captured and made an institution of indoctrination.

3. "Academic freedom," the rallying point of traditional liberalism in education, must be stated to the community positively, not negatively—that is, not as pleading for special privilege, but as necessary freedom of inquiry for the benefit of the ongoing community.

4. Education carries on its function for the community by two activities, the honored twins of teaching and research.

5. If our society is to use realistically the function of education, research must be subsidized in education and must be granted complete freedom of inquiry into any subject, area, or ideas.

6. Sponsored inquiry—for the purpose of determining answers to special problems, primarily in technology—must not be considered the true research function of education.

7. Teaching activity, likewise, is devoted to freedom of inquiry, in the classroom and out.

8. Both teacher and student are inquirers; neither is equipped to provide, beforehand, the final products of inquiry. The class is a group activity of inquiry in which each member, teacher and student, brings special abilities and interests. The teacher's responsibility, as a mature, accomplished person, is to aid in the inquiry and to offer guidance, not to provide by rote the end products of his thinking as the end products of the inquiry.

9. The teacher must realize, in his bones, as it were, that the significant result of his activity *as teacher* will be the activity of others, perhaps after he is dead. He depends in his role as teacher upon the minds of others; he lends himself to the future of others.

A MAGAZINE FOR THE WEST?
Inland, Autumn, 1957

I have placed a question mark at the end of my title because I wish to offer, not pronouncements, but some speculations I have been mulling over for several years. What would be the nature of a magazine from our region which could achieve national influence upon the direction of people's thought? What would be the grounds of such a magazine? Are those grounds, are those conditions, coming to be?

During the generation just past, undoubtedly the most influential group of writers has been the Southerners. The Southern Agrarians and their followers, and Faulkner and his imitators, have had a pervasive influence upon our thinking about poetry, about fiction, about literary criticism, and also about social philosophy. I shall not try to argue the quality of this influence—but merely remark that I have not been in agreement with a great deal of it; yet the power of the influence is readily demonstrable in our books and magazines, our colleges and universities.

Although *The Fugitive* magazine and the early Agrarian symposium *I'll Take My Stand* touched off much of this Southern influence, the pervasive power of the influence centered in the magazine *The Southern Review*—and, of course, many books. Edited by

Cleanth Brooks and Robert Penn Warren and published from 1935 to 1942, *The Southern Review* was surely the best and the most influential literary magazine ever to appear in America. If it was not the best and most influential by itself, it need share those adjectives with only one other magazine, the somewhat earlier *The Hound and Horn*.

In speculating about a possible magazine from the West which could speak with similar power, we would do well to learn lessons from *The Southern Review*. It spoke ably for a whole attitude which had roots in a certain region. How did it do so? May the conditions which made it possible come soon to the West?

These are my speculations upon those questions.

First, one would need to sense that a possible creative flowering were upon us, as it was upon the South thirty years ago. I sense that this may be true for our region today. Recently there has been much public noise about a so-called cultural renaissance in the San Francisco Bay area. I must confess that I don't think much of what it has done so far. In that climate, it seems that anyone who can holler rather loudly is considered a new evidence of the renaissance. But, fortunately, we need not call upon this offensive publicity and the work behind it to judge that we are moving a bit; the good evidences are elsewhere.

One impressive matter to me is that we are no longer losing so many of our talents to other regions. Although these talents are scattered over a wide geographical area—and frequently suffer as a result of this—they are remaining to work here, that is, a higher and higher proportion of them. And at many places there are growing centers of purposeful activity in writing, frequently centered about the critical leadership of an individual. And we are creating more and more opportunities for the voices to be heard. Our number of magazines devoted to creative work primarily grows regularly—this new *Inland*, *Talisman*, several other little magazines on the Coast, my own *PS*, and a number of college and university sponsored quarterlies. I should judge that few of these are yet of high rank, but they are preparations and published from a sense of something stirring. As they become better, their influence will grow; only thus will the convictions of their editors that something *is* stirring be vindicated.

Second, the lesson of *The Southern Review* is that we need a group of creative writers with homogenous ideas. This is a great stumbling block to us in the West. Without it, we shall probably never have the greatest impact upon the national culture; yet we are so diverse geographically and intellectually that I doubt we shall become homogenous.

I have reflected a good bit upon this, and as I have met writers from all over the West, the famous and the struggling, I have tried to sound out any common areas of thinking. It has seemed remarkable to me that these people are in some way alike, in friendliness, in skepticism of the national trends, in doubt of the "official" attitudes of the Eastern intellectual circles. There is a common ground, even among persons of diverse beliefs.

It seemed to me at one time that the common ground swept down to a basic Western belief in what I shall call Rationalism—a feeling that man must make his own destiny with his own faculties. I should like very much to feel that this is common among our intellectuals: in the famous phrase of Yvor Winters' book, "in defense of reason." Yet to feel that there is that common element in all of us as Western intellectuals is foolish. There is, indeed, a great deal of reliance on the anti-rational (an example: the so-called cultural renaissance of the San Francisco area); there is hearkening after the symbolist, or after the wayward, or after the anti-intellectual; and sometimes there is a decided interest in the mystic.

Thus, although I feel that if there is to be a common ground among Western writers which can convey much to the national direction of our culture, it must be the rationalist spirit, I do not think we are very near to it and may never achieve it.

Third, from the lesson of the Southerners and especially of *The Southern Review*, we need persons of diverse interests who are yet caught up in the homogenous direction. We need—as they had—the good economist, sociologist, historian, as well as the creative writer and the literary critic. People's ideas are not exclusively literary or concerned with the arts; they are rooted in philosophy and play in the arenas of social behavior as well. When a new book or some other source suggested an article for *The Southern Review*, Messrs. Brooks and Warren could turn to one or another of a considerable number of persons in many "disciplines" who could be relied upon to do a very good job of writing and work within the cluster of ideas which characterized the magazine and the Southern group.

Perhaps such a hope is farthest of all from realization in the West. I have looked, as among writers, among persons in various studies to find homogenous character. Interestingly enough, I found more give-and-take among such persons in a limited group in Denver than elsewhere in the West. But diversity is the general keynote.

As I see the matter, then, we are well-intentioned to find every means of sponsoring sound creative work in the West. It has its satisfactions; it is preparation for something else, as well. But we are not yet ready for that something else and would not be able even to define it. As a region we suffer too greatly, still, from our common plagues: distance, isolation, colonialism of dependence upon what is the fashion outside our region, the movement of our people elsewhere. Our efforts, however, are gradually changing this. We are finding voice—here and there, in a leader, in a writer, in a particular place. Out of this may be forged the common ground on which may rest a character of our own. If this occurs, I think it will be detectable in the three characteristics—the three lessons learned from the Southerners. Perhaps our various work can then be linked into a major outlet for the whole.

Meantime, I hope we shall rally round the voices, little and great, which we have. I hope, also, that sometime a foundation or other source of footing the expense will make possible a grand gathering of the serious writers from all parts of the West. Face-to-face, I think we have much to talk about, much indeed, to discover about our common ground.

THE MAVERICKS
Critique, Winter, 1959

1.

Ten years ago one of the most able executives in New York commercial publishing told me that 58% of the authors on his list lived west of the Mississippi River. And just a few months ago, I had the opportunity to speak with the senior editor of the trade department of one of New York's largest publishing houses. When I asked him about such a proportion of his authors, he at first thought the proportion would be small. On further thought, however, he confessed that since most of the manuscripts accepted came to him from the hands of New York agents, he had just automatically assumed most were written east of the Mississippi. His considered estimate was that more than half were, in fact, written west of the river.

I do not know that one should make a great deal of this fact. But it is a simple way of estimating something which is happening in American letters, and that something is, I think, of considerable importance; more than that, it is a something which is not being recognized in those places which marshal our intellectual life, which create our literary fads, which make us think we are keeping up on cultural affairs. I am sure that these places are out of touch with reality in a measurable degree.

Surely much of this development I can demonstrate by considering my immediate topic, the novelist in the West.

2.

In the Twenties we had a literature dominated (if *dominated* is the correct word) by the expatriates. In the Thirties the domination was chiefly by those with social concerns. During the last two decades, probably the single most potent literary force has been that of the Southerners—the Southern Agrarians and those others from the South who, if not Agrarians, were within nodding distance of the Agrarian attitudes. The power of this literature is still by our sides, so that it is difficult to assess it well. However, it seems clear that the basic creative urge is scattered by the winds, through the fact that the South did not harbor well its own creatures. Last summer a reunion of some of the Southern Agrarians was held, of all places, in Boston! This fact is indicative of a great shift, and some seeds have been uprooted. The cult of Faulkner, the biggest name in fiction among the Southerners, is dying gradually, and properly so. I say "properly," for we ought to correct our intellectual fads as rapidly as possible. And "properly," also, because he is not worth so much as all that. Once misunderstood and unfairly attacked, Faulkner deserved attention for those brilliant works of a decade or so; now, nearly as badly understood (although with idolatry), perhaps some sound sifting of his worth can be done.

We are not done with the work of the past four decades. But we are nearly done with it as creative source. Recently many have remarked that our literary horizon, particularly in fiction, seems to be flat and dull. The partial truth in such an observation demonstrates, I think, the pastness of those decades.

I believe, just as a matter of cultural direction, that the next two decades, if our world will permit us to live them, shall see a gradual dominance (in the same sense in which I referred to the dominance of the other forces) come to our intellectual life, and particularly to our poetry and our fiction, from the West. The seeds have been sowed, and they have sprouted. The yeoman work has been done already by persons who will in the next decade be recognized for much more than they are now. The movement is on.

3.

It would be silly to assume that there is a vast similarity of creative spirit in the West. The comments on the fiction, below, will remove any such tendency to infer. It would be silly even to assume that there is a kind of "movement," comparable to that of the Agrarians, now arising in the West. But as I have thought of these problems over the years and have talked with many writers in the West, I have become willing to hazard two hunches or guesses about basic characteristics of the hypothetical Western writer.

First, he is almost without exception at odds with all the evidences of intellectual dominance of the past two decades. He is mostly on uneasy terms with the fashions of book publishing today. He is frequently berated or ignored in the reviews. He is not among the honored "men of letters" who have risen to great recognition in this period. Furthermore, he is so much at odds with those official recognitions that he appears an individualist. Indeed, he *is* an individualist; these writers almost all are. For that reason, I have called them, collectively, "the mavericks" in the title of this essay.

Second, although they vary a great deal in philosophy—say from the vehment rationalism of Vardis Fisher to the incipient mysticism found in works of Frank Waters and Walter Van Tilburg Clark—I detect some common qualities. One of these is nothing more (and yet how significant) than the observation that all of the six I shall treat in most detail are wonderful, warm, superb human beings. Although they may occasionally suffer from the biting that has been done on them, or plain neglect, I have detected none of the bitterness, the backbiting, the jockeying for position which one detects so much in our cultural life. These people are down to earth, they have greatness as persons and as friends. And with this goes a rooted rational approach which will, I think, be important in our coming literature.

4.

One can mention with respect and admiration quite a number of novels and works of fiction from Westerners. Indeed, no one person can have read all of them and know all the good ones, I am sure. I shall not try to make assessments of a large group but shall name some which, I believe, form at least a core of work which has speaking acquaintance with greatness, in one small or large regard or another; and these are some of the seeds and sprouts of which I spoke: Wallace Stegner's *Big Rock Candy Mountain;* the Rio Grande novels of Harvey Fergusson; *The Big Sky* by A. B. Guthrie and *Johnny Christmas* by Forrester Blake, both dealing with the same Mountain Men era; *Orange Valley* by Howard Baker; the work of Donald Wetzel, transplanted Southerner, and the work of Mark Harris, transplanted Easterner. There are more I should name, I am sure, but these occur most readily to mind and perhaps suggest the flavor and breadth of some of this work.

But for more extended comment, I have chosen six.

5.

It is common enough to speak of "woman writers," as if they were a race apart and not to be judged by the same standards as "men writers." I shall follow suit only to try to suggest judgment of worth. There are three women writers of fiction whom I admire greatly: Katherine Anne Porter, Caroline Gordon, and Janet Lewis. By marking them off as women, I do not mean to suggest inferiority. Indeed, I do not believe I could name three living men writers of fiction who are their equals.

Of the three, it seems to me unfortunate that the least known has been Janet Lewis. Her virtues are rare, indeed, today, and they are to be commended as corrective to the inflated reputations of our times. Janet Lewis's first novel was published in 1932 and is named *The Invasion*. I must remark a continuing gratitude of more than two decades to Robert Penn Warren for calling my attention to this book. It is a very special book in American letters, one hard to characterize.

Recently I saw in manuscript an article by a British author now in this country, Donald Davie, in which he has tried to link *The Invasion* and William Carlos Williams' *In the American Grain* with a particular, special American literary tradition, a tradition which stems out of Fenimore Cooper, the later novelists and historians who dealt with Indians and with other peculiarly American experience, and to the interesting intuitions D. H. Lawrence offered about our literature. I think Davie may have hit upon a significant characterization.

In brief, *The Invasion* is the story of the Johnston

family of St. Mary's in upper Michigan, the story of a family intermingled of white and Indian. In movie parlance, it is a "documentary." It is based closely upon documents of the Johnston family and is often very close to the language of those documents. With this is welded one of the most perfect eyes in literature for the detail which captures the sensory data and the emotion, the exactly right selection of the significant. The style is quiet, impeccable; it has none of the rhetorical flashes or the fancy-dan stuff which goes for "brilliant writing" today. But it is assertive of true brilliance. Janet Lewis learned almost impossibly well from the styles of the great historians and fiction writers of the nineteenth century—if one must point to sources of individual style.

And with these qualities goes Janet Lewis's "womanly" (and I mean this as a term of respect and admiration) feeling for the basic issues, for the significant meanings, for the universal insights in the story she is telling. This quality, by the way, is characteristic of her poetry: it goes to the true root of human concern, to the sometimes simple (but not simple-minded, which, it seems to me, characterizes so much of our writing today which tries to find hidden meanings) but the always sound and penetrating insight.

Janet Lewis's next novel would not "go" in New York commercial publishing. We shall meet this theme often. It appeared in 1941 in a very limited edition from the Colt Press in San Francisco—most beautifully presented, too. It is *The Wife of Martin Guerre* and is the first of three novels Miss Lewis has written based upon documented court cases of old times. It is a "short novel," a form in which some excellent fiction has been written, and *The Wife of Martin Guerre* stands with the select best.

Here again we find the impeccable, quiet style; we find immense richness of detail offered, as in a fine poem, with the exact and meaningful eye. The insight into the problems of Bertrande de Rols, the wife of Martin Guerre, is precisely set in the culture of sixteenth-century France yet is the universal story of a woman beset by unusual conflict. Without equivocation, it is one of the truly distinguished pieces of writing of our time.

The Wife has been followed by three works: another short novel in the court record series, entitled *The Trial of Soren Quist*, again a jewel like *The Wife;* Janet Lewis's only novel with a contemporary setting, *Against a Darkening Sky;* and a book of short stories, *Goodbye, My Son*. I am writing this in early February, and late this month Doubleday will publish the third of the court-case novels, *The Ghost of Monsieur Scarron*. It is, I understand, a long novel, not the short novel one might have expected as companion to *The Wife* and *The Trial*. Its publiction should be looked forward to eagerly by everyone interested in American letters.

Janet Lewis has never been popular, nor has she won critical regard. *The Wife of Martin Guerre* has appeared in France in translation, and I understand that *The Trial of Soren Quist* sold well in Canada. Other than this modicum of attention, near silence! She is a maverick today, for her style is exact, impeccable, and just, but it does not shout for attention. She is *quiet* in a day when the threshold of our hearing is that of the noise of jets in flight.

Yet I have tried an experiment over the years. I have often handed *The Wife of Martin Guerre* to people or recommended it highly—to people of most diverse interests, women and men, professionally in "literature" and casual readers. I have never found one who did not admire the work, genuinely like it. Let us hope that this spring some attention for *The Ghost of Monsieur Scarron* will begin to set us right with the fiction of Janet Lewis.

6.

As of this early month in 1959, Vardis Fisher has published twenty-four novels. He is at work now putting the finishing touches upon the twelfth volume (a gigantic volume it will be, in itself) in his Testament of Man series, and Doubleday has him under contract for a volume of his short stories.

His public career has been that of a true maverick —or "orphan," as Fisher will say in his last volume of the Testament. His relationships with the large publishers have been most uneasy. Twice they have quit him in his work, and he has had to seek publication with a small Western publisher. In the Thirties, Caxton Printers, Ltd., of Caldwell, Idaho, published him when the New York firms would not. The other case I shall discuss in speaking more about the Testament of Man series.

Some of Fisher's trials and tribulations as a writer are recorded in his book of advice for writers, *God or Caesar?* He has had only one relatively big success: the $10,000 Harper Prize for his *Children of God,* which, in addition to winning the large prize, sold quite well. Unlike many other writers whom my readers can name under their breaths who squandered a much larger bonanza from a novel or two, and seemed ever after to have lost their punch, Fisher parleyed his modest good fortune into some small property on which he built, with his own hands, a beautiful place to live; and he managed most sensibly to set up for a full devotion to writing.

There have been a few other small successes. When his Vridar Hunter tetralogy had to be published in the West, its early volumes caught hold of some public attention and some of the merchandising was large enough to demand a New York firm. The cheap-reprint publishers have been quietly picking up various properties among his novels; indeed, in reprint form, he has sold amazingly well in comparison with any attention accorded him as a "new book" author.

Several of his books have been read avidly in Europe: only this past year one of the most popular books in Germany was Fisher's *Pemmican*.

During the Thirties, Fisher attacked both Marxism and Freudianism, so that he was persona non grata with the reviewers and critics of the day who made literary reputations, being as badly handled, then, say, as was Faulkner. But Fisher has never been a "fine" writer— devotee of elaboration of style, the "well-made" fiction, or the other icons of fiction criticism of the past two decades. So he has always been at odds with his literary environment. Indeed, I know that some of his former friends and admirers feel that he went off the deep end when he tackled his Testament of Man and threw up their hands in a gesture of hopelessness; and no one of them has made a peep for his works since then.

Fisher also had his troubles with the critics because he is a political reactionary and makes no bones about it. This is a source of serious amusement to me, for I am a political liberal. Yet Fisher is one of the best political reactionaries I know—not consorting with the Libertarians, the modern reactionaries, and such groups. His reaction is based, as I see it, on one principle which makes all serious political thinkers one: the assertion of individual liberty. He has reason, because of what he has seen of our intellectual life as well as of our governmental life, to fear what is happening to us in our suburbanite, institutionalized, organizational-man culture. In his sense, all men of good faith are reactionaries and ought to know it.

Fisher is also a rationalist, a humanist. These directions contrast so much with the trends in contemporary literature concerned with the irrational, the mystic, the surrealist, the symbolic, the mythic, that here, again, he has been a maverick in the culture in which he writes.

This at-odds quality has gone pretty far. I am convinced in my own mind that many review media do one of two things: they ignore the work, deliberately, as a means of keeping notice from it; or they hand it to a hatchet man. Two little stories from these few years I have been publishing some of his work will illustrate the matter, perhaps. It would appear that one of the Fisher-haters is the book editor (or one of his important assistants) of *Time*. This magazine has chosen to ignore most of the Fisher novels for quite a time. It did review *Pemmican* viciously, from the tone of the review. When one of the recent Testament novels came out, I forget whether is was *A Goat for Azazel* or *Peace Like a River,* the magazine had, of course, received the usual review copy. I later received a special delivery letter from *Time* asking that a second copy be forwarded immediately; the letter indicated that *Time* possibly would review. No review did appear. My inference is that they used the second copy (or one of the copies) to hand to their research man, and that they expected he could break down the scholarship of the volume. When they could not, as I infer they could not, they chose to ignore the book. Then a couple of years ago the *Reporter* magazine published an article by a woman critic in which she spoke of a British novelist who had undertaken a long series of novels and decried the fact that no American novelist undertoook such large-scale efforts. I wrote a letter to the editors of the *Reporter* pointing out that their author was in error, that, in fact, Fisher had undertaken a most gigantic project, perhaps the largest in the history of fiction. The reply to me was to the effect that my letter had come up in a meeting of the editors of *Reporter,* but, as I knew, they had not published my letter. I infer that they had little regard for fact.

So much for the trials of a maverick of stature and industry. Fisher's twenty-four novels fall readily into three groups: the biographical and autobiographical works based on his own experience as a child and young man; his historical novels of various aspects of Western history; and the Testament of Man series.

His biographical work includes novels about people who lived near the Snake River valley in Idaho. These characteristically have sombre human interest, but one of my favorites is the short novel *April*, which, I think, Fisher wrote to show some of his detractors that he need not always be sombre. Better known of the novels in this general group is the autobiographical Vridar Hunter tetralogy, *In Tragic Life, Passions Spin the Plot, We Are Betrayed,* and *No Villian Need Be.* The series of four started off powerfully. If you have a stomach for the sombre, even the bitter, you will find, I think, *In Tragic Life* one of the most effective novels available. As the series went on, it thinned out—largely through "talk." Fisher is an intellectual novelist, primarily, and, as he himself recognizes (and the Testament of Man largely grew out of this problem) the later novels in the tetralogy increasingly became debate upon intellectual currents and philosophical positions.

I suppose Fisher's novels on Western history can hardly be called evidences of his quality as an intellectual novelist. But in taking particular historical materials (and he most often has done exactly that), he has been scrupulous in his scholarship and has been amazingly successful in making the "true" story work as fiction. There are too many to list here, but I particularly recommend *The Mothers,* a novel based on the Donner Party disaster and, I think, a book with tremendous power. Published last year was *Tale of Valor,* his novel upon the Lewis and Clark expedition. To my mind, this appeared intractable material; I did not think a novelist could turn it to good fiction. But the result, *Tale of Valor,* is amazing; it is a novel of great stature. I find a kind of bitter irony in the fact that this novel of immense quality upon a "big" American story could have been virtually ignored by those dedicated to official "Americanism"; and in the fact that it will appear in paperback form and undoubtedly will sell extremely well in such form.

The Testament of Man series is Fisher's effort to probe the origins and roots of human thought and behavior. It is a series of twelve novels, of which eleven have now appeared, the twelfth to appear late in 1959 or early 1960. Fisher did a tremendous job of scholarship in preparing his work for these volumes, investigating all the best that is known by the scholars about man's development. Then he chose crises, in a sense, in human development, as he saw them, and built novels which tell those crises and resultant directions. The first five were based upon man's prehistoric eras—*Darkness and the Deep, The Golden Rooms, Intimations of Eve, Adam and the Serpent,* and *The Divine Passion*. These volumes were published by Vanguard Press, which was also in the early Forties publishing some of Fisher's Western historic novels. The series was not well received and sales were poor, and Vanguard dropped the project. Then Abelard Press published the next two, *Valley of Vision* and *Island of the Innocent,* based on Old Testament and ancient Greek times. Abelard abandoned the project after that, and the series languished for many years. Fisher, indeed, finished writing the next four volumes and much of the last, but they could not be sold to the New York firms. Meantime, those firms were anxious to get his novels upon Western history, and Doubleday has issued two since then. A few years ago, I became conscious of the fact that Fisher's big series was not continuing and that even Caxton Printers, a firm which had come to his rescue earlier, was not going ahead with the Testament. So one day I wrote to Fisher to inquire about it and found this story of failure at the commercial level. I then determined to do all I could to see that the series should be completed, in print, and subsequently issued volumes eight through eleven—*Jesus Came Again,* on New Testament times; *A Goat for Azazel,* upon the times of the formation of the Christian church; *Peace Like a River,* upon the asceticism which befell the Christians; and *My Holy Satan,* a novel upon the early Middle Ages and the human drive toward "humanism." The twelfth volume, which I shall be proud to publish, is Fisher's testament of modern man, to some extent a rewriting of his tetralogy in view of his two decades devoted to writing the Testament of Man.

In any work so vast as the Testament, one should expect unevenness. There is some here, true, and differing types of unevenness. But in this series Fisher has had perhaps his largest "odds" with his artistic culture. For he is, as I said, primarily an intellectual novelist. We once honored such, in old Sam Johnson's *Rasselas,* in George Meredith (whom Fisher studied closely in his graduate work at Chicago). But, no, the the dominant trends in our creativity of the past generation or so have been anti-intellectual; we like "guts" writing, like Faulkner and Hemingway. We feel that civilized man, who writes with direct style and can conjure up interest in idea and concept, is not truly at grips with the world. I think the drifts of correction will change this. We shall provide those critics who, to my mind, dodged their jobs and politely declined to say anything about a "work in progress" until it might be safe to do so, will some time have to deal with a vast, imperfect, but truly imaginative work which looks like a giant of humanistic endeavors among the pygmies of "fine" writings.

7.

For a man who has published only four books—*The Ox-Bow Incident, The City of Trembling Leaves, The Track of the Cat,* and *The Watchful Gods*—Walter Van Tilburg Clark has won a considerable success. Two of the books were honored, of course, by becoming the bases of relatively good movies. So it would not appear that Clark is among the mavericks listed here.

Let it be said at once that these books have deserved all the attention they have secured. They were not cut to any of the contemporary fashions; their boldness is interesting and useful. I remember once that J. V. Cunningham said to me that we ought to discover what constitutes excellence in the "western story." Such comment is not mere play: the traditional western story, like the mystery, has many patterns, and within the patterns much inept writing has "got by." What all of these patterns are I am not the one to say. But it is clear that the typical western story has at least two virtues. First, it tries to see human behavior (as does the mystery) in simplified terms; in Empson's term, I suppose it is "pastoral." Even the shoddiest makes virtues of brotherhood, of helping the downtrodden, of asserting the right. True, these virtues are sentimentalized unbearably; yet I suppose the sentiment is not so vicious as false sophistication, or at least no more so. And most often, true, the characters are sticks in dimension, if not in action.

Second, the western story does translate its themes into action. There is much to be said for "psychological" fiction, but there is also much to be said for action fiction, for the ability to raise the important problems in terms of overt struggle. And sometimes, especially in what we think of the "best" western fiction, we see the struggle in both psychological (internal) and overt terms.

What constitutes the true worth, the possible excellence, of western fiction is something upon which Walter Clark can best testify, as a working writer. In his two spectacular novels and in some of his stories, he has at least used some of the ingredients of the "western story" and seen fit to raise them to serious levels. (I should mention that Frederick Manfred's recent *Riders of Judgment* is a similar attempt of entirely worthy proportions, and that we have a good many novels of only slightly smaller accomplishments within the general pattern.) I think Clark has more to testify on the subject.

Despite the big "success," Clark's relationships with New York publishers have not been altogether peaceful. I do recall that there was considerable reluctance at one time to publish a volume of his stories, on economic grounds, and that the success of the novels aided this publication. This is, of course, an old economic story in writing today.

But a matter of chief concern has been that Clark has not produced more. There has not been a new book in many years. It seems that every month I hear someone ask, "When is Walter Van Tilburg Clark going to get out a new book? What's the matter that he is not producing more?"

I have little testimony in the matter, and much of what I shall say is clearly labeled conjecture.

The first thing to be noted is that Clark is, within the terms of his own insight, a perfectionist. I say "within the terms of his own insight," for I have never known a writer more averse merely to producing something for the market. Here is the staunch virtue of a man who must see something himself before he believes, one of the great virtues in American letters. It is clear that Clark is perfectly willing to throw away ideas for books, parts of books, even perhaps whole books in manuscript when they do not come up to his own notion of what they should be. What a great contrast to, say, a Caldwell or a Steinbeck or Faulkner, who can so indifferently publish ghosts of themselves!

The second *is* my conjecture: I once heard Walter Clark give a talk to a class of writers in which he used, I judged with great intensity, the terminology found in the books we are all so familiar with, the anthologies with commentary which seek to help us analyze, explicate, and understand the novel and the story. I confess that this surprised me coming from Clark, and that it has worried me a great deal. This is not the place to debate the validity of those concepts. I don't deny their considerable usefulness, perhaps to critics, chiefly to the pedagogue. But I do not believe they belong more than on the periphery (if even there) of the consciousness of the creative writer. This reminds me too much of the old writers-conference story of the girl who was questioned about what Mr. So-and-so Leader had said about her story. "Oh, he liked it and thought it was a fine story. Now I have to go home, he told me, and put in the symbols."

There are bigger fish to be caught than these terms; there are larger critical concepts. There are more important helps for one who, as Clark has demonstrated his intention, wishes to probe human behavior for its meaningful patterns and to offer us a fictional insight in which the style becomes that "simple" exposition, **in fiction, of what he knows.** I confess a troubled fear that Clark has bound himself in the net of the critical sleight-of-hand; and since he is so terribly conscientious as to offer only what has become real and good to him, the net perhaps is a great hindrance.

Enough of conjecture, and I hope I am badly mistaken. My personal feeling for Walter Clark is extremely great, for I think, like the others of this special list, he is one of the "good guys" of the world who make our existence tolerable; and that our American letters would be measurably poorer without the work he has done. This feeling is expressed in part in a poem of mine in which the following stanza was addressed to Clark:

> Walter, I think there's gold dust on your trail
> Or some black-banded ore your gentle pace
> Discovers veined within the rock.
>   I talk
> To wish sun-warmth upon the mountain shale,
> Sun-warmth forever on your face.

8.

One must picture Frank Waters as a lean, bronzed inhabitant of the mountains who knows the earth and its people. And this is true, but he has also, in his active life, been all over the Southwest and knows all of it, I suppose, better than any other person. He is a challenging, I should say even bull-headed, writer of non-fiction about this great area, as well as a novelist of significance. He has done a good many different kinds of writing, even scenarios, and has acted as consultant upon scenarios. His knowledge of the Indians of the Southwest is intimate and based upon active friendship and deeds done.

Apart from the miscellaneous writing, whose interest I in no way pass off, his reputation primarily rests on six novels arranged in two trilogies. The first trilogy written was more of a "true" trilogy than the other. The three novels were *Below Grass Roots*, *The Dust Within the Rock*, and *The Wild Earth's Nobility*. These novels have, unfortunately, been out of print for quite a time. They constitute a serious effort to write about mining, the search for gold, in the West.

The best comment I know upon these novels is that of a friend who came from the East and who, in Providence, had been one of the editors of *Smoke* magazine. After a thorough study of the literature which had grown up about this interesting aspect of American experience, this critic said that Waters' trilogy was the "epic" of mining. The analogy serves a useful function. The trilogy has sweep and ambition and, of course, length. I personally think that it can stand condensation, and I hope, as he knows, that he will return to this trilogy and make for us a single big book. I do not belittle the past accomplishment. But I feel that when these books are condensed and made available again, we shall recognize that we have a great novel about something which is specially American and especially interesting, a spirit by very broad analogy (and unfair to Waters) similar to what

Steinbeck was trying to grasp in his story "The Leader of the People."

The other trilogy by Waters shows greater maturity, greater compactness, a style more exactly suited to its purpose. The three novels deal with the "dark-skinned" peoples of the Southwest. *The People of the Valley* is "about" the strain of pure Spanish blood left in the New World of the Southwest; *Man Who Killed the Deer* is "about" the Indian, particularly the Pueblo Indian; *The Yogi of Cockroach Court* is "about" the half-breed found particularly upon the U.S.-Mexican border (where Waters worked for the telephone company for some time).

These are interesting and good novels, all; but the supreme one, to my mind, is *Man Who Killed the Deer*. Here, I think, is easily the finest of the novels about the Indian, a book to be placed alongside Janet Lewis's *The Invasion* on the broader canvas of Indian-White relationships. For *Deer* is concerned with the man we used to call the "marginal man," the man caught between two cultures. The treatment is knowledgeable; it is incisive and fundamentally enlightening; and the style has no particular pyrotechnics but is rich with the impeccable touch for the right tone and the right detail, quietly assertive.

Like many another who has known the Indian well, Waters has developed a touch of mysticism. I do not know where this will take him, of course. It was, the last time I saw any of his new work, well modulated and not anti-humanist. Waters, like Clark, is a searcher, and he has showed no interest in the parlor game of getting out books which are repetitive of his own insights. He moves to additional ones. He has not had a new book for quite some time, that is, a novel; and I know that he would like to finish up a very ambitious project. I hope he will be able to do so, and the others of which he is capable, and also return to his mining story. But, frankly, I fear the market; I fear here is a maverick, like Fisher, whose most ambitious work may rub the wrong way in New York. I hope that the publishers shall prove my fears mistaken.

9.

As I write, I am aware that an interview with Frederick Manfred will be a part of the issue of *Critique* for which I am writing; and that the reader will be able to sample something of Manfred's attitudes directly. To anyone who has known him, it is very nearly impossible to talk of Manfred except in personal terms. There appeared on my doorstep one day, unannounced, this veritable giant. He introduced himself as Fred Manfred and said that he wanted to talk with me about his publishing problems.

Manfred has already become something of a legend, and it is well to review that legend for a moment. His early books had to come from a small publisher in the Twin Cities, a publisher now gone for some years. He was then writing under the name Feike Feikema. Some of his later works were published in New York; these include an autobiographical trilogy, which he now calls *World's Wanderer,* published in New York under the titles *The Primitive, The Brother,* and *The Giant.* They won him some reputation as a sort of Thomas Wolfe character, perhaps effusive, certainly sensitive and omnivorous of experience. Unfortunately, as Fisher indirectly noted in *God or Caesar?,* the reception was rather blind to the true qualities of the writing. Manfred's knowledge of his people was great and sound.

Then Manfred turned from this direct material to his first historical novel, *Lord Grizzly.* I do not know for sure, but I suspect this was his most "successful" novel in earning ability, for it sold relatively well and went into a large paperback edition.

Then he wrote his most ambitious work, a long novel entitled *Morning Red,* which was his insight into many of the contemporary directions he saw in the northern plains area. He had already evolved his idea of an area he calls Siouxland and his further idea that he would investigate it in all its aspects, from pre-history of the Indian life to contemporary times. But *Morning Red* was not the sort of material on which Feike Feikema had built a reputation, nor was it the Western historical material of *Lord Grizzly.* The New York publishers were anxious to get some more Western historical novels, but they wouldn't have *Morning Red*. So he wished to talk about his publishing problems.

Now I am sure that Manfred is the kindest, most honest, most sensitive, and most intellectually able giant anywhere around. I ask my reader: When a man of genius stands before you and says that his most ambitious, most important novel to date won't be published by the New York houses, what the deuce do you do? I did the only thing I knew to do, and that was to publish it.

This was an interesting experience. The book has a great deal of interest, it is a very large book physically but also in conception. It has the double plot which Faulkner and Warren have made, in a sense, popular. It has many characters, and interesting ones, too. It was a big piece of food to get into the mouth and chew, but Manfred chewed masterfully. And it had the type of insight which he has importantly been developing in his new projects. It has a fault of going a bit for pyrotechnics of style—some coined words, some deviations from sound English in favor of "expression" and freshness. I am not alone in thinking that Manfred must learn a somewhat better style, a purity of style in the sense that it is adapted more closely to exactness of meaning and perception. But, like so much of his work, it has bigness of heart, large compass, joy in being alive and seeing the world.

So what happened when it appeared? A considerable silence. A few key places to achieve best Manfred sales went against it. Manfred, like Fisher, has apparently earned the enmity of *Time* and some others. Some of the reviewers, who ought to know better, really, cried out that *Morning Red* was not like the other books of his they had liked; why didn't the big oaf give us another book like the ones he had already done?

The pattern now seems to be that his historical novels will be welcomed in New York. Since *Morning Red,* there has appeared *Riders of Judgment,* a very good job upon one of the famous Western historical events, with an interesting style. Late this spring is to appear *Conquering Horse,* also from a New York house, a novel, which, I understand, fits within his Siouxland saga, being a story of the Indians in the land before the coming of the Whites. As soon as I am able to accomplish the work of production, I shall issue *Arrow of Love,* a book composed of three novelettes, one of these stories reaching back to Indian times, also, and the other two being farm settings of recent times. This book did not receive acceptance in New York. In all of the later work I have seen, Manfred has been developing a beautiful style.

The summary is surely clear: Here is a man of prodigious labor and prodigious ability. The mere publishing scene has been difficult. It marked him as a sort of second Thomas Wolfe and then condemned him for developing. But this is precisely the point. Ten books—to be twelve by the end of 1959—is a lot of accomplishment in less than two decades, and they are worthy books. But the last ones have showed us than Manfred has a very great deal, indeed—not alone in the values of those books but also in the demonstration that he is on the move. I hope a lot of silly reviewers are going to cry out often because Manfred doesn't write what they expect him to write! He has a very great deal to tell us, and an inherent sensitivity which is making that telling rich and good.

10.

In some contexts, it certainly would be an error to talk of a writer with practically no reputation, but since I am not writing a scholarly paper, rather an expression of some considered attitudes built out of my experience, I am glad to hazard the error. My sixth maverick is a young writer, Edward Loomis.

I first heard of Loomis through some mutual friends, and, as I recall, I asked to see a manuscript they had seen. It was a short novel entitled *The Charcoal Horse*, a novel about some army experience. I admired it greatly, but I thought that there was some hope it would be taken by a New York house. I encouraged Loomis to try a multitude of submissions but guaranteed publication if his submissions were unsuccessful. The manuscript went the rounds, was rejected, and I gave him a contract for it, publication to come as soon as a difficult schedule (and the difficulties of publishing fiction by a small publisher) would permit.

Meantime, Loomis had continued writing. He looks to be a hard and steady worker, a most important matter. He had finished two other novels which an agent was sending about New York unsuccessfully up to that time. He had also done some shorter work and sent me two long stories or novelettes for consideration for my magazine. I really was tremendously impressed by these two long stories. On one of those apparently silly ideas which hit us occasionally, I sent the two off to a New York firm which was doing fairly regularly, an anthology of short novels. Back came the reply that they were impressed with this short work and wanted to know more about Loomis's work. I told them what I knew and even sent the manuscript of *The Charcoal Horse* as a mere suggestion of his style and worth and suggested they get in touch with his agent about the two novels he had done. As I understand it, this house had previously read and rejected at least one of those two novels. But the new combination in some way, plus, I understand, the special interest of one of the readers, swung matters the other way and Loomis was given a three-book contract—for the two novels and for a collection of the shorter works.

The first of those novels appeared a year ago under the title *End of a War*. I tried in a feeble way, since I do not see all the main reviews by any means, to watch what would happen. So far as I could tell, almost complete silence except for one very appreciative review by Granville Hicks in his column in *Saturday Review*.

As I understand the schedule, *The Charcoal Horse* will appear next, for I shall be able to get it out late this spring; another novel shall appear from New York late this year, and the volume of short stories in 1960. Meantime, again, Loomis has continued on and has more stories and has nearly completed another novel. He *is* a worker! I mention these matters because, begging pardon for including a book from my own list before publication and assessment by others, I ask that the reader look into Loomis's work. I think it will be a revelation.

Clearly the virtues I see in his work are the virtues I have stressed throughout this essay. Here is a man who takes fiction quite seriously as a job to be done well. One of the stories I saw was of a wild mustang hunt. I have never been on such a hunt, but I was in that story, clearly and calmly immersed in it, with the sensitivity of meaningful, human experience arising from it. *End of a War* is no big blast like *The Naked and the Dead* or *The Young Lions*. By almost exactly its difference in tone would I measure its better quality of writing—and I do not mean to belittle two books in which I found enjoyment or two writers who I think have a great deal. But they rarely show the control one finds already in Loomis. I suspect, but I do not know, that he learned much from Janet Lewis and from some of the nineteenth-century writers of history and fiction, particularly in style. This is the revelation: to see so much quiet mastery of significant detail, sound emotion, and emerging theme in one who has written three novels, only one of which has so far been published, and some stories, none of which has appeared. Loomis in this sense belongs with my other five mavericks in our culture who, I feel, demonstrate the cultivation which is going on in the West today.

PROFESSIONAL LETTERS AND THE TEACHING OF ENGLISH
College Composition and Communication, May, 1960

When Professor Albert R. Kitzhaber suggested this topic for a talk to the annual meeting of the Conference on College Composition and Communication, I accepted almost eagerly. The reason is that to my mind came, not a single impression, but a multitude of impressions. As one who knows that the shortest distance from one point to another point is not necessarily a straight line, I shall not pretend to a tightly organized talk ending with a single thought. Rather, being earnest and dedicated to these various impressions, I have decided to classify them under four headings.

1. *Profession.* Both the profession of letters and the profession of teaching are, in our culture, something of a joke. A profession is a *calling*, a calling at which we make a living. There are thousands making a sort of living at teaching, of course, but often not a very adequate living. In letters, there are probably not more than 2500 persons in the United States who make a full living as freelance writers, although the general estimate is that there are some 100,000 persons who are semi-professional or amateur in that they provide

a steady stream of manuscripts filling certain needs in our magazines and publishing houses.

Our two professions, then, are lacking in the economic reward which is one of the touchstones of a "profession." But when we compare our professions with those of medicine and law, I think we find many other ways in which the "joke" is apparent. For both, we must surely make every effort to raise ourselves by our bootstraps and see to it that we make our ways of life truly professional. As I see the lacks, here are things we must do:

a. Neither for writers nor for teachers is it apparent that we meet the primary assumption of a profession: that we can codify our interests and intentions. Our ideals are not known to us, and those we most often profess stand on shifting grounds of various community and financial pressures. It is high time that in these matters we declare our interests and our ideals and brook no compromise with forces outside our professions.

b. Nor does either of our professions provide another essential—that of codification of professional practices and of internal discipline. In letters today, we know that the phenomena of publishing and reviewing are such that, to a large extent, the unworthy shall march first among us. Teaching is much the same. We are familiar with the frequency with which our heads of departments, for one example, are not chosen from the most vigorous or creative teachers.

We do not have an adequate means of determining and recognizing worth.

c. Neither do writers nor teachers have adequate professional control of their fees and income. In letters, we are stuck with the requirement of single submissions of a literary work, and the individual author is most often in very little position to set his fees or even to bargain for his payment. When James M. Cain, some twelve years ago, proposed a means of providing a better bargaining ground for authors, his proposal was not taken seriously. Teachers are in much the same situation. A former student of mine, a true wit, now teaching in a small college in Los Angeles, wrote me recently that he had become tired of living "poormouth." So he finally approached his administration and suggested a raise in salary. This was granted, even with a sort of commitment that there would be a further raise next year. As the teacher wrote, he could now live, not "poormouth" but merely "threadbare."

d. In neither profession do we have adequate access to knowledge essential to our professional roles. True, in our professions the problem is more difficult than for other professions, where a scholarly press can provide the means within a reasonable compass. In the teaching of English, particularly, all new works of genuine literary value are our province, as well as the old works. But we do not have reliable guides to that literature. Our review media are close to being contemptible, and no one of them provides even a decent guide. When the U.S. government attempted for some years to offer at least a serious overview of American publishing, the effort was killed by the present administration. (I am pleased to note, in an aside, that the *Library Journal* comes within shouting distance of the objective, providing reasonably sound brief notices and reviews of about twice as many books as are covered by any other review medium.)

My summary thought on this topic is that, proud of the responsibilities of our "professions" and proud of the serious potentialities of both ways of life, we must work to become proud of the ways in which we conduct the two professions.

2. *Writers as teachers.* During the generation of which I count myself a part, we have witnessed a great change upon the campus in that many writers have become teachers. If we think for a moment of the writers of 60 or over—Dreiser, Anderson, Fitzgerald, Frost, Stevens, Hemingway, Eliot—we know that the teaching profession did not once harbor many writers. But at the present time, a very large proportion of the serious writers are on college campuses. In the case of the critic, this is quite understandable: he has no other place to go for a living, and his work properly has considerable basis in academic scholarship. In the case of the poet, he also has no other place to go, in a sense, to make a living; yet his acceptance of the teaching role has been at least nu-

merically avid during the last twenty years. In the case of the fiction writer, since his chances of earning larger sums on the literary market are greater than for the critic and poet, we do not find quite so high a proportion on the campus. But we do find a startling number of the good ones.

There are serious pros and cons in this movement to the campus on the part of creative writers. Among the "family" of writers I had the pleasure of having in my classes in writing, the pros and cons are argued most vigorously. Last year an attack upon the academic writer was made by Donald Wetzel, and a defense was made by Mark Harris.

In favor of the trend, I think, is this chief factor: Since the serious creative writer only by a kind of luck can make a living in his primary role as writer, it is necessary for him to think of some means of livelihood which can be useful to him. For many, it is a good feeling to know that this work is itself a good and proud work, not a mere means of getting a few dollars. Teaching is a serious profession, or should be so; in teaching, one can feel that he is doing something vital and good; the work itself can be creative, or at least teaching should be so; the profession provides some security and some chances for advancement. But on the negative side is the fact that often the academic way of life is stultifying, that it is sometimes inbred, that it is most often accompanied by jealousies and pettiness. When a writer feels the encroachment of these sides of the academic life, he must spend much energy in trying to improve them, with consequent loss of his creative energy; or he will find the encroachment deadening upon his creative intentions.

After observing this trend of the writer to the campus with close interest for twenty years, my advice to the individual writer is that he must probe himself carefully. If he finds that his personality and creative ability are such that teaching can provide a serious challenge, and a rewarding way of life, to him, while he is able to carry on with his writing quite seriously, then the campus can be a beneficial thing to him and the combination of the two professions a heartening thing. But if his personality and ability are such that he feels stultified on the campus, then perhaps even the menial job is the best choice for him as a means of keeping body together while he works his creative intentions.

My advice to the profession of teaching is that it should continue to make a place for the writer. He has demonstrably, I think, liberalized and in many ways vitalized teaching; he has proved, often, a most worthy colleague. But the writer must, in return, honor the profession of teaching. It is dishonest for him not to accept and perform the duties of the profession. He must not assume that his position as writer gives him a privileged position in itself (and I have heard of this far too much, with resultant and justified resentment). He must consider that he earns his way in the profession as a teacher, not as a writer.

In summary of this second cluster of impressions, I feel that the movement of the writer to the campus has been, on the whole, a very good thing. It has added something to the profession of teaching. And teachers may be proud that some place has been made for those in the most difficult of the professions economically, that of the creative writer. But there are many problems here which must be dealt with intelligently by members of both professions.

3. *Teaching of creative writing.* Again, during what I have considered the generation of which I am a part, we have witnessed a considerable revolution upon the college campus. Thirty and forty years ago, we can judge by such attacks as those of James T. Farrell and many others upon their college teachers of writing, very few adequate courses in writing were being offered. But now we have gone to the other extreme and have made room in our academic procedures even for the advanced degrees of M.A. and Ph.D. with a considerable emphasis upon creative endeavor.

There is an old adage, "those who can't do, teach." I think this was to some extent true a generation ago—that our courses for the creative writer were conducted by persons who could not write and knew little of the problems involved. I would not be one to assume, however, that a person who does not write could never teach writing well; indeed, I am aware of some exceptions. But with the coming of the writer to the campus, we are doing this job somewhat better. And there has been some truly distinguished teaching of writing, by such men as Yvor Winters, Robert Penn Warren, Wallace Stegner, Allan Seagar, Andrew Lytle.

Just as the academic halls have made a haven for the serious writer, so also have they provided a helping hand in many ways to the young writer. There are some "cons" in this matter similar to those mentioned in my second cluster of impressions, but on the whole it seems clear that both the profession of letters and the profession of teaching have benefited from the trend. And I believe that the effect of this little revolution upon the work we shall see in the next two generations will be very great, indeed.

4. *Teaching of composition.* Perhaps in speaking to this group, I should have devoted more of my talk to this topic. But when I come to it, my thoughts tend to go helter-skelter. This problem has been with us a long time, and we have been trying a long time to do the job well. I have had the pleasure of working wholeheartedly in a bold experiment in "communications"; I have taught in the traditional freshman composition course. All I really know from these experiences is that there is no single way to teach composition well. I can respect the experimenter; I can respect the traditionalist. Both have done adequate jobs. Both have failed miserably.

But let me try to be more positive:

a. Because the teaching of English, and, specifically the teaching of composition, appears a narrow profession within a large profession of all teaching, the English teacher sometimes lets himself be put in too narrow a confine. By all means the teacher of English must make it clear that his department is not a "service department." He must not perform a job whose shots are called by other departments or professions. He must teach for the growth of his students. Indeed, it behooves every department upon the campus, of whatever sort, to aid their students to learn the organization of their thoughts, to build self-expression into something communicable. Until the English department has made this clear to the entire college, I do not think it will ever teach composition well.

b. I know that teachers of composition worry a great deal about "motivation," how to motivate the student to learn to write. I confess that this has seemed to me a relatively simple problem; I am probably too simple-minded to see all the complexities. But the truth is that it is not too difficult, I think, to sell the concept of writing. If we truly believe that the students in our classes will sometime fill positions of leadership, professional or otherwise, in our communities, after they have gone from our classes, then we know that the problem of writing reasonably well will be with these students far into the future. There is not a one among them, if he is ever "successful," who will not have need of it. And it simply is not true, as I heard was once bruited about a college of business, that the "executive" need not ever worry about this for the reason that he can get a secretary for a pittance who will take care of it for him. Indeed, the man of some success who is called upon, as he must be, for some writing and yet who cannot do it with any adequacy whatsoever is a pathetic sight. We need only to present this concretely; we do not need to use it as exhortation. I recall that my father, a farmer, but an excellent one, a man of profound abilities but relatively little school education, had need to contribute to a professional journal. Having seen him and others in similar circumstances wrestle with the problems of writing, I confess that selling the concept of writing has seemed relatively simple to me.

c. The lesson from professional letters and from the teaching of creative writing which can be carried to the teaching of composition is, I think, something like this: Do not emphasize too strongly at first (or even at any time!) the self-consciousness of form and grammar. Let the student try to capture his thought. Let him try expression as freely as he needs. Let him experiment. Then in a *social* context of the class, in reading aloud, in group criticism, let him begin to see where he failed in communication of his thought. At judicious times, the concepts of composition, such as outlining, documentation, paragraphing, and the concepts of grammar will insert themselves as helps to the student in his effort to capture and communicate his thought.

And let him rewrite. I look with some horror upon the phenomenon of a new theme a week. In creative endeavors, we know that sometimes a student learns more from rewriting one piece nine times than from writing nine new things and doing, as he knows, incompetently, similar things over and over.

I think the teacher is justified in holding before that student the relative certainty that he will sometime, indeed, be doing this for a professional editor.

Out of a multitude of thoughts generated by my topic, I have collected and divided by four topics. But my main thought is this, that if I have told you that our professions are in a kind of infancy, and that we have a chance to make ourselves and our professions more worthy, then I shall be pleased.

AMERICAN PUBLISHING AND THE AMERICAN WRITER
Chicago Review, Autumn-Winter, 1960

Several quiet but serious attacks upon American publishing have appeared since World War II and post-war inflation "shook up" the publishing industry. With the industry going through virtually a revolution in these years, it is indeed time that we try to assess the primary method by which we have contact with our literary and cultural heritage and with the additions our contemporaries are making to that heritage.

Under optimum conditions, we might presume that the great creative works of the past, and the non-"literary" writings of greatest impact upon human development, should be continuously available to the citizens of a democracy in editions relatively easily secured by anyone interested. We also might presume that the person of creative talent who has something genuinely valuable to offer, in new ideas or in new "literary" works, should find such support in the publishing industry that his best work would also be readily available to its intended public.

Our question is, "How well does our publishing industry approximate these optimum conditions?"

I

I should first like to take a quick glance at the criticisms I have seen in the post-war period.[1] In 1946 *New Directions* published a James T. Farrel pamphlet entitled *The Fate of Writing in America*. Farrell's genuine concerns grew out of one economic fact: he detected forces at work in publishing which would lead to an increase in size of our publishing firms and combines, and possibly to monopoly. At first glance his analysis seems premature. True, some firms have grown mightily in the last decade and a half, and some combines (of "original" publishers, of reprints, of book clubs) have grown somewhat larger. But the nature of publishing in America has so far resisted what would appear to be a natural economic development. Fortunately for us, books are not automobiles, and something about them resists the complete trend toward sameness which reduced our automobile offerings to the absurdity of no more than a couple of types of cars.

But Farrell's fears are not ungrounded. This possible growth of monopoly is ever present. Today it takes a somewhat different form from what Farrell observed—namely, not in the financial combinations among firms (which may well follow other develop-

---

[1] My own analysis of publishing situations in the 1940's appeared in *Berkeley* magazine in 1948, and my articles upon the problems of publishing *Poetry* magazine in 1949 and in *Poetry Broadside* in 1957. These three essays are reprinted in this volume.

ments) but in the development of merchandising methods which may well, in time, split the industry into the "haves" and the "have-nots."

Consequent upon his primary observation, Farrell saw difficulties which to a limited extent have come to pass. He feared what he called Hollywoodization in publishing, that is, the development of the "star" system, the development of patterns and types of work with well-known box-office appeal. To some extent this has developed in American publishing more than before. A part of this growth is the result of the fact that our post-war fiction, particularly, has not provided the manuscripts with which one might break such always-present, incipient possibilities of the industry.

Farrell also feared other consequences. He noted the growth in importance of the "idea man" in editorial offices and in literary agencies. Such men, comparable to editors of a large magazine who need to adapt a year's contents to a conception of a "family magazine," or whatever, are charged with the responsibility of finding the idea for a new book which could be put over. The hack writing talent is available, but the "idea man" is prized because of his knowledge of the situation, and his inventiveness (as opposed to creativeness) is at an economic premium. Personally, I do not view this with too much alarm, that is, so long as we keep it in perspective. There is a place in our lives for the ephemeral, like the newspaper we throw away as soon as we put it down. "Topical" and "idea" books are needed in publishing. What should be our concern is that they should become dominant, either in an individual publishing firm or in the industry. There are too many publishers, it is true, who have this uppermost in mind, and the "idea man" has been supplanting many of the best minds in publishing. But the trend has been serious, I think, only in some operations.

(As an aside, I remember that the man placed in charge of a new trade publishing activity of a wealthy text and technical firm contacted me several years ago in Denver to ask me to scout for manuscripts. He explained his situation with candor. His training had been in advertising. Of his staff, more than a majority was trained in promotion and advertising. They naturally commanded Madison Avenue perquisites, including salary. There was almost one man for each title to be done each year. So the problem of this executive in publishing was quite clear; he had to come up with books into which these high-powered men could sink their teeth, and each title had to earn such a high salary in addition to all the overhead and production expenses and the profit expected by a management used to making profit with their text and technical books. The man confessed that he was pleased if the book could be a "good" one, but his charge was to find the type of book for these men to work on. Goodness or badness was not an important criterion in his judgments. I was personally pleased that this firm never made as much in trade publishing as they apparently thought they would!)

Farrell's other prime concern was that developments in publishing would bring on intellectual stultification. "The area of literary freedom will become narrowed, bottle-necked. The serious writer will be pressed into his bohemia, that cultural ghetto of bourgeois society." He thought that this effect would apply more for new ideas than it would for creative literature. His fears certainly are in part justified; to say that book publishing does enjoy greater freedom of thought than other "means of communication" does not entirely absolve publishers from permitting economic and other pressures from letting intellectual freedom narrow at all.

In the February, 1959, issue of *Author & Journalist* magazine appeared an article "The Crazy Publishing Business" by "John Grapevine," frankly indicated to be a pen name for someone in publishing as well as author of a number of books. Mr. Grapevine stresses that publishing is an "unbusinesslike business." He sees certain problems in publishing which so far have "resisted all attempts to reduce them to manageable difficulties." Among these he lists the following: inadequate payment for the producer of books; the absurd advertising problem of the publisher; and that book publishing, because it depends upon its profits from income from subsidiary rights, "is a business which does not live on the sale of its main product." Mr. Grapevine does mention one other matter, that in publishing books, although we have many persons of taste and ability, we often have people who do not really like books and know little about them in a quality sense. This also applies to much retailing of books, where, unlike the retailer of underwear, there are tens of thousands of "models" to be sold, and one supposes that the retailer ought to have some smattering acquaintance with the broad segment of these products. His task is great, however, because of this multiplicity, and because of the poor economic return found in retail bookselling.

We may chortle with a little glee that publishing is not an industry in which all problems are to be reduced to "businesslike" proportions. Frequently we see a successful businessman in manufacturing or retailing take a look at publishing and think, "Those people don't know how to run a business. Let's show them how to produce books and *sell* them efficiently." Fortunately for the book business, to my knowledge none of those persons ever became a successful publisher.

Of the recent criticisms of publishing I have seen, the most serious (although least developed) is an article "On the Art of Book Publishing" by Emile Capouya which appeared in *The Nation* (October 24, 1959). Mr. Capouya poses the question, "As a matter of common experience, and theory aside, doesn't the system [of commercial trade publishing] work more or less well?" His answer, without illustration or argument, is no. He qualifies with "It is cause for amazement that it works at all."

What Mr. Capouya proposes is the development of three additional sources for publishing methods. First, that a government agency, such as the Government Printing Office, which is already engaged in publication of a great deal of material, extend its work into other fields, even creative literature—"a publishing TVA." Second, that the system of subsidy publishing which we know as the usual pattern of university and denominational presses (subsidy by tax support of the institutions, by groups, and by foundations) be extended beyond its present range. He proposes that the "moral commitment" to better things by such presses be subsidized further by public funds. Third, that the present pattern of vanity publishing be regulated to prevent overcharging and gouging for services and that, indeed, such a prototype be extended to operation of cooperatives in the publishing industry.

Mr. Capouya has some excellent suggestions. I would look at it this way: We are aware that in the most commercial of all our means of communication—radio, TV, newspapers, magazines—we cannot expect serious, quality work. In radio, as a corrective to out and out commercialization, we support the small FM station devoted to programming good music, lectures, readings. In TV, we provide, through taxes or otherwise, for "Educational TV." And in the magazine field we know that even the most "literary" of our commercial magazines such as *Saturday Review, Harper's, New Yorker, Atlantic,* cannot do a truly intelligent and quality job. So we work with "little magazines" all the way from the large university quarterlies through the great diversity of efforts we know in this engaging, less formal field.

I myself became interested in little magazines early in my life. I have edited and published in the field and will continue to do so. By publishing the *Index to Little Magazines,* I try to aid them somewhat. We have a great many such efforts, at times perhaps even more than we need. True, we always need new ones, to highlight a new talent or new trend; we need new ones to "correct" the tendency of established ones to become stuffy and hidebound; we need the continuation of the best. But I observed that in book publishing, we somehow feel that the commercial publisher should fill all the needs fulfilled in the analogous area of magazines by both our large commercial journals and our little magazines. This, I think, is shortsighted. As Mr. Capouya has said, it is surprising that commercial publishing could provide us with any excellent work. We do not expect it of *Saturday Evening Post,* say, or *Atlantic,* or *Saturday Review.* So an analogous effort is needed. Part is supplied by the university and institutional press, which, however, is usually more confined in what it can do than the comparable university-supported quarterly magazine. The other part must be the small publisher devoted to bringing out works of quality which do not have a chance to make their ways in commercial publishing. My feeling was that book publishing needed the "little publisher" the same way that the world of magazines needed the "little magazine."

"Vanity" publishing as presently done is really a commercial thing, vicious in many of its aspects. Better is the tradition of the "private edition." But, as Mr. Capouya says, this could be developed by regulation and by the introduction of cooperatives. They would have to be done well and with some knowledge, for publishing has pitfalls, of course. Further, the pattern of government subsidized publishing could be well extended, from state support of university presses to enlarging the federal publishing arm, so that we may supplement and challenge the commercial publisher.

II

We are witnessing quite a revolution in commercial publishing at the present time, that is, the impact of paperback publishing. In the history of this development as it is being written, I feel that not enough credit is being given to those who solved some of the technical, manufacturing problems (especially Staley Thompson, who was with Armed Services

Editions and later made Rinehart Editions possible from the technical side), and to Rinehart Editions, the first to open the college market to paperbacks. But, be that as it may, paperback publishing is certainly quite young in present forms in this country, and it is loud and vociferous. It would be foolhardy to predict what will come, for this is contingent upon the personalities and ideas of men as well as upon economic facts. But we may discuss some of the problems and possibilities.

In speaking of paperback, at the present time we need to keep clearly in mind the difference between the cheap paperback and the higher-priced paperback. The two are to be differentiated not only by price but also by many other factors, chiefly the factors involved in merchandising.

The cheap paperback is distributed to the customer through a network of agencies which involve wholesalers covering the "accounts" of many retail outlets. There are reputed to be more than a hundred thousand outlets for these books. They are serviced purely upon speculation of the publisher: he "floats" his edition out to the wholesaler in quantity, that wholesaler then distributes to the retail outlets in his geographical area; when a sale is made, the retailer is then obligated, on next report time, to pay the wholesaler, and the wholesaler, on his next report time, is obligated to pay the publisher. No money is received by the publisher until this movement of books is made out from plant to retailer, and movement of payment is made back through the channels. Thus, the publisher has his capital tied up for periods of many weeks, and some of it for periods of many months. He is the speculative person primarily: the wholesaler speculates only his immediate space and employee cost, and the retailer speculates only his space (which he might give over to cosmetics or something other than books) and his time. Neither wholesaler nor retailer pays for merchandise handled until he is paid; he does not speculate capital invested in merchandise.

I am continually amazed at the vast opportunities for the cheap paperback publisher. It seems to me that they are greater than for the high-priced paperback publisher. By contrast with every other type of publishing, his outlets are numerous; he has contact with almost every citizen, in contrast with the outlets for other types of books. His outlets are almost exactly the same number as his minimum printings need to be; in theory, he need sell only one copy of a title in each outlet to be in a successful business. All things being equal, with such contact with the public, it would seem impossible to think of any reasonably good title which would not sell at least one copy per outlet!

Of course the problems are not so simple as this. The outlets are short of space, and competition is great for that space. A single copy of a book could very possibly get buried on the racks used for merchandising.

My point, though, is that in contrast to other publishing, the cheap paperback firm has great control over its merchandising methods. It is not so haphazard, so dependent upon inefficient and inadequate outlets, as are the other publishers. The possibilities seem limitless.

But the cheap paperback publishers have been hampered in many ways. One of the ways, of course, is the development of the outlets into an efficient system. Competition for space in these outlets is keen from other industries as well as from fellow publishers. But I think they have been hampered more by their own attitudes. In the "mass market," they seem to feel that they must act in the tried ways of the mass market. To use James T. Farrell's word, they suffer from "Hollywoodization." When a pattern of successful titles appears, then everyone must get on the bandwagon and produce similar titles. When that runs its course, like a series of movies or TV shows based on a momentarily popular pattern, then another one has to be picked up. The independent judgment in this field, I believe, will eventually pay off handsomely. The problems of publishing, *per se*, seem to me more adequately solved in this realm than in any other aspect of publishing, except textbook publishing.

Cheap paperback publishers can learn to reward their authors a bit more; but actually they do better by their authors, in relationship to capital investments, wholesale returns, etc., than do other publishers today. This is an industry which, like items we buy in the grocery store, is calculated on costs to split pennies, and the author's share of those split pennies, while not handsome, is at least decent.

However, one serious fault of the cheap edition publisher lies exactly in his merchandising. Clearly he operates upon a mass basis by a particular method, as described. It is uneconomical for him, most of the time, to service individual orders for particular titles. The cheap edition publisher cannot keep his good titles indefinitely in print, or keep them out for display indefinitely, or service the individual need. The customer must pick from the stands. Something he saw there two months ago may now be gone, and his retailer can't do much about it. And in the sense of making the good work reasonably available to all, at all times, the methods of the cheap paperback publishers are not yet adequate. I feel that he can solve this problem by supplementing his present method by joining to his edition perhaps a slightly higher priced one which will be available more like the high-priced paperback, that is, have sufficient margin to handle the extra labor involved in servicing greater individual choice and keeping editions in print and available to the regular bookstore or the "special order" buyer.

More in the news recently is the "quality" or high-priced paperback. Even the review media are beginning to pay particular attention to these books, by devoting special issues to them or by devoting regular review space to them as well as to hardbound books. College communities have particularly welcomed these books.

What the high-priced paperbacks have done is this: they have brought into print some excellent books which otherwise might be out of print, in other words, have promised to aid in one serious problem of publishing; they have made often very good books available to the public. In the first of the two optimum conditions—making serious work of the past reasonably available to everyone—these paperbacks show great promise of solving a real problem. One cannot deny their many satisfactions.

Yet the high-priced paperback has a number of problems yet to be faced, or, to say it alternatively, has a good many faults at this time. The faults so far are these:

1. Pay to authors is inadequate. Up to now, the high-priced paperback has shared less royalty with authors than has either the cheaper paperback or the regular hardbound book. Of course in the excitement this has been overlooked to a great extent. If one had a book which neither the cheap paperback publisher could do nor the "original" hardback publisher keep in print, and thus had no income from some old literary property, then the chance to have the book

in print, even at low royalties, would seem a godsend. But the truth is that the quality paperback has to do better by authors if it wants to feel mature and able. Some persons may make a bit in the spadework of editing new combinations (anthologies, writing prefaces, etc.), but the problem of support for the author has to be faced in this publishing.

2. The high-priced paperback is primarily what I call "leech" publishing. That is, it does not depend upon the assertion of new talent, the discovery of new talent; instead, it depends primarily upon reprinting of works already published and judged. In making those works available in good editions at a decent price, it certainly is publishing which has the elements of greatness. But if one were to follow this to a logical conclusion we would find no place for the new author, or at least not more than a five or ten percent place among our titles. And once we had got into print all the good books of the past (and our book outlets become almost a nightmare of evenly spaced shelves showing mostly the uninteresting spines of thousands of paperbacks!), we would be hard up indeed—for further titles to reprint, and little way in which to develop the talent which would provide titles to reprint!

3. The possibility for the "small publisher" (analogous to the little magazine, as I have mentioned above) is smaller in paperback publishing than in hardback publishing. Whereas an individual, perhaps

with help of friends, could issue an occasional hardback in "corrective" competition to the commercial publisher and by devoted labor perhaps do something of benefit, the structure of paperback publishing and distribution is against him. For paperback publishing is going even more strongly than hardback to the emphasis upon "merchandising" whereby the small title, the small press, will have even greater competitive problems; further, capital investment is greater, with little chance that it can be alleviated, as in the case of a hardback, by personal labor or cooperation.

There is much experimentation going on in paperback publishing at the present, so that answers are not complete. Perhaps some of my objections to the high-priced paperback (objections not to what is offered, for that is a real and important gain; but objections, I hope it is clear, to what is not offered) may be solved. Those persons most involved tend to think that at least they can solve the problem of introducing new talent. And quite a few new works, new authors, are being published in paperback form. But no effort, so far as I can see, is as yet critical. Aside from a few foreign authors, from a few momentarily popular authors (primarily the Beat), and from a few authors already known through hardback books but offering new work in paperback form, no truly new talent has been discovered and furthered in paperback publishing as yet. Perhaps it can be. The next five years should tell us much. Indeed, experiments of some of us in offering poetry, by other than the momentarily popular poets, may be a useful indication in the next year or so.

My feeling is that perhaps the cheap paperback, if it would get infused with some new blood and a few adaptations, may well be better for this than the high-priced paperback. But, brilliant and useful as paperback publishing is right now, it has not demonstrated the equally important ability to put us in touch with the best developing work of our own comtemporaries. If it does so, I thing it will require editorial talent quite different from that which is now dominant in paperback publishing.[2]

---

[2] Two and a half years ago, for my own firm, I faced the problem of entering the high-priced paperback field, and, because of the objections I have detailed, decided to stay out of it. A year and a half later I reversed the decision and did enter it. Now it happens that, as a small publisher in the sense I have used above in analogy with the magazine field, I feel that the particular role I must perform is the assertion and development of new work, that is, quality work which does not seeem to have an immediate attraction for the large commercial publisher—although, once established in at least a small way by such efforts, it may have later. The patterns of paperback publishing seemed to be a side-track from that endeavor. But why the change of decision? The reason was this: with a backlist of some very fine work, I felt an obligation to the work and to the authors to try for this newly developing market for them. This market is real and important. I felt that to do justice to this work, this effort had to be made, although it involved bending some attention away from new work to the problems of the reprint business. I had to assert the importance of fiction in this field, also; and, like others doing the same, attempt poetry as a paperback item for the quality poet whose reputation must almost always grow steadily instead of burn fast like an explosion.

There are some anomalies in this business. For some reason, the firms working hardest at paperbacks in the quality field, tend to use European talent for their "new" works. Of course these are *not new*; they have been proved elsewhere. Like *New Directions*, these firms seem to be less interested in what is going on in American development than in the foreign author. I would not assert any "patriotism" or that American work must come first! The introduction of foreign works to American audiences is important, very important. But there is a matter if editorial judgment involved; there is still the failure to face the

III

For many of us in publishing the chief concern is less that of seeing important work of the past continue to be available, than it is the situation for the talented new writer. We are concerned with the poetry, the fiction, the literary criticism of inherent significance. How does it fare as work newly offered? And what of the book offering completely new, perhaps even radical, ideas in the realm of politics, economics, philosophy? Here again, we must feel misgivings although marvel a bit that the system works as well as it does.

The truth is that publishing in the United States does one thing very badly: it does not support its best authors. On the average, a good book of poems will earn the author a few dollars up to a few hundred dollars. On the average, a good novel will earn anything from five hundred dollars to a couple thousand dollars. In the face of present-day inflation and living standards, this is very bad, indeed. The rewards, of course, are out of all proportion to inherent worths. In a commercial society, with, as an example, bad TV programs earning some persons a

---

full problems of making the qualitative judgment. In the Twenties and Thirties at least two prominent firms made vast reputations here for their introduction of foreign authors. They deserved these reputations. But it is interesting, I think, that their steady list was often thin, and neither of the firms I have in mind seems now to have a distinguished list. I feel that, per the remarks in the next section of my essay, the person interested in the most serious way in the problems of our awareness of fine work, a "corrective" vision must always be applied to any publishing firm which seems to commercialize the newest development.

great deal of money, one must expect much of this. But the fact that the best talent is poorly supported or, in Farrell's phrase, consigned to bohemia, is a true blight upon our publishing picture.

Indeed, we have things backwards. There is a great deal of money being provided to talented authors these days. But publishing is less the earner of this money than it is the occasion for trying to get the money. The money comes from university jobs or from the gifts of various foundations, fellowships, grants. That a good writer can earn his living by teaching is not necessarily a bad thing. At least the teaching itself may be creative and rewarding. And for the literary critic, his work is close enough to the academic, with occasional exceptions. The poet and the fiction writer may even live on the campus with some relative ease. Yet we ought to have some concern for a culture in which the publication of a talented person's work may be most helpful *to him* in securing a teaching appointment or preferment on the campus.

This situation seems especially unjust with all the money available in grants—a great deal of it these days. The publisher becomes necessary as a means to such money: it isn't available to the unpublished writer, usually (and more's the pity, sometimes!). Matters have gone so far that we know of writers who go from fellowship to grant and back again year after year; this is their livelihood. And nothing very productive has been the result. The rewarding of conscientious, dedicated work which has won only mild acclaims with a chance for the talent to work unhindered upon a project for a period of a year or however long is required is a good thing. But we have moved far beyond this into a kind of political game in which the money dropping like manna is the prize for adequate maneuverability. It would seem to me that only very occasionally have we seen concrete benefit from this system; it is a kind of blind, unthinking patronage. For its few real benefits, perhaps we can put up with it as one of the excesses of a wealthy culture. But the culture is somehow sick that it must make its provisions in this way rather than through the legimate functions of rewarding excellence in work. Aside from this major fault of publishing, the other faults are fringe and relatively minor. Let us examine the various types of work.

Poetry has been making a strong comeback in publishing. During all but the last couple of years of the last two decades, it definitely was on the fringe. Most commercial houses felt they need not bother themselves, or their reputations, with showing poetry on their lists (except perhaps those often damnable things called anthologies). Fortunately, a few firms, still cognizant of long-range values and of quality in some of their decisions, felt it necessary to keep up a bit of poetry publishing. Perhaps such a firm (and there were relatively few) would offer one book of verse a year. Each few years it would be a new poet with his first collection; the other years, new volumes by poets already published previously, sometimes by some other firm which had taken the task of getting the poet started in his reputation. But at least an equal number of volumes (and probably more than an equal number) had to be done outside the methods of commercial publishing. The little press or little publisher, the cooperative group, the occasional tentative exploration into publishing by some well-meaning individual—these had to assume the functions of discovering more than half the genuine talent. I say more than half, for the commercial publishers who did publish poetry were often marred by bad editorial taste. One can confirm this by taking some representative list of the best poems of the last two decades and run a bibliography upon the publishers sponsoring their work. In this country, I should estimate that something like 75% of them got at least their starts, and often much more than that, from the publishers outside the usual commercial pattern.

Recently the situation has been changing—at least quantitatively. Commercial publishing has realized that, in long-range planning, poetry has a place, even an economic place, in its activities. But much more than that, the institutional press has forged into the field. For years, of course, Yale University Press sponsored its one volume a year. A few years ago Indiana University Press began a steady publication of poetry. Now the University of Minnesota Press, which had done occasional volumes, has announced several; the new effort at Wesleyan University Press offers quite a number of titles. Then the experiments of some of these presses and commercial firms in offering poetry in the high-priced paperback method have lifted the poet high. Simply speaking, a lot of books of verse are thus being published under good auspices. Indeed, whereas a few years ago one would have to conclude that the poet's opportunities for a decent volume were small, today they are almost at the other extreme. There are not that many good books of verse in a year—as being offered at the present time. The feeling of institutional responsibility may well continue, and I hope it does; the paperback development may prove a true boon. But there must come some shakedown, for whereas we corrected one extreme, we must ultimately correct another.

Those of us who have struggled with this problem for some time may feel relief in these developments, however. The individual responsibility may be lessened and the hard work may be lessened. The matter to be watched is the swing of the pendulum: if there is a reaction against this making publication of poets much easier than before, then perhaps there will be even greater need than before for the effort which supplements the marketplace.

Fiction, on the other hand, has never had quite the problems of poetry. The eagerness for talent within a context in which the publisher knows that he may get his real reward some years hence has been real and authors have been seen through many little-paying volumes time after time. I have been asked often if I ever saw a novel of really fine quality which was not published. And I must reply no—but with my fingers crossed. Many good manuscripts have gone begging for some time, as we all know; and ultimately they have sometimes had to be published outside the normal publishing industry. I have to say no because when I have found such a manuscript, I have gone ahead to do it myself, even though the patterns for publishing fiction are strongly against success outside those patterns. But the borderline cases have been many; I have heard, without seeing them personally, that some excellent manuscripts even by established writers have not been published; and the type of sacrifice to author and sponsor in doing such work outside the normal channels is often considerable. Obviously our patterns are not adequate, and especially is this true of short fiction or fiction of lengths outside normal "packages"; but one cannot, on the other hand, say flatly that commercial publishing never does the quality piece of fiction. It can say with pride that it has.

The critic has sometimes had it nearly as bad as the poet in the past. But in some ways this seems changed. The institutional press has recognized responsibilities in this realm faster—partly, I think, because criticism is close to the academic and because most of the critics have been on college faculties. The truth seems to be that there is almost too much opportunity, for the amount of bad criticism published in books today is appalling. I mean by "bad criticism" that which is repetitive, quite without new resources of concept or intellectual development. Some that have these qualities may be going begging, indeed; in that case, our touted critical revival would seem sad.

We have been going through a period of relative "safety" in intellectual ideas—under the impact of McCarthyism and a certain tameness in intellectual life. Hence, it seems to me that publishing has not truly been tested for some time regarding its resistance to the book of radical ideas.[3] There has been enough publishing of the informal sort, outside commercial firms, so that the "dangerous" idea has not arbitrarily been denied. And commercial book publishing is certainly the most free of the mass communications methods, to its great honor. But when tests really come strongly, as undoubtedly they will sometime, I believe that the support of corrective publishing will be absolutely necessary if our culture is to grow healthfully and strongly.

---

[3] I do not here consider the ideas of the Beats to be a true test of this problem. The ideas thus fostered seem to me not "radical," and surely less dangerous to our culture than to the individuals who hold them.

IV

Now we may return to our original assumptions, that under optimum conditions our publishing industry would provide continuous and easy contact with the great works of our heritage, and that it would provide support for the genuinely good new talent and make the work of that talent available to its intended public. That publishing also has other functions—from the great value of "how-to" books to "quickies" upon the latest political candidates—is true; but we are ultimately to test the value of publishing with these touchstones. How does publishing in America fare?

Only so-so. It does better by the first of these functions. For with the development of paperback publishing, our public does have reasonably ready contact with the great work of the past, even that of yesterday. Hardback publishing has in part failed in this—as we were shocked to realize when the paperback titles started pouring from the presses and we saw much brought back into print which was valuable. There are plenty of holes even yet, however. Often lost in this new publishing is the sanctity of the individual writer and the individual work. We are making a fringe career for two types of persons: the editor of anthologies, the preparer of digests and "selections," the idea man for searching bypaths for the partial work; and the "professional" writer of introductions to new editions. We may look upon this with some horror and upon the persons involved with some intellectual reservations. We have tended to lose something also valuable—the "nice edition" of a work or an author. If one, for example, wished to secure the works of Conrad (a writer recently high in the mobile parthenon of critical journals), where would he turn? Our publishing is just not providing these sets of complete works any more. Instead, we would hunt a dozen or more paperback and hardback lists to pick up a title here, a title there; and we would end up without the complete works, probably, except over a period of time—and each would be different and probably in some measure inadequate. Or what if we wish to secure that old prize, a decent one-volume edition of the works of Shakespeare or Dante or some others? Gone is that decently readable book, good type and paper with first-class text, complete and unselected. Instead now we must be satisfied with somebody's selection of five tragedies, or someone else's presentation of the best of Keats. We have made gains, but we also are sustaining some losses in this aspect of publishing in which, as I have said, we seem to be doing better than the other.

Except in the case of poetic talent with its current (and very likely temporary) spurt in support from various types of publishers, our publishing industry is quite inadequate in its handling of new creative talents. There is a small but doubtful chance that paperback publishing may aid this. But it is clear that, if we are seriously concerned about this matter, as we should be, we must give every encouragement to some supplements or "correctives" to commercial publishing, both hardback and paperback.

In his *Nation* article, Mr. Capouya classified these possibilities as government publishing, the university and institutional presses, and the subsidized publishing he would like to see extended into cooperatives. These do at the present time offer some correctives and supplements, and I think that as public policy we must seriously consider extending these modes.

I would add still a fourth—and, to date, I think the most effective corrective. I refer to what I have pointed out as the small, dedicated publisher analogous to the "little magazine." Perhaps we need to coin a new term and speak of "little publishing." There is one great virtue in it: in the estimation of new work, the matter of critical judgment becomes paramount. The difficulty with commercial publishing is that the judgment can be blunted by many factors, including notions of the possible economic picture for the book. The difficulty with government or institutional or cooperative publishing is that the judgment may be blunted by the "group process." Excellent things come to light thus, but often the book chosen is the result of compromise of taste—like the winners of awards, who are only half the time truly distinguished. The "little publisher," like the editor of a little magazine, can assert his taste and judgment. He need not compromise so much. And although no one taste can do the whole job, by any stretch of the imagination, if his taste is strong, he will bring to light some excellent work. Some excellent work missed by him may be brought to light by another "little publisher" of different taste and judgment.

Hence the correctives to an inadequate "commerce" of publishing lie in the supplements to commercial publishing methods.

But correctives lie equally, I must conclude, with our reading public. Indeed, I think they shall lie more than equally with the public in the decades to come. For the fears of a James T. Farrell, premature as they seemed, are real. The greater efficiency of the paperback leads to some of the problems. The bookstore will, by merchandising methods now being tested by the publishers, both hardback and paperback, choose its stock less by choice of the owner; instead, it will be stocked much more impersonally by certain wholesaling and other sales methods. This is inevitable, I am sure. And as this happens, the possible "correctives" of the other publishing methods will be lessened. We will be worse off, probably with regard to our contact with the great works of the past, and certainly with regard to our contact with possible new genius. We need not visualize very many steps in this direction to know that the situation for the American writer will worsen markedly, and we will also find the stultification, by economic methods, comparable to the stultification by law and fiat of undemocratic nations.

How do we assure ourselves of means to fight these tendencies? Basically by being intellectually awake and enquiring. For an example, as bookstore frequenters, we can examine the offerings. Then as we step to the cash register with our selections, we can say, in effect, "I have looked over the new titles from Anchor Books, and I have found these three excellent titles I want. Now then, what else can you find for me? What publisher in Keokuk, Iowa, offers some work in poetry or fiction or philosophy which would interest me? I don't want to be confined in my selections by what you have here in the store."

Or for another example, we can consider book reviews merely as news about a few books published. A large review paper can cover only perhaps 15% of the titles offered. Many that it covers are newsworthy in an immediate sense, and they must be commented upon. That is a part of the function of the review which is competently edited. But there is little time in the press of deadlines and multitudes of books to read and note all. So we must go beyond these sources. The serious critical magazines must think beyond the moment and the books already under public discussion in our bobby-soxing intellectual life.

What books are being missed which might have values? Why must these presumably more "critical" journals, in their pages, comment upon what already has been commented on? Let them perform another function. The assertions of these "correctives" by the public must be continuous and devoted, just as the "correctives" in publishing itself must be continuous and devoted. What is at stake is our intellectual fibre.